METHODOLOGIES OF MOBILITY

Worlds in Motion

Edited by Noel B. Salazar, University of Leuven, in collaboration with ANTHROMOB, the EASA Anthropology and Mobility Network.

ANTHRO
MOB

This transdisciplinary book series features empirically grounded studies from around the world that disentangle how people, objects and ideas move across the planet. With a special focus on advancing theory as well as methodology, the series considers movement as both an object and a method of study.

Volume 1
KEYWORDS OF MOBILITY
Critical Engagements
Edited by Noel B. Salazar & Kiran Jayaram

Volume 2
METHODOLOGIES OF MOBILITY
Ethnography and Experiment
Edited by Alice Elliot, Roger Norum, & Noel B. Salazar

Methodologies of Mobility
Ethnography and Experiment

Edited by

Alice Elliot, Roger Norum, & Noel B. Salazar

berghahn

NEW YORK · OXFORD

www.berghahnbooks.com

Published in 2017 by
Berghahn Books
www.berghahnbooks.com

© 2017, 2019 Alice Elliot, Roger Norum, & Noel B. Salazar
First paperback edition published in 2019

Library of Congress Cataloging-in-Publication Data
Names: Elliot, Alice (Social anthropologist), editor. | Norum, Roger,
  editor. | Salazar, Noel B., 1973- editor.
Title: Methodologies of mobility : ethnography and experiment / edited by
  Alice Elliot, Roger Norum & Noel B. Salazar.
Description: New York : Berghahn Books, 2017. | Series: Worlds in motion ;
  volume 2 | Includes bibliographical references and index.
Identifiers: LCCN 2016054959 (print) | LCCN 2017008869 (ebook) | ISBN
  9781785334801 (hardback : alk. paper) | ISBN 9781785334818 (ebook)
Subjects: LCSH: Ethnology--Methodology. | Migration, Internal--Social
  aspects. | Emigration and immigration--Social aspects.
Classification: LCC GN345 .M485 2017 (print) | LCC GN345 (ebook) | DDC
  304.8--dc23
LC record available at https://lccn.loc.gov/2016054959

British Library Cataloguing in Publication Data
A catalogue record for this book is
available from the British Library.

ISBN 978-1-78533-480-1 (hardback)
ISBN 978-1-78920-060-7 (paperback)
ISBN 978-1-78533-481-8 (ebook)

Contents

Illustrations

Acknowledgements

A number of scholars contributed ideas and effort to this project from its very outset. We are grateful, in particular, to Siew-Peng Lee, John McManus, Kira Allmann, Nayana Bibile, Paolo Boccagni, Kathrine Cagat, Jessica Chu, Guillaume Dumont, Yasmin Gunaratnam, Miia Halme-Tuomisaari, Ines Hasselberg, Haosen Hu, Annette Idler, Mari Korpela, Anna Lipphardt, Raluca Nagy, Sean O'Dubhghaill, Branwyn Poleykett, Marilou Polymeropoulou, Jonah Rimer, Joris Schapendonk, Valerio Simoni, Katja Uusihakala, and Katarzyna Wolanik-Boström. For their time and critical engagement, we are also indebted to Michaela Benson, Dace Dzenovska, Eric Meyer, David Mills, Jonny Steinberg and David Zeitlyn. We are especially indebted to the ideas, energy and commitment of Jamie Coates, who was a co-conspirator of the book project from the beginning. The manuscript has also benefited greatly from the input of Simone Abram and Alison Macdonald.

The book is the result of a collaboration between the European Association of Social Anthropologists Anthropology and Mobility Network (ANTHROMOB) and the University of Oxford's Centre on Migration, Policy and Society (COMPAS). At COMPAS, we received priceless support from Mikal Mast, Ida Persson, Emma Newcombe, Bridget Anderson, Michael Keith and Nicholas Van Hear, who was particularly instrumental in early planning discussions. We are thankful for the continual engagement of ANTHROMOB with this project, as well as for its important work on the themes of mobility and anthropology. We are also grateful for the support received from Pegasus Marie Curie (FWO) and Leverhulme Trust Early Career Fellowships, as well as HERA (Humanities in the European Research Area).

Berghahn Books have been exceptional in their support for this book project from its very outset, as well as its different stages of production. We would like to thank in particular Sasha Puchalski and Duncan Ranslem for shepherding reviewers and offering editorial suggestions, Caroline Kuhtz for copy-editing assistance, and of course Marion Berghahn herself for championing the idea throughout.

Finally, we want to thank the volume's authors, many of whom have now become research colleagues and friends, for their exciting ideas and their undying dedication to seeing this project through.

Studying Mobilities
Theoretical Notes and Methodological Queries

Noel B. Salazar, Alice Elliot, and Roger Norum

Xavier de Maistre was born in 1763 at the foot of the French Alps. At the age of twenty-three, he became fascinated by aeronautics. De Maistre and a friend fashioned a pair of giant wings out of paper and wire and planned to fly to America. They did not succeed. Two years later, de Maistre secured himself a place in a hot air balloon and spent a few moments floating above his native Chambéry before the device crashed into a pine forest. At the age of twenty-seven, while under arrest in a modest apartment room in Turin as the consequence of a duel, de Maistre pioneered a mode of mobility that was to make his name. In his *Voyage Autour de Ma Chambre* (A *Journey around my Room*), soon followed by *Expédition Nocturne Autour de Ma Chambre* (A *Nocturnal Expedition around my Room*), de Maistre proposes 'room travel', a way of being mobile that is infinitely more practical for those neither as brave nor as wealthy as the explorers. How does it work? Simply lock your door and change into your pyjamas. Without any need for luggage, walk to the various pieces of furniture in the room. Look at them through fresh eyes and rediscover some of their qualities. The story's moral: the mindset we journey with is far more important than the destination we travel to.

This historical anecdote serves to contextualize how mobility, as a concept-metaphor, captures the common impression that our lifeworld is in flux. Mobility, as de Maistre's story confirms, entails more than mere motion. It can be understood broadly as 'the overcoming of any type of distance between a here and a there, which can be situated in physical, electronic, social, psychological or other kinds of space' (Ziegler and Schwanen

2011: 758). As a complex assemblage of movement, social imaginaries and experience, mobility is infused with both attributed and self-ascribed meanings. In addition, de Maistre's narrative descriptions of his peculiar travel experience illustrate how people are moved by movement: emotional processes shape mobilities, and vice versa (Svasek 2012).

Mobility research calls attention to the myriad ways in which people, places, and things become part of multiple networks and linkages, variously located in time and space. Some scholars, mostly in sociology and geography, have drawn attention to a 'mobility turn' in social theory to indicate a perceived transformation of the social sciences in response to the increasing importance of various forms of movement (Urry 2000; 2007). The 'new mobilities paradigm' they propose incorporates novel ways of theorizing how people, objects, and ideas travel, by looking at social phenomena through the lens of movement (Hannam, Sheller, and Urry 2006). This can be seen as a scholarly critique of both theories of sedentarism and deterritorialization, trends in social science research that may confine both researchers and their object(s) of study.

Proponents of the 'mobilities paradigm' have also called for novel research methods that are concomitantly 'on the move' and 'simulate intermittent mobility' (Sheller and Urry 2006: 217). Proposed methods include, for example, interactional and conversational analysis of people as they move, mobile ethnography involving itinerant movement with people and objects, keeping of textual, pictorial or digital time–space diaries, various methods of cyber research and cyber ethnography, and so on (Sheller 2010: vii). While these methods are being increasingly deployed to understand mobility, critical reflections on their drawbacks are also emerging in parallel. Peter Merriman (2014), for example, has warned about some of the methodological pitfalls of mobility studies, questioning the underlying assumption that mobilities research is necessarily a branch of social science research, and highlighting the production of overanimated mobile subjects and objects such research tends to produce, its inherent prioritization of certain kinds of research methods and practices over others, and the over-reliance on specific kinds of technology.

Anthropologists, too, have taken a particularly critical stance of late towards the analysis of the contemporary world through the lens of mobility (Salazar and Jayaram 2016). Regardless of this position, many of the issues raised within mobility studies are relevant to current debates within anthropology, for instance regarding the role of ethnography in the study of mobile subjects and objects (Amit 2007). Despite the extensive literature on the instability of 'the field' and anthropologists' relationship to it (e.g. Gupta and Ferguson 1997), there has been little scholarship that speaks to the implications of this theorizing for methodological considerations such as participant–observation, the participant–research relationship, and the logistics, depth and breadth of data collection – or 'creation' (Lucht, this volume) – and of ethnographic thought.

The aim of this volume is to rise to the specifically methodological challenge that mobility-related research poses to our field(s). How can we, through our research, observation, and analyses, best capture and understand a planet in flux? What methods does a mobile world require us to design and reinvent? What are the challenges posed, and the possibilities offered, by novel methodologies of mobility to the production of engaged socioscientific theory and practice? As the chapters comprising this volume testify, the answers to these questions are not as straightforward as we may expect. Indeed, by bringing together scholars grappling with very different forms and scales of mobility, this volume reveals that engaging methodologically with mobility goes well beyond a mere methodological exercise, bringing to the surface issues of scale and ethics, geographic boundaries and social imagination, class and gender, material culture, and interdisciplinarity.

In this Introduction, we provide a background to the rich chapters to come, and the complex questions they pose, by reflecting on the multiple conceptual and methodological challenges that researchers – anthropological and otherwise – are facing when engaging with subjects, objects, and ideas 'on the move'. Using our own discipline's engagement with methodologies and mobility as a point of departure for our overview, but also moving beyond anthropology and disciplinary boundaries to develop a more adequate picture for the complex matter at hand, we reflect on the ways in which mobility acquires, and requires, specific forms of methodological thinking and acting.

A Moving Discipline

Ideas concerning mobility have a long history in anthropology. They are already present in late nineteenth-century transcultural diffusionism, which understood the movement of people, objects, and ideas as an essential aspect of cultural life. In a very different context, physical movement was a focus also of the first ethnographies of human dance, which, dating to the late nineteenth century, analysed the meaning of culturally derived movement and patterns through elaborate descriptions of steps, surfaces, and spaces. An important aspect of dance ethnography was (and remains) the ethnographer's participation in the dance itself, generating informed anthropological knowledge through intimate bodily practice (Davida 2011; Neveu Kringelbach and Skinner 2012).

However, the tendency throughout most of the discipline's history was to treat mobility as a concept describing physical or abstract movement, rather than as an ethnographic object in its own right, or something implying sociocultural change (or stasis) in and of itself (Salazar 2013). Human mobility was mainly understood as a defining characteristic of specific groups, such as hunter-gatherers or traveller-gypsies and, overall, the study of mobility remained subsumed under broad concepts such as class, social structure, kinship or geographic space. Anna Tsing remarks that 'if older anthropological frameworks were unable to handle interconnection and mobility, this is a problem with the frameworks and a reason for new ones but not the mirror of an evolutionary change in the world' (2000: 356). While Tsing is correct, it is equally important to note that there have been key technological and social changes that affect how people, things, and ideas move – even if such movement was present in other forms in the past.

Bronisław Malinowski is credited for moving anthropology beyond armchair philosophizing and putting notions of movement at the heart of ethnographic practice (Wilding 2007). In 1915–1916, Malinowski found himself stranded in the Pacific due to the outbreak of World War One. Prevented from returning to Europe (as with de Maistre, an exemplary case of 'involuntary immobility'), he embraced the opportunity to conduct research on the *kula* trading cycle of the Trobriand (now Kiriwina) Islands. Malinowski's participant-observation is often assumed to present the methodological ideal for studying a territorially bound culture (see Walton, this volume). But, as Paul Basu and Simon Coleman point out, 'in fact he was describing a "migrant world", albeit a very particular kind of one, where the significances of exchanges were articulated within an outwardly ramifying yet also confined sphere, constructed by the players in a system of exchange that spread across different islands' (2008: 322). Indeed, 'was Malinowski not a "multi-sited" ethnographer when he dealt with the Kula', Ghassan Hage asks, 'if all that is meant by multi-sitedness is this circulation between geographically noncontiguous spaces? Was he not an ethnographer of movement rather than stillness?' (2005: 467). From Malinowski's pioneering fieldwork onwards, the notion of ethnographers as itinerant and 'going somewhere' has been reinforced and reproduced.

Although the history of ethnography is thus intertwined with (technologies and practices of) travel, Claude Lévi-Strauss famously argued, after beginning *Tristes Tropiques* (1961) with the dictum 'Je hais les voyages et les explorateurs' ('I hate travelling and explorers'), that this has no place in the written work of anthropologists. Rather, he emphasized, travel should merely serve as a method to gather the empirical material necessary for writing ethnographies. In direct contrast to this, in his book *Routes,* James Clifford (1997) advocates for travelling as a way of doing ethnography; he argues that anthropologists need to leave their preoccupation with discovering the 'roots' of sociocultural forms and identities behind, and instead trace the 'routes' that (re)produce them. If our objects of study are mobile and/or spatially dispersed, being likewise surely becomes a form of participant-observation – 'fieldwork as travel practice', as Clifford (1997: 8) puts it. This is an approach to ethnographic fieldwork as a movement back and forth between desk and field, and as an ongoing translation between social and spatial locations (Gupta and Ferguson 1997).

Rather than focusing on the local anchorage of peoples and cultures, the notion of Clifford's routes points toward their mobility – their movements, encounters, exchanges, and mixtures. Malinowksi's work on the *kula* ring, for instance, becomes from this perspective an illustration of how people in Melanesia move through the places (i.e. things) that they cause to travel (Strathern 1991: 117). It is precisely this kind of thinking that finds further elaboration in Bruno Latour's (2005) actor-network theory, which transforms the social into a 'circulation', following actors in networks – something urban anthropologists have also been doing for some time now (Smart 1999; Wolch and Rowe 1992).

It is important to remember that anthropology also has a long tradition of research on (semi-)nomadic people, and that this so-called traditional field of study contributes in fundamental ways to a more general understanding of mobility. Take, for example, the now-canonized work of Edward Evans-Pritchard (1940) on the Nuer, which presented in striking ethnographic detail how the mobility of cattle herding generated both contact and conflict among transhumant individuals and groups unconstrained by settlement and compelled to follow the movement of the seasons. More recently, Joachim Habeck has proposed a shift in the perspective from the potential of movement (or motility) to mobility 'acted out' in order to 'obtain more nuanced insights in how nomads and transhumant herders see the world that surrounds them and how they interact with the surroundings while doing their work' (Habeck 2006: 138).

Methods on the Move

How, then, to study mobilities, which can be inherently transient and unstable? As Jo Vergunst writes, 'ethnography is an excellent way to get at important aspects of human movement, especially in relating its experiential and sensory qualities to social and environmental contexts' (2011: 203). But while notions of culture and its relationship to place have been dramatically revised in anthropology, ethnographic methods have been slower in catching up with changing objects of study (Olwig and Hastrup 1997). Given that traditional ethnography relied on a rather sedentary approach, with a tendency to privilege face-to-face relationships, permanent residence, and fixed boundaries while overlooking mediated interactions, movements, connections, and connectivity (Wittel 2000), ethnographic techniques have needed to be adapted and sometimes radically rethought to be of use in mobilities research.

A range of anthropologists have creatively innovated various modes of research in order to be able to productively use multiple movements within their field sites (see, e.g. Kirby 2009). In her study of the mobilities of an island community in Melanesia, for instance, Katharina Schneider adjusted four familiar ethnographic methods to the purpose of learning about movements: (1) employing the senses to detect movement; (2) paying attention to verbal as well as nonverbal expressions of movement; (3) moving along with people; and (4) strategically deploying the researcher's own movements and recording people's reactions (Schneider 2012: 17–19). In his research on how places in the Bolivian Andes become intertwined via circuits constituted by the movement of people, goods, and information, Stuart Rockefeller adds to the mix 'a dialectical approach to movement and efforts to control or constrain that movement' (2010: 27). This tension is also taken up by Birgitta Frello (2008), who analyses the discursive constitution of movement in the Danish media.

In his 'anthropology of movement', Alain Tarrius (2000) proposes a 'methodological paradigm of mobility' articulated around the space–time–identity triad, along with four distinct levels of space–time relations, indicating the circulatory process of migratory movements whereby spatial mobility is linked to other types of mobility (informational, cognitive, technological, and economic). What he describes as 'circulatory territories' are new spaces of movement that 'encompass the networks defined by the mobility of populations whose status derives from their circulation knowhow' (Tarrius 2000: 124). This notion reaffirms that geographical movement is always invested with social meaning.

Ethnographers have often been concerned with the movements of their interlocutors. As Marianne Lien (2003) points out, anthropologists' unease in relation to rapidly changing global connectivities may be understood as a direct result of the way their discipline has traditionally delineated its object of study in time (synchronic studies, the use of the ethnographic present) and in space (a community, a small-scale society). In other words, a discipline which builds its epistemology around one's immersion in a single place (over a period of a year or more, usually) can hardly be well suited to dealing with translocal connectivities and flows – at least not without some creative reimagining and innovation of this epistemology. The single-sited methodology, its sensibility and epistemological presuppositions, are by many in the anthropological community no longer felt to be adequate for the realities of an increasingly mobile, shifting, and interconnected world (Ong 1999).

To this end, Michaela Benson (2011) revisits the centrality of mobility to fieldwork methodologies which investigate mobile formations. She proposes a multi-faceted approach that embraces innovative thinking and flexible ways of building rapport with the subjects by engaging in mutual forms of everyday-life mobilities. There exists some excellent ethnographic work on everyday mobile practices (Wolch and Rowe 1992) and the actual processes of movement rather than the systems of mobility (*Journal for the Anthropological Study of Human Movement*; Ingold and Vergunst 2008). Here, much of the discussion on movement draws on nonrepresentational approaches that emphasize the importance of mobility not only as a defining feature of contemporary everyday geographies, but also in its capacity to transform social scientific thought – think, for example, of the way in which Tim Ingold (2004) has not only written extensively on the comparative anthropology of hunter-gatherer and pastoral societies, but also has offered a more general approach to human movement as a whole, and socioscientific thought about it, sensitive to embodied skills of footwork.

Ethnographies of mobility necessarily draw researchers into a multitude of mobile, material, embodied practices of making distinctions, relations, and places. Rarely is this more acutely experienced than through mobile video ethnography, 'where people's moves in interaction with others and their environments have to be anticipated by the positioning of the camera's viewfinder' (Büscher and Urry 2009: 105). The use of mobile technologies, especially for recording image, as well as soundscapes, is well established in anthropology. In the 1950s, for instance, the portable film camera reshaped ethnography's ongoing investigation and recording of 'exotic peoples' (e.g. the influential work of Jean Rouch; see Vium, this volume).

In the early days of such recording, the aim was to capture an objective representation of people's natural behaviour. Applications of these technologies are now 'more reflexive, participatory, and experimental and seek to capture on film the systems of signification of different cultural groups' (Lorimer 2010: 243). Film can approach the mobility of ordinary movement from a variety of vantage points and provide a way of creating ethnographic data collaboratively (Pink 2013). Employing mobile video ethnography, of course, requires engagement with a range of practical, epistemological, and ethical issues (Fincham, McGuinness and Murray 2010). For example, equipment choice, camera set-up and positioning, gaining access to and consent from participants, 'literacy' with respect to particular visual cultures, protecting the anonymity of 'incidental' participants, breaking the law on camera, and so on, are all key considerations when creating mediated narratives of observation and analysis. Indeed, digital 'record-ing' has now progressed far beyond techniques of audiovisual film/ing, as Daniel Miller's comparative anthropological projects on 'new' technologies and social media have shown (Horst and Miller 2012).

Follow Me

Mobility scholars track in various ways the many and interdependent forms of movement of people, images, information, and objects (Sheller and Urry 2006). Such approaches are not particularly new in anthropol-ogy; they were in large part what diffusionism was all about. This type of research is also linked to Arjun Appadurai's call three decades ago to 'follow the thing' – a method that is still very popular in the study of commodity chains and consumption. For Appadurai, following specific objects is important because 'their meanings are inscribed in their forms, their uses, their trajectories' (1986: 5). In his work, the focus on objects rather than people is a methodological intervention, not a theoretical one: 'even though from a *theoretical* point of view human actors encode things with significance, from a *methodological* point of view it is the things-in-motion that illuminate their human and social context' (1986: 5). Within studies of science and technology, scholars such as Latour (1987) have used a similar approach, studying how the interactions and movements of humans and nonhumans alike enact scientific realities (see also the Matsutake Worlds Research Group (2009) for cutting-edge work on the concept of 'following the thing').

Following 'things in motion', as Appadurai (1986) originally suggested, has proven a productive strategy for pursuing diverse empirical and theoret-ical concerns (see Österlund-Pötzsch, this volume, for an example of early 'following methods' employed in nineteenth-century ethnographic expe-ditions). 'Following' has taken two main methodological forms. The first, perhaps more immediately intuitive, mode of engagement with 'things in motion' requires the researcher to travel alongside the moving things that are being studied. The second mode, or form, of methodological engage-ment, draws on the researcher's observations, interviews, mapping, and other techniques of tracing aimed to capture the complex mobilities of the 'thing'. In the latter case, following things requires imaginative mobilities (cf. Walton's 'digital travel', this volume) and methodological and ana-lytical attention as much as it does physical travel. Though this approach may miss out on some detail of the mobilities involved, for various practical reasons it can provide a solid option when being co-mobile is not possible or desirable (Hui 2012). Julia Harrison (2003), for example, found that her desire to interview Canadian tourists in Hawaii was mitigated by their reluctance to give up their leisure time, and she opted to focus instead on the integration of travel experiences into the daily lives of tourists who had returned home. Another approach, with its own advantages and drawbacks, is auto-ethnography, employed for example by Shahram Khosravi (2007), who describes his own 'illegal' border-crossing journey from Iran to Sweden.

Studying mobility whilst remaining 'in place', so to speak, 'offers a type of perspective that is concerned more with the social organization of mobility than with particular circuits, more with a system than a place of origin or a specific destination' (Lindquist 2009: 10). Much ethnography of mobilities has been located at sites of passage, transfer points, where populations and things are temporarily contained and arranged within stations, waiting rooms and baggage systems (see Andersson, this volume). Mobility infrastructure, then, is being increasingly seen, no longer as 'non-place' (Augé 1995), but as 'the ideal place where an anthropologist can perceive, study, and even touch the various dynamic transnational and fluid sociocultural formations, literally in the making, from both below and above, and on the move' (Dalakoglou 2010: 146).

Although the value of remaining 'in place' when studying movement has received increasing recognition (a point we return to below), the first mode of engagement with mobility, built on the idea of following one's subject or object of study, often remains the most alluring methodological route for anthropologists of mobility. Anthropological studies of mobility conducted through multi-sited methods are generally less directly concerned with the physical traces of movement, but rather tend to re-examine the ontological status of the local and offer a more careful contextualization of sites within networks and flows across diffuse time space.

Mobile ethnography involves 'travelling with people and things, participating in their continual shift through time, place, and relations with others' (Watts and Urry 2008: 867). George Marcus's celebrated 'multi-sited ethnography' deals with the following of numerous objects of study, by tracing their 'chains, paths, threads, conjunctions, or juxtapositions' (1998: 90). According to Marcus, multi-sited ethnographies may focus on persons, things, metaphors, stories, allegories, or biographies. In her early work on Indonesia, Anna Tsing, for instance, abandons the fixed locale of the 'out-of-the-way' village to follow her interlocutors, whose communities can be understood only 'within the context of ... mobility – from daily visits to annual field movements to long-term trajectories across the landscape' (1993: 124).

It is worth keeping in mind that such multiple, multi-variant voyaging is nothing new in anthropology. As Cordula Weissköppel writes, for many years:

> mobile research, in the sense of a multi-sited strategy, existed alongside
> stationary fieldwork. It even flourished in the first half of the twenti-
> eth century as anthropologists, cultural relativists especially, required
> comparative data in order to back up their arguments with empirical
> evidence ... Later, Lévi-Strauss's many short trips to various countries
> and continents helped him demonstrate the universal character of
> the structures underlying patterns of behaviour and meaning systems
> (2009: 252).

Indeed, as mentioned above, traditional ethnography also 'gave rise in
practice to works which were as mobile and, in some senses, "multi-sited"
as the *Argonauts of the Western Pacific* or those arising from the Manchester
School's "extended case method"' (Candea 2007: 169–70).

Although Marcus (1998) promotes multi-sited ethnography as a way of
investigating culturally connected, but geographically dispersed, phenomena, he is less clear about how such investigations should take place 'on the
ground'. Clifford (1997: 57) has noted that there is a difference between
the concept of multi-sited ethnography and its implied practice of multi-
locale fieldwork; where the former recognizes the many locations of culture, the latter requires culturally cognisant field study in many locations.
This raises unresolved questions about whether one should spend less time
in each site (Lucht, this volume), and whether this implies forgoing some
of the depth often considered the main strength of ethnographic fieldwork
– crucial questions addressed by many of this volume's contributions. Nor
is it clear if one should apply the same criteria for 'good' fieldwork of traditional ethnography to multi-sited ethnography – an open query which
reveals how mobility may require us not only to think of new methodologies, but also to rethink the very methods through which we judge and
asses 'research' itself.

Alongside Coates, Andersson, Walton, and Leivestad (this volume),
Susan Frohlick (2006) has challenged notions of multi-sited methodology
that conceive it simply as a matter of systematically following the circulation
of people, objects, or practices within globalized worlds. Frohlick highlights, for example, how it is not always the researcher who follows mobile
interlocutors – sometimes it can be the latter who follows (or bumps into)
the researcher, in contexts other than the conventional field, leading to very
new understandings of both research participants and of the process of
research itself. Indeed, while from a certain point of view some multi-sited
work may be criticized as 'shallow jet-set ethnography' (Olwig 2007: 22), it
all depends on what one is actually researching, and on the ways in which
'the field' is allowed to intrude into one's methodological infrastructure.
Karen Fog Olwig, for example, argues that while her multi-sited ethnography of migratory family networks produced 'limited data on the local sites

where the research took place', it did nevertheless produce 'rich data on the family relations that were the actual field site' (2007: 23).

A number of methodological and theoretical efforts have been made to develop the by now near-classic multi-sited method to capture the mobile field. Marianne Lien (2003) suggests a complementary approach to the field, one based on multi-temporality, where instead of juxtaposing field sites that differ in space, she juxtaposes the configurations of a single field site as it differs over time. Vergunst (2011), on the other hand, seeks to reconcile the embodiment of ethnography in the (mobile) field with various technologies of field noting: paper, typing machines, laptops, audio and video recorders, GPS, digital applications, and so on. He also warns, however, that the excessive attention paid to high-tech devices employed in ethnographic and mobile practices tends to distance both ethnographer and participants from the immediate experience of movement which these research methods seek to seize in first place (cf. D'Andrea, Ciolfi and Gray 2011). And while ethnographers may be moving together with some people in physical space, their interlocutors' communication and movements in digital spaces are often not easily available – the recording, logging, and capturing of digital activities in combination with analysis of ethnographic experiences are one way of tracking and making sense of the multi-sited, collective or collaborative action of distributed mobile participants (Büscher, Urry, and Witchger 2011).

In sum, a mobile set of methods based on 'following' – broadly conceived – resonates among anthropologists, but such methods are never entirely free from a concern with the possible fragmentation of research they may entail (Sorge and Roddick 2012). As Matei Candea (2007) notes, it is useful to ask how much following is necessary, and whether too much of it detracts attention from the emplaced. However, as many of the contributions to this volume testify (see e.g. Vasantkumar, or Lucht), following need not come at the expense of emplaced research, and indeed the two may be combined for a more refined view on the scales along which sociocultural phenomena might articulate.

Weighing Scales

A fundamental methodological challenge that studies of mobility pose to anthropology is one of scale. Presenting the researcher with an inescapable quantity–quality nexus (Holbraad and Pedersen 2009; Strathern 1991), the concept of 'scale' at once encompasses and exceeds that of size and measurement (Tsing 2000). In the study of mobility, it has often to do with the presence or absence, and relative efficacy, of overarching institutions, networks, and processes, rather than with merely geographic

or demographic scope. Scale, in this sense, requires researchers to simultaneously focus on the macro-processes through which the world is becoming increasingly, albeit unevenly, interconnected, and on the way subjects
mediate these processes – it requires, in other words, what Noel Salazar
(2010) terms 'glocal ethnography' (and Michael Burawoy (2000) calls
'global ethnography'). Other methodological modes of engagement with
the issue of scale and mobility exist, from Anthony D'Andrea's 'nomadic
ethnography' – which he defines as 'a methodology that tries to integrate a nomadic sensibility toward routes and rituals of mobility, with a
notion of macro-ethnography that deploys methods of multi-sitedness and
translocality in context' (2007: 33) – to Sverre Molland's (2013) 'tandem
ethnography' – ethnography that allows a methodological oscillation
between the policy domain and the social world, which Molland proposes
as a solution to the methodological difficulties resulting from the destabili-
zation of bounded territory and 'sitedness'.

> Glocal, nomadic, tandem ethnography all represent attempts to
> develop a methodological 'double gaze', capable of capturing both
> descriptively the lived cultures with all their subtleties and analytically
> the global which structures them, both people's experiences and the
> social environment in which this experience is grounded, both the expe-
> riential surrounding that people are aware of and the macro-global
> structures that are well beyond their reach (Hage 2005: 474).

Indeed, according to Molland (2013), the task is neither to deconstruct nor
to essentialize 'site', but to investigate empirically what 'sitedness' means
to different actors, and how it becomes privileged in different contexts. As
such, the pivotal anthropological principle of comparison can be productively brought into fieldwork itself, and to mobility studies more generally,
hereby illuminating discrepancies and inconsistencies (Gingrich and Fox
2002).

Together with a major focus on comparison, the perspectives offered by
glocal, nomadic or tandem ethnographies, which Xiang Biao (2013) terms
'multi-scalar', lead also to a more nuanced understanding of the relation
between mobility, established institutions, and multiple ethnographic experiences. In Biao's words:

> Multi-scalar ethnography follows flows and connections, but more
> importantly traces people's concerns, calculations, and strategies. It
> seeks to explain why certain changes take place and others don't, and
> identify the interfaces between mobility and institutions where inter-
> ventions are feasible and productive. Multi-scalar ethnography does
> not at all discount the importance of sites, but articulates the meanings
> of sites to the actors ... [W]hat is at stake is not the expansion and

contraction of physical scope of mobility, nor the jumps up and down between pre given levels, or the actors' defiance of established boundaries. What matters is the creation of new scales. The emergent scale can be undefinable and unmappable in the given scalar schema (Biao 2013: 296–97).

Together with Mika Toyota, Xiang (2013) has presented important methodological experiments that explore the interfaces between individuals' migratory experiences and institutional, structural, and historical forces that are themselves constantly changing.

Such ethnographic approaches incorporate two major ways of addressing the conundrum of scale. First, they scale vertically ('scale up'), by providing close-grained studies of how a 'field' is connected locally, regionally, nationally, and globally (Rockefeller 2010). If the goal is deep system awareness, traditional fieldwork, and the method of participant-observation may be just the beginning, and will need to be reinforced with other, complementary ethnographic methods and conceptual tools. Gupta and Ferguson, for instance, call for introducing a multitude of 'other forms of representation' alongside fieldwork as it was traditionally understood in anthropology: 'archival research, the analysis of public discourse, interviewing, journalism, fiction, or statistical representations of collectivities' (1997: 38). The presence of these new types of material 'may require, and also provide openings for, new skills of composition and synthesis' (ibid). Vertical scaling can also include a multi-temporal (longitudinal or historical) dimension (Dalsgaard 2013).

The second strategy to deal with issues of scale is to scale horizontally ('scale out'), by including more than one site in an analysis. Multi-local or multi-sited research (Marcus 1995) might sometimes prove an inadequate description as many places are linked or networked to each other – what Ulf Hannerz calls a 'network of localities' or 'several fields in one' (2003: 21). A single site within a complex society may be conceptualized as a multiple one, whereas multiple localities can be seen as 'a single geographically discontinuous site' (Hage 2005: 463). Hannerz therefore advocates 'translocal' research (2003: 21), clarifying the nature of relations between localities. While the analytical entity may be translocal or glocal, fieldwork is unavoidably multi-local, because the ethnographer is always somewhere. Sally Engle Merry, on the other hand, proposes a 'deterritorialized ethnography' (2000: 130), not restricted to predefined sites, but rather one that follows patterns of circulation. Naturally, the more complex the levels of analysis become, the more necessary collaborative, interdisciplinary and creative research methods need to be (Coleman and Von Hellermann 2011). Such notions clearly open interesting questions for anthropology, a discipline that long distinguished itself from other modes of social scientific research by its very (rich, deep, empirical – and often highly individual) method. Indeed, it is precisely these sorts of questions that animate the contributions to this volume.

Moving Forward

As the chapters in this volume show, mobility can take myriad different forms. However, it is important to reiterate here that mobility research does not refer to a new subject of scholarly investigation, much less a new discipline. Rather, it directs new questions towards classic anthropological subjects. As this Introduction has outlined, and the chapters to come testify, mobilities – be they physical or digital – can be thought of as an entanglement of movement, meaning, and practice. The effects of these mobilities are multiple (and by no means necessarily beneficial); new boundaries are constructed even as borders are crossed, and such boundaries are multiple and multi-faceted. Mobility remains formidably difficult for many; sometimes more so than before. To understand mobility, we thus need to pay close attention also to immobility, to the structures (which, once again, shift and move in their own right) that facilitate certain movements and impede others (Salazar and Smart 2011).

How mobilities should be studied clearly remains a methodological and theoretical challenge. Anthropological methods in general have had a significant impact on mobility studies (D'Andrea, Ciolfi, and Gray 2011). While direct participation in analysing mobile practices is nothing new in anthropological research, what emerges as innovative in recent scholarship on mobilities is a concern with mobility as a *sui generis* mode of phenomena requiring particular methodological and conceptual work. As a polymorphic concept, mobility invites us to renew our theorizing, especially regarding conventional themes such as culture, identity, and transnational relationships (Glick Schiller and Salazar 2013; Salazar 2011). Interestingly, mobilities research remains rather methodologically homogenous, with a focus on qualitative studies and few examples of quantitative studies or mixed-method approaches (Ricketts Hein, Evans, and Jones 2008). Despite the long tradition, 'the impact of movement (and motility) upon a researcher's own research remains largely unproblematized at the level of analytical representation' (D'Andrea, Ciolfi, and Gray 2011: 154). For one, the often exhausting nature of multi-sited travelling remains undiscussed (Hage 2005). This is why, with this volume, we aim to broaden the terms of methodological engagement with mobility, as well as initiate a constructive reflection on the challenges and possibilities of the methods of mobility.

Over the past few decades, numerous anthropologists have criticized the discipline's traditional approach to ethnographic fieldwork (Faubion and Marcus 2009). However, despite the effort spent moving the ethnographic imagination into 'shifting locations' (Gupta and Ferguson 1997) and 'non-places' (Augé 1995), most models of fieldwork still evoke the ethnographer's entry into a discrete 'field' (Hume and Mulcock 2004). If beginning scholars receive any methodological training at all (Stocking 1992: 14), they are being taught that medium- to long-term participant-observation (alone) is and should remain the norm. In addition to dictums about the necessity of (and time required for) cultural and linguistic immersion, this is also inherently linked to the epistemic value of serendipity (Rivoal and Salazar 2013). This, as suggested above, stems from the idea that anthropology as a discipline only distinguishes itself from other disciplines by virtue of its methodology. Even Marcus shies away from endorsing a 'thinner' model of ethnography by suggesting that field study, although framed by a 'multi-sited imaginary', should for the moment remain a 'site-specific, intensively investigated, and inhabited scene of fieldwork' (1998: 15). Mobile fieldwork that does not fit disciplinary norms – or worse still, mobility-related projects without any field component – can be easily marginalized within anthropology. There may, at times, be good reasons for such deviations. However, what is often forgotten in such disciplinary identification with fieldwork is that the crucial, fundamentally ethnographic, question anthropology should be compelled to ask, and that the volume contributors explicitly, and indeed boldly, address, is how to make meaningful research whilst allowing research problems to guide which methods we use. And not the other way around.

Sociocultural anthropologists are well equipped to challenge the assumptions embedded within much current mobility theory. Founding fathers such as Franz Boas and Bronisław Malinowski, while perhaps ignoring the extent to which their own epistemological project was predicated on their own mobility, showed how the liminal positioning of anthropologists among the humanities and social sciences, with constant methodological and theoretical boundary crossings, offers promise for a fruitful holistic and grounded ethnographic analysis. Anthropology – with its interest in holism and scale, methodical scepticism, and focus on the primacy of ethnography – holds the potential to act as a catalyst for the establishment of novel horizons in the study of mobility, bringing different fields together in creative ways. As the chapters of this volume show, a processual, collaborative, and creative ethnographic focus enables anthropologists to document the many ways in which mobility transforms social life, both for 'movers', 'stayers', and those in-between.

'Methodologies of mobility' here become more than mere technicality, but rather a gateway to radically rethink mobility, its protagonists, and our continual engagement with them. Rethink is the operative word here, but such rethinking should not be seen as a means of doing away with so-called traditional, bread-and-butter ethnographic method. Rather, the 'experiment' employed in the title of this volume refers precisely to the chapters' experimental engagement with classic anthropological, and broader social-scientific, methodologies (from participant-observation, to snowball sampling, to archival research). Even if anthropology's traditional(ist) roots long maintained rather fixed ideas about what proper ethnography should entail – and what type of research card-carrying ethnographers should (and should not) engage in – the ethnographic methods used by even the early anthropologists were always experimental, and necessarily so. This holds true even if anthropologists, themselves perpetually (self-)conscious of the contested 'scientific' nature of their discipline's core methodology, may have been less ready to embrace the necessarily exploratory or untested nature of many ethnographic research tools. But reflective work on the discipline's experimentation with ethnographic method – and its intrinsic theoretical potential – is emerging (e.g. Estalella and Criado, forthcoming; Marcus 2013; Berghahn's *Ethnography, Theory, Experiment* book series). Indeed, the reflective writing in this volume speaks explicitly to a need within the social sciences more broadly to be continually rethinking and reimagining what investigative research methods are and what they can do.

The Chapters

The opening chapter of the volume provides a historical perspective on the themes outlined in this Introduction. Susanne Österlund-Pötzsch delves into historical records of Finnish–Swedish ethnographic expeditions at the turn of the nineteenth century and reveals how mobility was at the methodological and sociopolitical heart of these trips. Drawing on fieldwork diaries of folklore collectors, Österlund-Pötzsch traces the extensive physical mobility of these early ethnographers throughout the vast Finnish countryside in search of Swedish-speaking peoples and traditions. In doing this, she shows how 'mobile methods' were not only constitutive requirements of these culture-collecting endeavours, but also fundamentally contributed to the creation of a Swedish-speaking 'ethnic group' in Finland in the cultural and national imagination of the time. Moving between contemporary theoretical perspectives and historical archives, Österlund-Pötzsch traces the deep social, political, and cultural implications of research methods in general, and of methodologies of mobility in particular.

Hege Høyer Leivestad also uses, in her chapter on the materiality of mobile homes, a peculiar form of archive-as-method, albeit of a different, contemporary, kind. Drawing on ethnographic fieldwork among British caravan dwellers in Spain, Leivestad introduces 'the inventory' as a specific research technique for studying social spaces constituted by complex layers of mobility and immobility. She traces how a co-created inventory of mundane objects and materials inside the caravan provides crucial insight in the material and social life of (im)mobile homes. In doing so, she powerfully draws our attention to the materiality of mobility, or 'mobile materiality', and the complex role it plays in contemporary forms of social, spatial, and imagined mobility. Interrogating the very analytical category of 'mobility', Leivestad argues that creative methodological techniques such as 'home inventories' reveal how the potential mobility of specific materials and objects – for example, the wheels of caravans – constitutes continual fodder for imaginaries of mobility.

Chris Vasantkumar also reflects on the concept of dwelling, in his discussion of mobile methods and their theoretical underpinnings. Vasantkumar draws, in particular, on the work of Tim Ingold, and his influential proposal of treating anthropological practices of dwelling as themselves mobile methods. In doing so, Vasantkumar offers both a conceptual tour de force on newly visible mobilities emerging in contemporary anthropological fieldwork, and a careful analysis of the specific ethnographic case of the Tibetan diaspora, whose members have increasingly lived as 'exiles in their own homeland'. It is through the peculiar existential and (im)mobile case of the Tibetan diaspora that Vasantkumar foregrounds the itinerancy of 'place' itself – both in methodological and theoretical terms. Indeed, attention to mobile methodology emerges here not only as a mobilization of new anthropological fieldwork techniques, but also as in-depth reconsideration of its very traditional objects, tools and loci.

It is precisely on questions of objects, tools, and loci that Ruben Andersson focuses his contribution. Relating to his work on what he calls 'the illegality industry', Andersson unpacks the distinctive methodological challenges raised by a phenomenon characterized by conflictive mobilities and immobilities and spanning multiple countries, contexts and domains – 'illegal' migration between West Africa and southern Europe, and those measures used to control and contain it. Explicitly drawing on the classic Manchester School 'extended case method', Andersson charts an original methodological perspective based on the idea of the 'extended field site', and shows how such methodological framing can bridge migrants' lifeworlds and the 'macro' features of a system. Arguing for a form of mobile fieldwork at the 'borderline' between groups and disciplines, Andersson proves how creative methodologies become crucial pathways for studying complex, dispersed, and mobile systems in the contemporary world.

Developing further Andersson's point on the crucial importance of 'strategic locations' in mobility research, the chapter by Jamie Coates, based on fieldwork with Chinese migrants in Tokyo, shows how picking a locale and 'staying put' is at times the best strategy for capturing those whose lives are transient, busy, and even hidden. Conducting 'immobile research' in a small Chinese hair salon in Tokyo, Coates traces how, from lunchtime businessmen, to afternoon students and late night adult entertainers, this tiny space served as a plateau of conviviality among Chinese migrant lives in the city, while also enabling Coates to weave a patchwork of mini-ethnographies within a single Tokyo neighbourhood. Coates shows how 'multi-sited' fieldwork often occurs within field sites as much as between them, and that due to the embodied limitations of the ethnographic researcher, staying in one place (what Coates terms 'strategically situated idleness') can reveal much about the movement in the city and beyond.

'Staying put' – for example, with a seemingly ineffective research assistant – emerges as a key 'mobilities method' also in the chapter by Hans Lucht. Looking back with a reflexive and critical eye at his ten years of research into transnational migration between Africa and Europe, Lucht writes about the methodological concerns, challenges, and possibilities this specific form of human mobility produces for the researcher. In engaging the virtues (and limitations) of classic socioscientific research methods, such as snowball sampling and reliance on local research assistants, he traces the fragmentation of his subjects across regions and continents to consider how social networks can be mined as fodder for research questions. Championing serendipity and embracing the 'forms of disturbance' inherent in fieldwork, Lucht calls attention to the value of simply 'waiting around' with research interlocutors in contexts of intense and multi-layered mobilities, mining 'breakdowns' in fieldwork for their own epistemic value and espousing the virtues of wading through unknown social waters.

Shireen Walton engages in a similar kind of recursive conversation between field and method in her chapter on Iranian photo bloggers. Walton addresses the dictum of geo-spatial (co-)presence that has long been mythologized as a defining aspect of anthropological fieldwork. In rethinking the various landscapes of 'the field', she shows that limited physical access for the researcher can present less a predicament of 'immobility' than an opportunity for methodological innovation. Walton's proposed methodology relies on physical and digital movements, both of which are rooted in the practices and circulations of

Iranian digital photography, her research 'subject'. In co-curating with her interlocutors a digital photography exhibition, Walton showcases the ability of 'remote' methods to build connective proximity to geographically dispersed research subjects, the virtue of developing site-specific methods, and the multiple layers of digital ethnographic investigation. In so doing, she reminds us that impactful ethnographic work can indeed take place in tandem with the development of new forms of methodological creativity.

The closing chapter, by Christian Vium, also draws on the method of photography to delineate novel horizons for mobility research and 'collaboration' in methodology and theory. Returning to the theme of transnational migration addressed by Andersson and Lucht, Vium shows how photography is a privileged methodology for analysing such a difficult, elusive, and ethically complex 'field'. Through empirical examples of 'interventions' in significant migratory nodal points, Vium argues that the camera can incite new forms of performative storytelling processes and discourses. Indeed, Vium suggests that the collaborative dialogue arising around the production of photographic images plays a crucial part in 'fixating' a 'fluid' context, rendering it comprehensible to both ethnographer and migrant. It is in this sense that Vium agitates for an approach to photography that acknowledges the inherently interventional nature of ethnographic fieldwork, which is able to open up to a more reciprocal, participatory, and enactive form of research of, on, and in mobility.

Finally, in her afterword, Simone Abram reflects on the promises (and pitfalls) of the very concept of mobility – in particular its potential for generating and informing modes of critical, comparative study. In doing so, she stresses the continued importance of manifold forms of immobility in, and to, mobility research, arguing that immobility and mobility need not be binarily opposed to one another, and that nuanced methodologies of understanding each are key in an increasingly complex and spatially politicized world of movement.

Noel B. Salazar is Research Professor at the University of Leuven. He is editor of the *Worlds in Motion* and *Anthropology of Tourism* book series, co-editor of *Keywords of Mobility* (2016), *Regimes of Mobility* (2014) and *Tourism Imaginaries* (2014), and author of *Momentous Mobilities* (2018), *Envisioning Eden* (2010) and numerous other publications on mobility. Salazar is secretary-general of the International Union of Anthropological and Ethnological Sciences and founder of the EASA Anthropology and Mobility Network.

Alice Elliot is Lecturer in Anthropology at Goldsmiths, University of London. Her research focuses on Morocco, Tunisia, and Italy, and she writes on the social and intimate dimensions of Mediterranean migrations, gender and mobility, Islam, kinship, and political imagination.

Roger Norum is an anthropologist based at the University of Leeds. He studies the changing roles of mobility, social exchange, and the environment, particularly among transient and precarious communities in both the European Arctic and South Asia. His recent books include *Political Ecology of Tourism: Communities, Power and the Environment* (Routledge 2016).

REFERENCES

Amit, V. (ed.). 2007. *Going First Class? New Approaches to Privileged Travel and Movement*. Oxford: Berghahn.

Appadurai, A. 1986. *The Social Life of Things: Commodities in Cultural Perspective*. Cambridge: Cambridge University Press.

Augé, M. 1995. *Non-Places: Introduction to an Anthropology of Supermodernity*, trans. J. Howe. London: Verso.

Basu, P., and S. Coleman. 2008. 'Migrant Worlds, Material Cultures', *Mobilities* 3(3): 313–30.

Benson, M. 2011. 'The Movement Beyond (Lifestyle) Migration: Mobile Practices and the Constitution of a Better Way of Life', *Mobilities* 6(2): 221–35.

Biao, X. 2013. 'Multi-Scalar Ethnography: An Approach for Critical Engagement with Migration and Social Change', *Ethnography* 14(3): 282–99.

Biao, X., and M. Toyota. 2013. 'Ethnographic Experiments in Transnational Mobility Studies,', *Ethnography* 14(3): 277–81.

Burawoy, M. (ed.). 2000. *Global Ethnography: Forces, Connections, and Imaginations in a Postmodern World*. Berkeley: University of California Press.

Büscher, M., and J. Urry. 2009. 'Mobile Methods and the Empirical', *European Journal of Social Theory* 12(1): 99–116.

Büscher, M., J. Urry, and K. Witchger. (eds). 2011. *Mobile Methods*. London: Routledge.

Candea, M. 2007. 'Arbitrary Locations: In Defence of the Bounded Field-Site', *Journal of the Royal Anthropological Institute* 13(1): 167–84.

Clifford, J. 1997. *Routes: Travel and Translation in the Late Twentieth Century*. Cambridge: Harvard University Press.

Coleman, S., and P. Von Hellermann (eds). 2011. *Multi-Sited Ethnography: Problems and Possibilities in the Translocation of Research Methods*. London: Routledge.

D'Andrea, A. 2007. *Global Nomads: Techno and New Age as Transnational Countercultures in Ibiza and Goa*. London: Routledge.

D'Andrea, A., L. Ciolfi, and B. Gray 2011. 'Methodological Challenges and Innovations in Mobilities Research', *Mobilities* 6(2): 149–60.

Dalakoglou, D. 2010. 'The Road: An Ethnography of the Albanian–Greek Cross-Border Motorway', *American Ethnologist* 37(1): 132–49.

Dalsgaard, S. 2013. 'The Field as a Temporal Entity and the Challenges of the Contemporary', *Social Anthropology* 21(2): 213–25.

Davida, D. (ed.). 2011. *Fields in Motion: Ethnography in the Worlds of Dance*. Waterloo, ON: Wilfrid Laurier University Press.

Estalella, A. and Criado, T.S. 2017, forthcoming. *Experimental Collaborations: Ethnography through Fieldwork Devices*. Oxford: Berghahn.

Evans-Pritchard, E.E. 1940. *The Nuer: A Description of the Modes of Livelihood and Political Institutions of a Nilotic People*. Oxford: Clarendon Press.

Faubion, J.D., and G.E. Marcus (eds). 2009. *Fieldwork Is Not What It Used to Be: Learning Anthropology's Method in a Time of Transition*. Ithaca: Cornell University Press.

Fincham, B., M. McGuinness, and L. Murray (eds). 2010. *Mobile Methodologies*. New York: Palgrave Macmillan.

Frello, B. 2008. 'Towards a Discursive Analytics of Movement: On the Making and Unmaking of Movement as an Object of Knowledge', *Mobilities* 3(1): 25–50.

Frohlick, S. 2006. 'Rendering and Gendering Mobile Subjects: Placing Ourselves between Local Ethnography and Global Worlds', in S. Coleman and P. Collins (eds), *Locating the Field: Space, Place and Context in Anthropology*. Oxford: Berg, pp 87–104.

Gingrich, A., and R.G. Fox (eds). 2002. *Anthropology, by Comparison*. London: Routledge.

Glick Schiller, N., and N.B. Salazar. 2013. 'Regimes of Mobility across the Globe.' *Journal of Ethnic and Migration Studies* 39(2): 183–200.

Gupta, A., and J. Ferguson (eds). 1997. *Anthropological Locations: Boundaries and Grounds of a Field Science*. Berkeley: University of California Press.

Habeck, J.O. 2006. 'Experience, Movement and Mobility: Komi Reindeer Herders' Perception of the Environment', *Nomadic Peoples* 10(2): 123–41.

Hage, G. 2005. 'A Not So Multi-Sited Ethnography of a Not So Imagined Community.' *Anthropological Theory* 5(4): 463–75.

Hannam, K., M. Sheller, and J. Urry. 2006. 'Editorial: Mobilities, Immobilities and Moorings', *Mobilities* 1(1): 1–22.

Hannerz, U. 2003. 'Several Sites in One', in Thomas Hylland Eriksen (ed.) *Globalisation: Studies in Anthropology*, trans. Daniel Winfree Papuga. London: Pluto Press, pp 18–38.

Harrison, J.D. 2003. *Being a Tourist: Finding Meaning in Pleasure Travel*. Vancouver: UBC Press.

Holbraad, M., and M.A. Pedersen. 2009. 'Planet M: The Intense Abstraction of Marilyn Strathern', *Anthropological Theory* 9(4): 371–94.

Horst, H.A., and D. Miller (eds). 2012. *Digital Anthropology*. London: Berg.

Hui, A. 2012. 'Things in Motion, Things in Practices: How Mobile Practice Networks Facilitate the Travel and Use of Leisure Objects', *Journal of Consumer Culture* 12(2): 195–215.

Hume, L., and J. Mulcock. 2004. *Anthropologists in the Field: Cases in Participant Observation*. New York: Columbia University Press.

Ingold, T. 2004. 'Culture on the Ground: The World Perceived through the Feet', *Journal of Material Culture* 9(3): 315–40.

Ingold, T., and J.L. Vergunst (eds). 2008. *Ways of Walking: Ethnography and Practice on Foot.* Aldershot: Ashgate.

Khosravi, S. 2007. 'The 'Illegal' Traveller: An Auto-Ethnography of Borders', *Social Anthropology* 15(3): 321–34.

Kirby, P.W. (ed.). 2009. *Boundless Worlds: An Anthropological Approach to Movement.* Oxford: Berghahn.

Latour, B. 1987. *Science in Action: How to Follow Scientists and Engineers through Society.* Cambridge: Harvard University Press.

_____. 2005. *Reassembling the Social: An Introduction to Actor-Network Theory.* Oxford: Oxford University Press.

Lévi-Strauss, C. 1961. *Tristes Tropiques*, trans. John Russell. New York: Criterion Books.

Lien, M.E. 2003. 'Shifting Boundaries of a Coastal Community: Tracing Changes on the Margin', in T.H. Eriksen (ed.). *Globalisation: Studies in Anthropology.* London: Pluto Press, pp vi, 236.

Lindquist, J.A. 2009. *The Anxieties of Mobility: Migration and Tourism in the Indonesian Borderlands.* Honolulu: University of Hawai'i Press.

Lorimer, J. 2010. 'Moving Image Methodologies for More-Than-Human Geographies', *Cultural Geographies* 17(2): 237–58.

Marcus, G.E. 1995. 'Ethnography in/of the World System. The Emergence of Multi-Sited Ethnography', *Annual Review of Anthropology* 24: 95–97.

_____. 1998. *Ethnography through Thick and Thin.* Princeton: Princeton University Press.

_____. 2013. 'Experimental forms for the expression of norms in the ethnography of the contemporary'. *Hau: Journal of Ethnographic Theory* 3(2): 197–217.

Matsutake Worlds Research Group. 2009. 'A New Form of Collaboration in Cultural Anthropology: Matsutake Worlds', *American Ethnologist* 36(2): 380–403.

Merriman, P. 2014. 'Rethinking Mobile Methods', *Mobilities* 9(2): 167–87.

Merry, S.E. 2000. 'Crossing Boundaries: Methodological Challenges for Ethnography in the Twenty-First Century', *Political and Legal Anthropology Review* 23(2): 127–34.

Molland, S. 2013. 'Tandem Ethnography: On Researching "Trafficking" and "Anti-Trafficking"', *Ethnography* 14(3): 300–23.

Neveu Kringelbach, H., and J. Skinner (eds). 2012. *Dancing cultures: Globalization, tourism and identity in the anthropology of dance.* Oxford: Berghahn.

Olwig, K.F. 2007. *Caribbean Journeys: An Ethnography of Migration and Home in Three Family Networks.* Durham: Duke University Press.

Olwig, K.F., and K. Hastrup (eds). 1997. *Siting Culture: The Shifting Anthropological Object.* London: Routledge.

Ong, A. 1999. *Flexible Citizenship: The Cultural Logics of Transnationality.* Durham: Duke University Press.

Pink, S. 2013. *Doing Visual Ethnography*, 3rd edn. Thousand Oaks: Sage Publications.

Ricketts Hein, J., J. Evans, and P. Jones. 2008. 'Mobile Methodologies: Theory, Technology and Practice', *Geography Compass* 2(5): 1266–85.

Rivoal, I., and N.B. Salazar. 2013. 'Contemporary Ethnographic Practice and the Value of Serendipity', *Social Anthropology* 21(2): 178–85.

Rockefeller, S.A. 2010. *Starting from Quirpini: The Travels and Places of a Bolivian People.* Bloomington: Indiana University Press.

Salazar, N.B. 2010. 'From Local to Global (and Back): Towards Glocal Ethnographies of Cultural Tourism', in Greg Richards and Wil Munsters (eds), *Cultural Tourism Research Methods.* Wallingford: CABI, pp 188–98.

_____. 2011. 'The Power of Imagination in Transnational Mobilities', *Identities: Global Studies in Culture and Power* 18(6): 576–98.

_____. 2013. 'Anthropology', in P. Adey, D. Bissell, K. Hannam, P. Merriman, and M. Sheller (eds), *The Routledge Handbook of Mobilities.* London: Routledge, pp 55–63.

Salazar, N.B., and K. Jayaram (eds). 2016. *Keywords of Mobility: Critical Engagements.* Oxford: Berghahn.

Salazar, N.B., and A. Smart. 2011. 'Anthropological Takes on (Im)Mobility: Introduction', *Identities: Global Studies in Culture and Power* 18(6): i–ix.

Schneider, K. 2012. *Saltwater Sociality: An Ethnography of Pororan Island, Bougainville (Papua New Guinea).* Oxford: Berghahn.

Sheller, M. 2010. 'Foreword', in B. Fincham, M. McGuinness, and L. Murray (eds), *Mobile Methodologies.* New York: Palgrave Macmillan, pp vii–x.

Sheller, M., and J. Urry. 2006. 'The New Mobilities Paradigm.' *Environment and Planning A* 38(2): 207–26.

Smart, A. 1999. 'Participating in the Global: Transnational Social Networks and Urban Anthropology', *City & Society* 11(1–2): 59–77.

Sorge, A., and A.P. Roddick. 2012. 'Mobile Humanity: The Delocalization of Anthropological Research', *Reviews in Anthropology* 41(4): 273–301.

Stocking, G.W. 1992. *The Ethnographer's Magic and Other Essays in the History of Anthropology.* Madison: University of Wisconsin Press.

Strathern, M. 1991. *Partial Connections.* Savage: Rowman & Littlefield.

Svasek, M., (ed.). 2012. *Emotions and Human Mobility: Ethnographies of Movement.* London: Routledge.

Tarrius, A. 2000. *Les Nouveaux Cosmopolitismes: Mobilités, Identités, Territoires.* Paris: Editions de l'Aube.

Tsing, A.L. 1993. *In the Realm of the Diamond Queen: Marginality in an Out-of-the-Way Place.* Princeton: Princeton University Press.

_____. 2000. 'The Global Situation', *Cultural Anthropology* 15(3): 327–60.

Urry, J. 2000. *Sociology Beyond Societies: Mobilities for the Twenty-First Century.* London: Routledge.

_____. 2007. *Mobilities.* Cambridge: Polity Press.

Vergunst, J. 2011. 'Technology and Technique in a Useful Ethnography of Movement', *Mobilities* 6(2): 203–19.

Watts, L., and J. Urry. 2008. 'Moving Methods, Travelling Times', *Environment and Planning D: Society and Space* 26(5): 860–74.

Weissköppel, C. 2009. 'Traversing Cultural Sites: Doing Ethnography among Sudanese Migrants in Germany', in Mark-Anthony Falzon (ed.), *Multi-Sited Ethnography: Theory, Praxis and Locality in Contemporary Research*. Farnham: Ashgate, pp 251–70.

Wilding, R. 2007. 'Transnational Ethnographies and Anthropological Imaginings of Migrancy', *Journal of Ethnic and Migration Studies* 33(2): 331–48.

Wittel, A. 2000. 'Ethnography on the Move: From Field to Net to Internet', *Forum: Qualitative Social Research* 1(1).

Wolch, J.R., and S. Rowe 1992. 'On the Streets: Mobility Paths of the Urban Homeless', *City & Society* 6(2): 115–40.

Ziegler, F., and T. Schwanen. 2011. '"I Like to Go out to Be Energised by Different People": An Exploratory Analysis of Mobility and Wellbeing in Later Life', *Ageing and Society* 31(5): 758–81.

'Few Are the Roads I Haven't Travelled'

Mobility as Method in Early Finland-Swedish Ethnographic Expeditions

Susanne Österlund-Pötzsch

Working with archival material presents challenges both similar to and different from those facing ethnographers engaging in contemporary fieldwork. An obvious problem that arises when dealing with historical material is that we cannot go back in time to collect additional information when we run into gaps, ambiguities, or unanswered questions (see e.g. Fenske 2007: 89–90). We can, however, try to increase our knowledge about archival sources in other ways. For example, studying the logic of the archive and how its collections have been compiled and organized can help us to put the material into context (Stoler 2002: 99–101). When it comes to archival institutions that collect and create material through fieldwork, such as ethnographic and folklore archives, this aspect tends to be crucial. In most cases, the researcher studying historical fieldwork material is interested in a different set of questions than those of the original collector. It is not merely a matter of academic fields being theoretically and methodologically mobile and that research questions change according to paradigms and trends, but also that seemingly similar research questions will take on different meanings in changing contexts over time and space. Consequently, conducting fieldwork in a historical field calls for an awareness of several layers of methodologies, ideologies, and power relations that might have influenced the composition of the collection (see e.g. Fenske 2007: 75–76, 89; Lennartsson 2010: 58). In this respect, the past is indeed a foreign country, where things are done differently (cf. Lowenthal 1985). 'Visiting' this country, the past, calls for a different kind of mobility than one offered by strictly physical movement.

This chapter builds on the critical analysis of historical fieldwork material, namely, fieldwork diaries kept by Swedish-speaking Finnish folklore collectors during collecting expeditions in the late nineteenth and early twentieth centuries. The theme of mobility as methodology is investigated on different levels. I suggest that mobility was central to the methodology and aspirations of these early ethnographers in several respects. Firstly, travel was an inevitable feature of the expeditions, as collectors traversed the countryside in search of unique items of folklore. Secondly, more localized and repeated movements became an integral part of the collectors' toolbox of methods, as they discovered the importance of following their informants in everyday tasks. Thirdly, the theme of mobility played another significant (but less obvious) role in the work of the collectors. Analysing the expeditions in light of the social, linguistic, and political climate in which they took place, reveals, I suggest, that the movements of folklore collectors across the Finnish countryside influenced and contributed to the consolidation of a Swedish-speaking 'ethnic group' in Finland, while simultaneously performing an 'othering' of the countryside population (Österlund-Pötzsch 2014). Fourthly, on yet another level, mobility, albeit of a kind involving considerably less physical exertion than what it required of my historical interlocutors, constitutes a crucial key to my own research methodology (see Introduction, this volume; see also D´Andrea, Ciolfi, and Gray 2011: 153); in this chapter, not only do I trace the itineraries and methods of the early folklore collectors, but also strive to move between an understanding of the historical context and present-day analytical perspectives.

In the Nordic countries, as elsewhere in Europe during the nineteenth century, the interest in folk culture was closely connected with the process of nation building. As Finland could neither draw upon a long history as a nation-state nor a cultural treasure of written literature in the majority language (Finnish), oral literature received special attention. During the time of autonomy under the Russian Empire (1809–1917), 'folk culture' became an important building block in the creation of a Finnish proto-nation.[1] In the eyes of many, an expedition in the Finnish countryside to collect folk poetry was tantamount to an act of patriotism.[2] Particularly during the latter part of the nineteenth century, it was not uncommon for students to undertake walking trips in order to collect folk culture, visit places of historical interest or study the national flora. Increasingly, walking trips were made not only for scholarly purposes but also for the enjoyment of hiking. Holidays on foot were heavily promoted as a sound activity and a way of learning more about one's own country and one's fellow countrymen. August Ramsay, an early and active proponent of Finnish domestic tourism, wrote in 1891 that 'the person who wants to get to know his country and its people, and this is a patriotic duty, should in order to gain insight go on a walking trip'[3] (Ramsay 1891: 64).

Several decades after Finland had been separated from Sweden (1809), Swedish was still the language of those in power, although the majority of the population was Finnish-speaking. Leading Finnish politicians and intellectuals, many of whom were Swedish-speaking, felt that the only way to secure and develop Finland as a nation was to strengthen the status of the Finnish language. Therefore, the interest in folklore collection in Finland initially did not extend to the folk culture of the country's Swedish-speaking rural population. However, during the latter part of the nineteenth century, there was a growing concern among members of the Swedish-speaking educated classes regarding the survival of Swedish culture in Finland. Until then, there had been no sense of common identity among the country's Swedish-speakers.[4] The upper and lower classes had minimal contact, and the Swedish-speakers were further divided among themselves by geography, culture, and linguistic difference and dialects. In the wake of the successful pro-Finnish movement, it became apparent that the small but influential group of the Swedish-speaking upper class now needed 'the common people' in order to substantiate the claim to the continued existence of a Swedish-speaking culture in Finland.[5] As in many nation-building projects, folk culture was employed as an adhesive in the consolidation process between the Swedish-speaking upper and lower classes.

On the Road

In 1860, the Swedish-speaking student society in Helsinki began offering small travel grants to students who intended to document local traditions in Swedish-speaking areas of Finland. This work was continued and expanded from 1885 onwards when the Society of Swedish Literature in Finland (Svenska litteratursällskapet i Finland) was founded. The collected folklore material had to be accompanied by a travelogue in which the fieldworker accounted for chosen methods and how the work had progressed, among other observations. A manual issued in 1887 by the Folklore Committee of the Society of Swedish Literature instructs the collectors to always include the place and time for each notation as well as the name of the person providing the information. However, no further personal details (such as age or occupation) were asked for. Consequently,

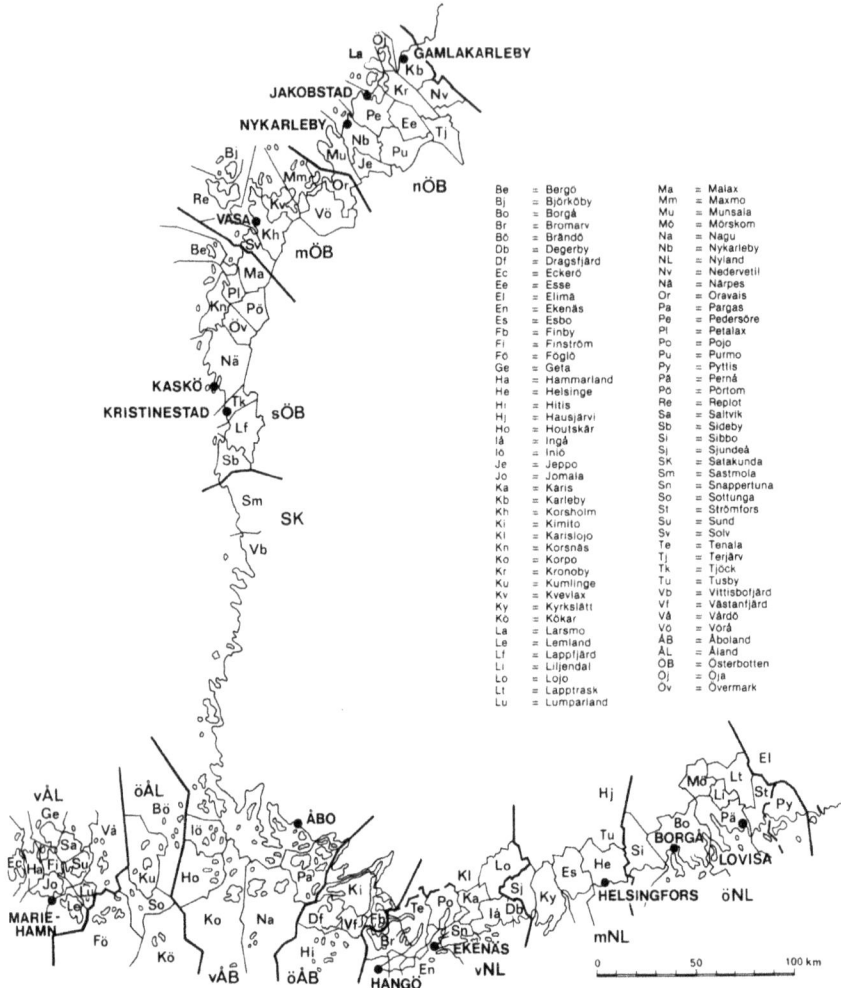

Figure 1.1 Map of all Swedish-speaking municipalities in Finland. Courtesy of the Society of Swedish Literature in Finland.

early collectors generally provided little information on the 'representatives of the folk' they had been in contact with. It was the ancient treasures of folk poetry that were of primary importance, not the individual 'tradition bearers' themselves.

Adhering to the guidelines, the reports over time became shorter and less motley. Whereas later travelogues mention very little about the details surrounding the fieldwork,[6] a number of the early collectors briefly refer to their mode of travelling. In order to reach the fieldwork destinations, collectors frequently had to walk long distances, though this in and of itself was nothing unusual in the late nineteenth century. The quotidian nature and matter-of-factness of these circumstances are one reason the collectors paid relatively little attention to their own movements and travels. Indeed, there was no particular reason for them to do so, as the mobility of the fieldworker was not a relevant research field at the time (cf. Frello 2008: 30; D'Andrea, Ciolfi, and Gray 2011: 154).

Nevertheless, bodily movement was an absolute necessity for the task of collecting folklore and assessing the language situation in all Swedish-speaking and bilingual regions in the country. The distances to be covered were often long and arduous. Several of the collectors describe using bicycles to facilitate their travels. The young student Filip Sundman noted with a hint of pride in his travelogue, 'on my bicycle I traversed Tenala in all directions: few are the roads I have not travelled' (SLS 72[7]). However, biking on poor roads and in difficult weather conditions was hardly less strenuous than lengthy hikes on foot. The collector Probus Karlsson wrote that he used his bicycle where the 'roads permitted' and walked the rest of the distance (SLS 79), while Maximilian Stejskal reported that his bike suffered no fewer than seventeen punctures while he was trying to take a shortcut through a bog (SLS 397). In the archipelago along Finland's west and south coast, the collectors used rowing boats to visit their informants. Isak Smeds recounted in his travelogue that '[in the archipelago] I rowed from skerry to skerry and from island to island and met Swedish-speakers on most islands' (SLS 7). It is clear that fieldwork was often physically demanding for the folklore collectors. Therefore, it is not surprising to find that the aforementioned Filip Sundman offered to produce a document certifying his healthy bodily constitution in his application for a fieldwork grant in 1899 (SLS Office Archives, board minutes 18 May 1899). Some of the more dedicated collectors seem to have pushed themselves to extremes. The assiduous collector V.E.V. Wessman, for example, who during a period of twenty years collected folk culture nearly every summer, wrote in a letter to the chair of the Folklore Committee that he could only manage five consecutive weeks of fieldwork before he became severely exhausted.[8] He explained that, when in the field, he worked relentlessly from early morning to late evening, often without breaks for food or rest. According to another letter, it was not unusual for him to work for sixteen or seventeen hours per day (Herranen 1986: 228). Despite despairing at times over his work, Wessman later described the days he wandered around in the Swedish-speaking countryside as the 'happiest of his life'. He added, 'it was always with a certain wistfulness that I ended my summer travels ... I still feel a sense of restlessness in my body when the summer comes around: I want out, out into the countryside to the simple, honest people' (SLS 1113). Despite complaints about the hardships, the on-the-road lifestyle clearly

Figure 1.2 Studio photograph of the folklore collector V.E.V. Wessman, posing with his bicycle and notebook. Photo by Natalia Linsén, courtesy of the Society of Swedish Literature in Finland.

attracted Wessman and many of his fellow collectors who embarked on repeated expeditions.

The general public took an interest in the folklore collectors' travels and the local papers reported on the results of the more extensive expeditions as well as on who had received grants for upcoming expeditions. For example, under the headline 'A harvest of fairytales and folk songs' the newspaper *Hufvudstadsbladet* reported that, 'Mr Wefvar has passed through our city [Vaasa] on his way home after having spent five months in the parishes of Närpes and Lappfjärd, diligently occupied with the collection of fairy tales, folk songs, traditions and so on. The tireless collector ... has collected 129 fairy tales and many folk songs in the local dialects, he has made notations of 50 melodies to folk songs and memorized another 25'. The newspaper commented on the achievement by adding that, 'one can hereby see that such findings can also be made in our Swedish-speaking districts, as long as a love for the endeavour and the aptitude to gain the confidence of the people are embodied in the person who visits the generally hospitable, tidy, and decent homes of our Swedish country folk' (*Hufvudstadsbladet* 28 April 1875). The statement reflects not only the romantic ideal of the honest and hardworking farmer, but also the wish to underline that, besides Finnish-speaking folklore, there was also folklore of Swedish-speakers to be found in Finland (Österlund-Pötzsch and Ekrem 2009).

On the whole, early collectors gave more detailed descriptions of their travels (and, indeed, travails) than what later became the norm among grant recipients. In the early travelogues, lists of the villages, parishes, and islands visited were a standard feature. The quote below from the travelogue of Selim Perklén gives the impression of a conscientious fieldworker trying both to cover as many places as possible and to make sure the result of the research – collected folklore – was rich and plentiful:

> I left Helsinki on 27 May [1892] and steered my course first towards Sjundeå, where I took up residence in the middle of the parish, in Purnus ... in the beginning of July I undertook my first trip to Kyrkslätt. Here, and likewise in Ingå parish, I had no specific place of residence but wandered around in the district. First I walked from the border of Esbo through the whole parish and made notations of fairy tales in Masaby and Ingvaldsby as well as taking down a few folk songs and riddles in Korkkulla and Hindersby. Walked on down to Kantvik and Strömsby and continued the journey by rowing boat to Svinö in Sjundeå, where I stayed for a few days and visited the neighbouring islands Kalfö and Vormö among others ... From the archipelago I walked through Pikkala and north of Viksträsk past Käla, Ängisby and Kynnar back to the vicinity of Sjundeå church. During this walk I had the opportunity to take down a few folk songs, words and superstitions etc.

After having written down the fairy tales 19, 20, 21, 22, and 23 as well as transcribing the harvest I had received so far, I made another trip to Kyrkslätt, this time to the northern part of the parish. I thus walked to Näsby, Bläsaby, and Andby in Sjundeå, where the folktales 59, 60 and 62 as well as some folk songs were taken down. The trip continued to Pettjärvi, where the folktales 26, 27 and 28 were told. From Pettjärvi I walked on to Kylmälä, Lappböle, and Leivasböle, where folk songs, especially, were taken down. From Leivasböle I returned by the way of Evitsskog and Karskog in Sjundeå to my place of residence, Purnus. In Evitsskog I took down the folktale 24. The harvest during this trip was by far richer than the previous one, as the civilization in these latter parts is still quite unknown. ... My intention was to walk from Strömsby to Porkkala, but I was informed that Dr Vendell had spent considerable time in the vicinity of Porkkala, and I therefore supposed that he had harvested everything of value. In this connection I want to emphasize that I during my collection of fairytales have not visited those persons whom I know the previous grant recipients student G. Lindström and *Magister* Wefvar visited. (SLS 26)

This was movement with purpose. As suggested by Birgitta Frello (2008: 29), movement cannot be understood outside the cultural meaning ascribed to it. Here, the extensive walking of the collector was a performance of the urgency and worthwhileness of a cause. The ambition was to cover all Swedish-speaking districts and to find all existing specimens of various folklore genres, and there was a belief that this endeavour was possible. 'Much is done but much still remains, as the aim is to gather all folklore', one newspaper commented a public lecture on folk poetry collection in 1890 (*Borgåbladet* 2 April 1890, 1). The same year, another newspaper, reporting on the collecting activities of the Swedish Dialect Society in Helsinki, stated that 'such work is with proliferating diligence continued without fail, and one can therefore safely predict that it will not be long before the hitherto unexplored Swedish-speaking districts in Finland will have been researched' (*Land och stad* 12 February 1890). The work was clearly seen as being finite – albeit pressing – carried out in what was believed to be the very last hour before folk culture would finally succumb to modernity. While the mobility of collectors was hailed and encouraged, the mobility of people was perceived as a threat (cf. Salazar 2010: 54) as traditional folk songs were being replaced by modern songs introduced by returning migrants and through increasing contacts with people outside the community. Another worry was Swedish-speaking youth's mass migration to North America, which had a considerable impact on many communities, especially in the province of Ostrobothnia and on the Åland Islands.

Figure 1.3 Pearls on a string. A few of Selim Perklén's collecting trips, summer of 1892. Map: Janne Rentola.

In the early twentieth century, folk-culture collectors had covered most of the Swedish-speaking districts (geographically an area of approximately 6,500 square miles) and a substantial collection of folklore material had been accumulated. It was becoming increasingly difficult to find new items of genres favoured by folklore scholarship, such as older folk songs and fairytales. As early as 1889, the schoolteacher and collector Henrik Ståhl noted in his travelogue that people in northern Ostrobothnia were familiar with ethnographic work due to the many collectors who had previously traversed the region (SLS 10). Experienced collectors, such as previously mentioned Wefvar and Wessman, recounted with contentment that they had visited every Swedish-speaking parish in Finland (The Tritonia Academic Library, letter from Wefvar to Rancken 14 May 1876; SLS Archives, Wessmann SLS 1113).

Movement as Method

These early collectors learned through trial and error and were met with varying success in their mission. Over time, as the practice of collecting folklore became professionalized, the instructions from the Folklore Committee became more specific and the collectors, more often than not, were no longer amateurs but experts in their fields and connected with the university or other teaching institutions. Many, though certainly not all, of the folklore collectors were students at the Imperial Alexander University in Helsinki. They came from a wide range of social backgrounds, although many of the initial collectors had an upper-class upbringing. Several of the collectors grew up in farming communities and were familiar with the countryside. Even so, for many, their fieldwork still entailed meeting people and engaging in practices with which they would not otherwise have had contact. The mobility of the collectors was not only geographical but also a matter of moving between social groups and classes.

The issued fieldwork instructions specified that folklore collectors should strive to 'primarily keep to the more remote and isolated villages, e.g. the attention should be directed to the outskirts of civilization' (*Förhandlingar och uppsatser 3* 1887: 103) as it was believed that old folk poetry and archaic customs had best been preserved in such places due to the perception of these places as frozen in time. Consequently, collectors often wrote about the degree to which the communities they visited were touched by civilization. Additionally, regions where the Swedish language was seen as threatened by the dominance of Finnish were considered a priority. The folk music researcher Alfhild Forslin, who collected for the Literature Society for many years, later observed that the Folklore Committee often encouraged their grant recipients to visit linguistic border regions (e.g. between Swedish- and

Finnish-speaking groups of people) but that the result from these regions, at least from her own experience, often turned out to be meagre in terms of material (Forslin 1976: 58).

The narrative style represented in the travelogues, especially in those of early collectors, was similar to that of the archetypical 'new world' explorer: the more exotic the traditions and the more remote the location, the more valuable the result was envisioned to be. Folk culture was regarded as proof of the long presence of Swedish-speaking culture in Finland (Bergman 1981). It became, furthermore, a way to bridge the gap between social classes. The collector's meeting with 'the people' was in itself a manifestation of this ambition. The successful folklore collector transcended boundaries and had access to both worlds. At the same time, the travelogues were often structured with binary oppositions between the mobile researcher and the static rural communities (cf. Vasantkumar, this volume, on the categories of mobile and immobile). However, this was in many cases more a trope of ethnographic literature rather than strictly true. In fact, many of the Swedish-speaking regions were far from immobile. There existed a long tradition of labour migration in Ostrobothnia, and on Åland, as well as along the south-eastern coastal regions; seafaring and trading across the Baltic Sea was a vital part of the local economy.[9] Nevertheless, as this excerpt from the fieldwork diary of Janne Thurman attests, the communities visited were often depicted as remote, isolated, and stationary (cf. Greverus 2003: 20; Salazar 2013).

> On the 27th of September [1889] I left the villages, accompanied by the memory of a warm welcome. The inhabitants and I had during our long time together become friends. They gave me their vernacular, their fairytales, while in the evenings, I told them about events from the history of the Fatherland, events from the world outside: 'If only the work will be good so that the fine gentlemen will be pleased' were the last words that reached my ears as I walked away with my pack. (SLS 13)

The description is filled with contrasts, juxtaposing the immobile with the mobile. The student Thurman takes on the role of a messenger, setting immaterial heritage in motion by delivering the frozen ancient treasures from the villages back to the 'fine gentlemen' in the capital and, in return, bringing stories from the outside world to the villagers. The collector thus portrayed himself as the true hero of the scenario. The villagers and the 'fine gentlemen' are, in this particular instance, equally locked in their locations – it is the mobile fieldworker 'walking away with his pack' who acts as a bridge builder between two different social environments.

On other occasions, collectors were met with open distrust by the countryside population. Towards the turn of the twentieth century, Russian policy towards Finland grew more aggressive. There was a great deal of suspicion regarding the intentions of unknown individuals, such as itinerant folklore collectors, as there was considerable fear of Russian spies. Alfons Takolander, who during the summers of 1898 and 1899 collected folklore on Åland, initially experienced great difficulty in convincing locals to share information:

> The population was sometimes reserved, suspecting that my notes about place names had some kind of connection to that I was 'working as a mole'. ... Regardless of how bitter it felt to be doubted, one could regardless be content to note how alert, how mindful and careful the population was even in these remote parts. A continued exchange of thoughts and a closer mutual acquaintance soon brought us closer, so that I gained their trust and the work could be carried out without disturbances. (SLS 70)

Consequently, collectors often had to work hard to win over their informants. A crucial part of the fieldwork was to overcome the dubiousness ascribed to community outsiders. The collector Karl Fredrik Juselius was able to use his own background as a farmer as a way of successfully connecting with the locals, when doing fieldwork in a very concrete sense of the word:

> In Pyttis I came along for threshing the rye at the farm of L. Wiiala in Kvarnby. Harvesting peas, stacking potato tops to dry etc. was work in which I often took part and [thus] tried to get close and through informal relations extract what I was looking for. Usually I was initially addressed as *magister* [Master of Arts/teacher], but when I explained in the manner of a country person that I was a farmer and not even an undergraduate, the knot was tied and the tobacco pouch produced accompanied by the words 'did you bring a pipe along too, then help yourself if you smoke tobacco leaves', and that I did and then we were as one people. (SLS 55)

In his seminal work on folk culture and landscape, Kent Ryden observes that folk boundaries arise from a strong sense of the local past, but also from the present daily round of living (Ryden 1993: 70). Although not all of the collectors were accepted as warmly as the farmer Juselius, many of them found that spending a longer period of time with the villagers and joining them in their everyday tasks was a good way of gaining their confidence. The teacher Isak Smeds, one of the very first beneficiaries of the Literature Society's grants, revealed that he made a point, in his mission to collect dialect words, of following locals in their work. Consequently, he joined them on the boats during fishing expeditions, to the hay meadows during harvest time and to the fields when it was time for ploughing (SLS 7).

The collector Selim Perklén describes that, in as much as was possible, he 'joined the people in various work' in order to take notes, but that he also made numerous excursions in the neighbourhood (SLS 26). Although the relevance of 'walking, not just talking' (Pink 2009: 21; see also Leivestad, this volume) has been long central to fieldwork methodologies, the early collectors had no formal training in fieldwork. However, the more success-ful among them seem to have employed a range of fieldwork techniques, including mobile practices, that yielded good results (see Vergunst 2011). The activity of 'following' did not only pertain to everyday life but could also involve a preparedness to embrace unusual circumstances and unexpected situations. For example, the energetic folk-tradition collector Maximilian Stejskal wrote that, during a shorter visit in the archipelago, he had joined a search for a man who had killed himself. Most of the fishermen in the community had gathered for the search party and Stejskal took the oppor-tunity to ask each participant about their knowledge of traditional games. 'The result was satisfactory', he succinctly commented in his travelogue (SLS 397). Reading the fieldwork diaries, one is left with the impression that the end result in terms of folklore notations was sometimes understood as justifying the means.

Much of the time, the collection work was based on the principle of 'learning by doing'. The devoted and attentive collector soon discovered which techniques gave the desired results in fieldwork. Going out of one's way to visit a potentially knowledgeable informant was a strategy among the more prolific of the collectors. The young female collector Vivi Peters seems to have had a natural inclination for fieldwork. On one occasion she describes visiting a small cottage away from the village and how she soon forgot all about the strange and filthy place that initially startled her, once an old woman living in the cottage started telling her stories. Peters noted in her fieldwork diary that 'experience told me that what a collector needs to be first and foremost is cheerful. Cheerful people are welcome every-where, and especially in the countryside' (SLS 277). She recounted a visit to a woman in the archipelago who had told her that she enjoyed talking to 'young miss' who was not 'uppity' but that she had not cared to talk to other collectors who had previously visited since they just 'sat at the head of the table and looked solemn'. Peters concluded that, 'It is much better to sit on the kitchen bench with the old women than to be treated like the parson during a household examination' (SLS 277). The widely travelled and industrious collector V.E.V. Wessman also took precautions so as not to come across as a 'fine gentleman'. He dressed simply, behaved unpreten-tiously and did not make reference to his education and social standing (as a teacher). In doing so, he was successful to the degree that he was at times taken for a vagrant – and often ended up living like one. In his unpublished memoirs he described sleeping in barns, in haystacks, in lice-infested beds, on kitchen benches and floors, under a large spruce and by the church wall (SLS 1113). For some of the collectors the road did, temporarily, become their home.

Movement as Performance of Space

Early folklore scholarship assumed a connection between places and the character of the people who lived there. Places were seen as separate entities and as arenas for human action. People were thus described as shaped by the locations in which they lived (Selberg and Gilje 2007: 13). Some of the collectors used the surrounding landscape to categorize not only people they met in their fieldwork, but also the particular types of folklore one could expect to find there. Johan Torckell, for example, writes in his fieldwork diary about the folk songs he collected on the Åland Islands in 1894:

> Naturally, also the exterior nature has here, as elsewhere, exercised its influence on the content and construction of the folk songs, and the melodies conform to a certain degree with the surrounding nature. A person from the mainland will thus find the melancholic and mournful basic sound of the Finnish folk song generally exchanged for a more happy, jaunty and lively mood. (SLS 40)

The folklorist Leiv Sem has pointed out that travel reports written by early Norwegian folklore collectors were often attempts to define national identity and national culture as well as the emerging disciplines of folkloristics and ethnology (Sem 2011: 53, 57). The same observation can be made about Swedish-speaking Finnish folklore collectors, whose travelogues often contain attempts to analyse and chisel out the character of people they met in different communities.[10] Right from the start there had been an additional aspect to the folklore expeditions – that of educating the people and informing them of the larger cause of preserving Swedish-speaking culture in Finland. In other words, the purpose of the expeditions was not solely to collect folklore, but also to collect Swedish-speakers. By being visited, people, and locations were brought into spheres of interest and literally placed on the map. There was mutuality in this, and although the informants may have feared ridicule from the educated upper classes, the majority seemed to have been pleased by collectors' interest and were happy to share their knowledge of traditions and customs. Through the practices and movements of the fieldworking folklorists, a Swedish-speaking folk culture map was brought into existence.

The interest in cartography and cultural regions was manifested early on within the disciplines of folkloristics and ethnology in the Nordic countries. The geographical tracing of traditions was far from unique to the Society of Swedish Literature in Finland but reflected Nordic folklore scholarship at large (Storå 1983: 23-24, Bringéus 2008: 160). However, the linguistic and political interests of mapping folk culture in this way gave the venture special applicability in the case of Swedish-speaking Finland. Maps are not empty mirrors, and they at once hide and reveal the hand of the cartographer (Pile and Thrift 1995: 48). While the fixating of cultural traditions on maps had scientific underpinnings, the practice simultaneously communicated a desire to organize and control space (Germundsson 2008: 111-13). The work of completing archive collections of different folklore genres and ensuring that no district was neglected was purposefully pursued during the first half of the twentieth century. Somewhat ironically, the result of this persistent work – the many cultural-geographical maps produced in the 1930s and 1940s – tended to emphasize the regional cultural differences between Swedish-speaking areas rather than indicating any intrinsic Swedish-speaking cultural commonality (Lönnqvist 1981: 70, 74). By this time, the cartographic approach to studying folk culture was already perceived as outdated. The disciplinary interest had moved away from quantitative to qualitative methods and materials. Yet, through the continued practice of collection expeditions, 'Swedish-speaking Finland' had been produced as a social experience and in this way become firmly established as a 'mappable' entity. While the borders between the Finnish and Swedish languages were evidently unstable and impossible to permanently delineate, the contours of a Swedish-speaking space emerged through the mobile fieldworks.

Many of the collectors reported having been remarkably thorough in their efforts to make sure they 'harvested' everything of interest. Movement, here, is taken as proof of the quality of the fieldwork. In their travel diaries collectors describe 'constantly wandering from village to village' and 'visiting every village and as good as every farm' (Alfons Iakolander SLS 69) and 'going in and out of houses like a peddler' (Henrik Kullberg SLS 201). Arguably, the encounters on a personal level this method of collection gave rise to had a galvanizing effect on the growing sense of a united 'Finland-Swedishness'. A vision of the world – a social imaginary (Taylor 2004: 23; Salazar 2012: 866) – was in effect being 'fieldworked' into public perception. By walking between villages and spending time with locals, the collectors became acquainted with rural populations in different parts of the country, at the same time that rural people became aware of the interest in folk culture and the Swedish-language question. 'It was immediately obvious that the ground was already prepared for the documentation of local traditions – the interest was aroused', Vivi Peters commented regarding her fieldwork on the island of Kimito in 1916. 'I was welcomed everywhere by happy countenances, and as soon I started talking with the old ladies they put the coffee pot on the stove' (SLS 277).

As observed by Salazar, Elliot, and Norum (this volume) as well as Andersson (this volume), the discussion continues unabated on whether multi-sited ethnography, and what kind of multi-sited methods, constitute the best ethnographic strategy to deal with the mobility, networks, and unboundedness of people. The folklore collectors of this chapter were more interested in the permanence, rather than the mobility, of their informants. However, without making mobility a significant research category (cf. Welz 1998: 192), the larger undertaking of gathering Swedish-speaking folklore in Finland was multi-sited in the sense that the fieldwork took the collectors to many different locales within the frame of the same study. Moreover, the process of documenting folk culture in this manner, in conjunction with the existing politico-social mobilization around the Swedish language, came to alter the understanding of the field itself. As 'the field' became an embodied reflection of the linguistic agenda and rhetoric of the time, the folklore collectors' itineraries tied together places and people – recalling what Hage describes as a 'single geographically discontinuous site' (Hage 2005: 465), or Andersson's 'extended fieldsite' (this volume). Increasingly, the expeditions were perceived not only as movement between places, but as movement within a single (Finland-Swedish) space.

Conclusion: Methodology of Mobility in Historical Materials

The fieldwork expeditions carried out in the decades around the turn of the twentieth century in Swedish-speaking regions in Finland did not comprise mobility research as it is understood in the contemporary sense. At the time, there was no intrinsic research value accredited to mobile methods. The communities visited were considered static and the travelling of the collectors was, simply, what was required to reach them, and thus was taken for granted. The purpose of these expeditions was clear: to collect the best examples of traditional folk culture and preserve them for posterity. This was perceived as a rescue operation in the final hour, as the old folkways had no place in modern life. Nonetheless, the various modes of mobility the fieldworks incorporated were not only central to the outcomes of the expeditions, but also had a social impact. Although it was a matter of several different collectors working during different times and in different locations (sometimes even taking care not to cross paths), these 'fields' were linked by a social imaginary, giving the venture of collecting all

Swedish-speaking folklore in Finland meaning and direction for the collectors, the funding institutions, and the general Swedish-speaking public. It was a project entailing 'several fields in one' (Hannerz 2003: 21), and for a specific cause. The sojourning and travelling on the part of the early folklore collectors were social practices that contributed to the emergence of a sense of a separate Swedish-speaking group regardless of social class.

Focusing on the theme of mobility in historical fieldwork diaries demonstrates how movement was a key feature of early ethnographers' work. On a pragmatic level, travelling was an inevitable part of the fieldwork, reflecting the mind-set and methodology of the time. Scholarly interest was directed towards the most remote and exotic locations. Moreover, the priority was to move on to the next location in order to find as many unique samples as possible, rather than doing in-depth studies of a particular place or person. On a more abstract level, and seen in light of the linguistic-political concerns of the time, the mobility of the fieldworkers appears as a community-building project and a claiming of (ethnic) space. Here, mobility was both a method in and a result of an ambition to establish a (Finland-Swedish) field.

An important but infrequently explored issue in mobile ethnography concerns the 'waves' set in motion by fieldwork. What are the implications of the fieldworker's contact with the groups of people under investigation? What traces are left by the fieldworkers and what stories do their itineraries tell? While a self-reflexive approach (see e.g. Caplan 1988: 12; Clifford and Marcus 1986) in modern ethnography (potentially) pays attention to short-term influences of the fieldworker's own mobility, any long-term effects can only be observed from a historical perspective. What might be suggested here is a temporal multi-sited ethnography that combines, contrasts, and moves between different kinds of historical sources and sites (Fenske 2007: 88), but one that also focuses on the relationship between sites in time, to reach a broader understanding of them (cf. Marcus 1995: 111).

In my study of fieldwork practices and mobile methods of the past, I was originally interested in the micro-perspective of the individual fieldworkers' experiences of mobility and the physical act of walking while in the field – it was, however, in the movement between the micro- and the macro-perspectives and between 'then' and 'now' that the combined impact of the multiple folklore expeditions started to reveal themselves to me. The call for self-reflexivity and decentring of analysis applies equally to historical fields (Lüdtke 1989: 14), and it is clear that my own interpretation of the early fieldwork diaries inevitably hinges on my own position in time and my awareness of the process of constructing Finland-Swedishness in the twentieth century. Studying mobility as method in a historical material, then, implies drawing attention to the dynamic interplay between one's own locality and mobility – both in temporal and spatial terms – in relation to the locality and mobility of the field.

Susanne Österlund-Pötzsch is an archivist and a folklorist affiliated (as docent) with Nordic Folkloristics at Åbo Akademi University, Turku. Her research includes everyday life, performance, food culture, island studies, and various aspects of mobility, such as migration and everyday walking practices.

NOTES

1. As a result of the Finnish War (1808–1809), Sweden lost much of its eastern stretches – present-day Finland – to Russia. Between the years 1809 and 1917 (when Finland gained independence), Finland was an autonomous part of the Russian Empire. Although Finnish was the majority language in Finland, Swedish was still the language of education, culture and administration. In 1880, Swedish-speakers constituted just over 14 per cent of the population. Developing and promoting the Finnish language was an important part of the work to expand Finnish independence. Members of the Swedish-speaking educated class took leading roles in this movement.
2. Collections of Finnish folk poems were already published during the latter part of the eighteenth century. However, the expeditions that were to become especially significant for the Finnish National awakening were those carried out by Elias Lönnrot during lengthy walking journeys in the 1820s and 1830s. Based on his vast collection of folk poems, Lönnrot compiled the Finnish national poem *The Kalevala* (first published in 1835). Particularly during the latter part of the nineteenth century, *The Kalevala* not only inspired researchers to undertake collecting expeditions and walking trips in the Finnish countryside, but it also became fashionable among artists, writers, and intellectuals to make pilgrimages to the district of Karelia, which had by then come to be seen as the cradle of Finnish culture. (On walking practices as a way of performing national identity, see Österlund-Pötzsch 2013.)
3. All translations from Swedish to English are the author's own.
4. Before 1914, when the term 'Finland-Swede' was coined, there was no common designation for Swedish-speakers in Finland.
5. Important to note in this context is that the proponents of the pro-Swedish movement in Finland felt themselves equally patriotic and dedicated to the Finnish nation as the pro-Finnish movement.
6. The folkloristic and ethnological tradition of fieldwork is both similar to and different from the 'classic' anthropological fieldwork. In general, the disciplinary tradition of anthropology developed in nations with colonies, whereas in countries without a strong colonial presence, as in Scandinavia, the disciplinary traditions of ethnology and folkloristics tended to focus on the 'primitives within' (see e.g. Frykman and Löfgren 2003: 2–3). However, also in the latter case the 'coloniza-

tion' aspect was present in the sense of bringing the more remote regions under the control of the nation (Sem 2011: 52). The early folkloristic fieldwork referred to in this chapter focused on gathering as many good quality samples as possible of the particular genre(s) asked for. These notations were the real purpose of the fieldwork and other ethnographic descriptions and observations were considered a side product. Consequently, the folklore collectors tended to move on to the next village when they felt that the repertoire was exhausted in one place. Any in-depth immersion in the community visited was not yet of interest (although many of the collectors were in fact locals and well familiar with the communities they visited). Many collectors did include ethnographic descriptions in their fieldwork diaries, although these were not specifically asked for by the fieldwork funders (in this case the Society of Swedish Literature in Finland).

7. The archive number (here, SLS 72) refers to the individual collection archived at the Society of Swedish Literature in Finland. The travelogues quoted in this chapter are archived together with the material (mostly folklore notations) from the fieldwork they describe.

8. As pointed out by Ghassan Hage (2005: 465), extensive travelling on the part of the fieldworker is one of the hazards of mobile fieldwork and can, in fact, lead to exhaustion and the inability to do efficient work also for the modern-day fieldworker.

9. For example, the collector Mårten Thors notes in his travelogue that the youth in many Ostrobothnian parishes spent their Sundays writing down the words to folk songs. Many of the folk songs were of Swedish origin and had been introduced by young people who during the summers found work in Sweden – across the Bothnian Sea (1891, SLS 19). Neither 'the folk' nor the folklore tended to be as static as they were portrayed in nineteenth-century scholarship.

10. Moreover, the particular life circumstances of people in different localities were seen to be reflected in the dominant folklore genres. The dangerous seafaring life of the inhabitants on the Åland Islands explained the local inclination for religious folk songs, as Torckell noted:

> Especially numerous are the so-called spiritual songs or folk songs with a religious content. A main feature of the Ålandic person's character is the strong religiosity. His adventurous life on the capricious seas, where he is often exposed to life threatening danger and where he risks his immediate death in the furious waves, has created a strong feeling of his own inferiority and powerlessness and a consequent need to entrust his life in the protection of a higher power. (SLS 40)

REFERENCES

The Archives of Folk Culture/SLS Archives, The Society of Swedish Literature in Finland, Helsinki.
Karl Frederik Juselius, 1896 (SLS 55)
Probus Karlsson, 1901 (SLS 79)

Henrik Kullberg, 1912 (SLS 201)
Vivi Peters, 1916 (SLS 277)
Selim Perklén, 1891 (SLS 26)
Isak Smeds, 1888 (SLS 7)
Maximilian Stejskal, 1929 (SLS 397)
Henrik Ståhl, 1882–1890 (SLS 10)
Filip Sundman, 1899 (SLS 72)
Alfons Takolander, 1898 (SLS 69)
Alfons Takolander, 1899 (SLS 70)
Johan Torckell, 1894 (SLS 40)
Mårten Thors, 1891 (SLS 19)
Janne A. Thurman, 1889 (SLS 13)
V.E.V. Wessman, 1973 (SLS 1113)

Bergman, A. 1981. 'Nyländska avdelningen och Svenska litteratursällskapets folkloristiska insamlingsverksamhet 1860–1908', in I. Nordlund (ed.), *Fynd och Forskning. Till Ragna Ahlbeck 17.7.1981*. Helsingfors: Svenska litteratursällskapet i Finland, pp. 7-43.

Borgåbladet. 1890. 2 April.

Bringéus, N.-A. 2008. 'Om förarbetena till Atlas över svensk folkkultur,' in L.-E. Edlund, A.-S. Gräslund and B. Svensson (eds), *Kartan i forskningens tjänst*. Uppsala: Kungl. Gustav Adolfs Akademien, pp. 159-74.

Caplan, P. 1988. 'Engendering Knowledge. The Politics of Ethnography, Part 1', *Anthropology Today* 4(5): 8-12.

Clifford, J., and G.E. Marcus (eds). 1986. *Writing Culture. The Poetics and Politics of Ethnography*. Berkeley: University of California Press.

D'Andrea, A., L. Ciolfi, and B. Gray. 2011. 'Methodological Challenges and Innovations in Mobility Research', *Mobilities* 6(2): 149-60.

Fenske, M. 2007. 'Micro, Macro, Agency. Historical Ethnography as Cultural Anthropology Practice', *Journal of Folklore Research* 44(1): 67–99.

Förhandlingar och uppsatser 3. 1887. Skrifter utgivna av Svenska litteratursällskapet i Finland: Helsingfors.

Forslin, A. 1976. 'Insamling av folkmelodier i Svenskfinland', *Budkavlen* 54–55; 52–65.

Frello, B. 2008. 'Towards a Discursive Analytics of Movement. On the Making and Unmaking of Movement as an Object of Knowledge', *Mobilities* 3(1): 25–50.

Frykman, J., and O. Löfgren. 2003. *Culture Builders: A Historical Anthropology of Middle-Class Life*. New Brunswick: Rutgers University Press.

Germundsson, T. 2008. 'Kartan som spegling och produktion av rumslighet', in L.-E. Edlund, A.-S. Gräslund, and B. Svensson (eds), *Kartan i forskningens tjänst*. Uppsala: Kungl. Gustav Adolfs Akademien, pp. 111–23.

Greverus, I.M. (ed.). 2003. 'Anthropological Voyage: Of Serendipity and Deep Clues', in *Shifting Grounds. Experiments in Doing Ethnography*. Münster: Lit, pp. 9–52.

Hage, G. 2005. 'A Not So Multi-Sited Ethnography of a Not So Imagined Community', *Anthropological Theory* 5(4): 463-75.

Hannerz, U. 2003. 'Several Sites in One', in T.H. Eriksen (ed.), *Globalisation: Studies in Anthropology*. London: Pluto Press, pp. 18–38.

Herranen, G. 1986. 'Med velociped, vaxdukshäfte och penna. V.E.V Wessman som insamlare av folkloristiskt material i början av seklet', Historiska och litteraturhistoriska studier 61: 213–30.

Hufvudstadsbladet. 1875. 28 April.

Land och stad. 1890. 12 February.

Lennartsson, R. 2010. 'Etnografiska utfärder i 1700-talets Stockholm. Etnologi, historia och metod', Kulturella perspektiv 3(19): 56–67.

Lönnqvist, B. 1981. 'Svenskfinland och kulturkretsläran', in I. Nordlund (ed.), Fynd och Forskning. Till Ragna Ahlbeck 17.7.1981. Helsingfors: Svenska litteratursällskapet i Finland, pp. 69–104.

Lowenthal, D. 1985. The Past is a Foreign Country. Cambridge: Cambridge University Press.

Lüdtke, A. (ed.). 1989. 'Einleitung. Was ist und wer treibt Alltagsgeschichte?' in Alltagsgeschichte. Zur Rekonstruktion historicher Erfahrungen und Lebensweisen. Frankfurt/New York: Campus.

Marcus, G. 1995. 'Ethnography in/of the World System. The Emergence of Multi-Sited Ethnography', Annual Review of Anthropology 24: 95–117.

Österlund-Pötzsch, S. 2013. 'Walking Nordic: Performing Space, Place and Identity', in P. Aronsson and L. Gradén (eds), Performing Nordic Heritage. Everyday Practices and Institutional Culture. Farnham: Ashgate, pp. 27–52.

―――. 2014. 'Bodies in Motion. The Peregrinations of Early Finland–Swedish Folklore Collectors', Journal of Folklore Research 51(3): 253–76.

Österlund-Pötzsch, S., and C. Ekrem. 2009. Swedish Folklore Studies in Finland 1828–1918. The History of Learning and Science in Finland 1828–1918. Helsinki: Societas Scientiarum Fennica.

Pile, S., and N. Thrift. 1995. 'Mapping the Subject', in S. Pile and N. Thrift (eds), Mapping the Subject. Geographies of Cultural Transformation. London/New York: Routledge.

Pink, S. 2009. Doing Sensory Ethnography. London: Sage.

Ramsay, A. 1891. På sommarvandring. Helsingfors: Söderström.

Ryden, K.C. 1993. Mapping the Invisible Landscape: Folklore, Writing, and the Sense of Place. Iowa City: University of Iowa Press.

Salazar, N.B. 2010. 'Towards an Anthropology of Cultural Mobilities', Crossings. Journal of Migration and Culture 1(1): 53–68.

―――. 2012. 'Tourism Imaginaries. A Conceptual Approach', Annals of Tourism Research 39(2): 863–82.

―――. 2013. 'Anthropology', in P. Adey, D. Bissell, K. Hannam, P. Merriman, and M. Sheller (eds), The Routledge Handbook of Mobilities. London: Routledge, pp. 55–63.

Selberg, T., and N. Gilje (eds). 2007. Kulturelle landskap. Sted, fortelling og materiell kultur. Bergen: Fagbokforlaget.

Sem, L. 2011. 'Kva fann du nå da? Folkloristane i eventyrland', in L. Esborg, K. Kverndokk, and L. Sem (eds), Or gamalt. Nya perspektiver på folkeminner. Oslo: Norsk Folkeminnelag, pp. 52–69.

SLS Office Archives, The Society of Swedish Literature in Finland, Helsinki. Caa 2: Minutes 18 May 1899.

Stoler, A.L. 2002. 'Colonial Archives and the Arts of Governance', *Archival Science* 2: 87–109. The Netherlands: Kluwer Academic Publishers.

Storå, N. 1983. 'Trends in Nordic Ethnological Material Research', in L. Honko and P. Laaksonen (eds), *Trends in Nordic Tradition Research*. Helsinki: Suomalaisen Kirjallisuuden Seura, pp. 23–45.

Taylor, C. 2004. *Modern Social Imaginaries*. Durham/London: Duke University Press.

The Tritonia Academic Library, Vaasa. The Library of Vasa Swedish Lyceum/The Rancken Collection. Capsule 104 (0481): J.E. Wefvar to J.O.I Rancken (14 May 1876).

Vergunst, J. 2011. 'Technology and Technique in a Useful Ethnography of Movement', *Mobilities* 6(2): 203–19.

Welz, G. 1998. 'Moving Targets. Feldforschung under Mobilitätsdruck', *Zeitschrift für Volkskunde* 94: 177–94.

2

Inventorying Mobility
Methodology on Wheels

Hege Høyer Leivestad

Introduction: Hidden Wheels

In a special edition of the journal *Mobilities* (2008), Paul Basu and Simon Coleman point to an apparent lack of literature that links research on migration with studies of material culture. As the authors put it, 'Whilst respective discourses on migration and material culture are abundant, there is remarkably little literature explicitly concerned with how these areas of study converge or how a focus on such convergences enables a rethinking of both material culture and migration' (2008: 313). Basu and Coleman's point can also be expanded to forms of mobility that are perhaps not so easily classified as migration, but that nevertheless involve an 'inter-relatedness of the movement of people and things' (ibid). In this chapter, I will address the intertwined discourses of mobility and materiality,[2] and trace several of the methodological challenges these evoke. More specifically, I engage with material expressions of mobility as we find them among Britons who have crossed national borders to live on a campsite in a caravan (or 'trailer' in the United States) or a motorhome[3] abroad. But instead of focussing exclusively on the mobility of human beings and their 'mobile' objects, I concentrate on the question of how we can methodologically approach mobility through the materiality of the house dwelling itself.

In pursuing the methodological possibilities involved in studying the material expressions of mobility – what Kevin Hannam, Mimi Sheller, and John Urry (2006) term 'moorings' – I introduce the home inventory as a research strategy that can be reinvented through the encounter with challenging practices and ideas of mobility within the domestic sphere.

In doing this, my aim is to illustrate that mobile methodologies do not necessarily imply multi-scale[4] physical movement, such as the strategies employed by Ruben Andersson (this volume) in his study of the illegality industry (see also Xiang 2013; Xiang and Toyota 2013), nor do they necessarily imply notions of following, as described in the Introduction to this volume. I show how research into everyday practices of homemaking can provide equally important insight into the ways 'mobile communities' are both constituted and contested. Although ethnographic studies that engage with people on the move have made important considerations on material aspects of these mobilities (see Cieraad 2010; Hecht 2001; Marcoux 2001a, 2001b; Savas 2014; Walsh 2006), my argument will be that parts of this work have tended to place objects within human life narratives. One result of this focus is an understanding of mobility that forefronts issues of life histories and migratory 'longing and belonging' rather than revealing how mobility is constantly socially and culturally constructed through everyday material practice. This chapter shows that a careful examination of the material culture of a mobile dwelling enables one to disentangle the very category of mobility itself. I will argue that what emerges in particular immobility/mobility intersections is not mobility in its realised form, but mobility as potential (Kaufmann 2002; Kellerman 2012; Leivestad 2016).

The travel of people unavoidably implies the travel of things (Savas 2014). However, in the case presented in this chapter, it is rather the dwelling itself that is movable, shedding yet new light on Martin Heidegger's near worn-out concept of *Heimat*, where home and homeland fluctuate and remain unclear. Caravans, and the campsites in which they are parked, thus offer particular possibilities and obstacles for the mobilities researcher, as they are social spaces both imbued with different meanings, imaginaries and aspirations of mobility, and at the same time constituted by and through deeply immobile practices. My suggestion here is that to understand the former, the mobile aspects of these social spaces, it might be just as useful to focus on the latter, the apparently immobile material manifestations that take place within it (Coates, this volume; Hannam, Sheller, and Urry 2006; Salazar and Smart 2011) – with the proviso that one does not lose sight of geographers Peter Adey's (2006) and Peter Merriman's (2014) warning against the employment of a simplistic mobility/moorings binary.

In the homebuilding processes of British caravan dwellers in Spain, expressed for instance through the refurnishing and extension of caravan living space, tensions between what is considered temporary mobility versus static permanence are crucial components. Caravan wheels are hidden behind wooden cladding and double-glazed awnings, whereas the temporality and mobile character of these homes on wheels simultaneously enable a life away from 'stuckedness' back home (Hage 2009). While a study of caravanning must involve mobile research methods, the everyday experiences of the residents of campsites reveal that while the caravans' wheels often remain still, the imaginaries of mobility are constantly on the move.

Caravan Homes and Potential Mobility

A trailer to live in that can also be towed behind a car – the caravan is an example of a dwelling that evokes strong, and multiple, meanings of mobility. Although caravans in the public discourse often have been connected to stigmatized groups in society,[5] they have had a visible position in the leisure and housing landscape of western Europe in the twentieth and twenty-first centuries. The increasing use of caravans, motorhomes or recreational vehicles as part of new waves of lifestyle mobility (Hoey 2014) resonates with a common and strong association between these vehicle homes and a perceived freedom of mobility, particularly in the context of North America and Australia. Although caravans were manufactured and in use in Britain as early as the 1920s, camping and caravanning had its great breakthrough in Europe during the 1950s and 1960s, following the expansion of private automobile use (Löfgren 1999). Today, camping is one of the most important sectors of tourism in western Europe, accounting for more than 20 per cent of tourist accommodation in the EU,[6] and caravanning – with increasingly advanced caravans and motorhomes[7] – remains an important leisure form, primarily among the working or lower middle classes.

Within the same leisure-related infrastructure of vehicles, roads, and campsites, we find extensive use of caravans and motorhomes as seasonal and full-time dwellings, too. In northern Europe, caravans are used as summer-season or second homes, but also as primary dwellings for people who have opted for other forms of lifestyle, whether in proximity to their original home area or, as is the case presented in this chapter, on a campsite in southern Europe. This variety of usage forms, and the complex blurring of domestic spheres, is also reflected in the lack of national and European statistics on the phenomenon: caravans are generally registered as vehicles, not as real estate, and alternative housing at campsites is often facilitated and accommodated in semi-legal ways. It thus remains difficult to pin down caravan use as a particular type of mobility, and dwelling, since the different forms of mobility this material category evokes alert the 'difficulties of extracting one category from another' (Basu and Coleman 2008: 316). The caravan and the motorhome represent examples of polyvalent material objects that can fall into categories of house/home, industrial leisure product and motor vehicle.

Figure 2.1 'Permanent' Caravans. Photo by the author.

In the context of caravan living, the material dwelling plays a crucial role in how mobility is understood, conceptualized, and practised. My British interlocutors at the Spanish campsite would frequently refer to their static caravan life as one of 'freedom'. Notably, they saw the caravan as a home that could be physically moved. It also allowed them the possibility, they argued, to be outdoors even when indoors, and it could easily be transformed into a 'real home'. When compared to the caravan, the house was a dwelling to feel 'stuck' in, or as one British woman in her sixties put it, it felt 'claustrophobic'. In order to understand how a life on the move can be both imagined and lived out in a seemingly static campsite context, it is necessary to turn to what the materiality of the caravan dwelling actually reveals about mobility. I argue in this chapter that the caravan holds an embedded mobile character because of its wheels. Its temporary (and sometimes permanent) static use is always challenged by the potential for mobility embedded in its very material form. In a similar way, campsites are also built on particular compromises between mobility and immobility, where notions of the private and the public take on peculiar expressions, and where imagined mobility and lived immobility meet in quotidian experience. What the material features of the caravan and its owner's engagement with it render visible, is mobility – not as realised geographical movement

– but as potential. By paying closer attention to the material features of the mobile dwelling, and how these are transformed, even altered, and at the same time become integral parts of larger discourses about people's life movements, it is possible to follow an analytical route that unpacks the very category of mobility itself. It is in the interface between mobile and immobile materials and practices that what I call 'potential mobility' (Leivestad 2015), sometimes referred to as 'motility' (Kaufmann 2002; Kellerman 2012; Leivestad 2016),[8] comes to the fore.

Through the mobility involved in the physical movement of people and things, and their own embedded potential mobility as dwellings on wheels, caravans, and motorhomes are mobile homes in more than one sense of the term. Engaging with mobile homes thus requires a shift in methodology, away from a narrative focus where material objects are used simply as props for human life stories and towards an approach that takes materiality itself as generative for insights into the production of (im)mobility.

From Mobile People to Mobile Dwellings

From the asphalted road it is well-nigh impossible to spot the wheels, covered as they are by panels and hidden behind the massive structure of a cladded caravan awning.[9] The original plastic awning windows have been replaced with versions in glass and there is a wooden door at the entrance. The front patio exposes plastic furniture and decorative garden animals. Only the exterior of the caravan body seems to be in its original shape and colour (white/beige). From its position, neatly parked on one of the campsite's pitches surrounded by leafy trees, the neighbouring caravan is only a few metres away.

Camping Mares, where I conducted extended periods of fieldwork between 2010 and 2015, is one of the fourteen campsites in Benidorm, located in the province of Alicante, along a stretch of the Mediterranean known as the Costa Blanca. Here, in caravans and motorhomes, hundreds of northern Europeans spend months (often the entire winter period) at the campsite – some have even made a permanent move. The majority of the full-time residents at Camping Mares are from the U.K. and from working-class or lower-middle-class backgrounds. Caravan life on Camping Mares is entangled with complex aspects of economy, retirement, and the aspirational 'search for a better life' (Benson and O'Reilly 2009; Fischer 2014; Hoey 2014).[10] Many of my interlocutors at Camping Mares had started off by touring in a motorhome or caravan as result of a wish to travel around Europe. A long-term or 'permanent' residency at Camping Mares at times had economic motives (staying put costs less than travelling around), but was also part of a multi-layered and elaborate withdrawal from a national context which a number of my interlocutors described as difficult, a difficulty articulated through frustration with a house-led life, national politics, an economic recession, and what they saw as a problematic multi-cultural society. While some campsite residents live year-round in their motorhome or towing caravan, others have purchased a so-called 'permanent' caravan on the site, paying the campsite owner an annual rent for the pitch. Caravans no longer in roadworthy condition have often spent twenty years on the same pitch and have had several owners throughout their lifetime. Sold for anything between £5,000 and £35,000, the caravan thus provides a relatively affordable and convenient entrance to home ownership in the periphery of the Spanish property market, in a campsite leisure context largely run by a local cash economy.

In the past few decades, anthropologists have criticized the tendency in ethnographic work to perceive the house as a manifestation of physical immobility, stasis, and permanence (Buchli 1999; Carsten and Hugh-Jones 1995; Dalakoglou 2009, 2010; Daniels 2010; Miller 2001). Here, however, I take the notion of the mobile home even further by addressing dwellings that are potentially mobile, due to their wheels. Containing coexisting notions of mobility and immobility, temporariness and permanence, the caravan presents an interesting and challenging site for the study of mobility, one requiring a rethinking of our methodological and theoretical tools. What are the methodological possibilities and obstacles when studying a home that can move and the human lives it enfolds? Let me begin by briefly addressing how a classic methodological strategy of home interviews centring on people's objects may contain critical pitfalls when examining 'mobile' domestic spheres.

The difficulties of conducting long-term fieldwork in domestic spaces have led to an extensive use of home visits and qualitative interviews in studies of the domestic sphere (Daniels 2010: 20). In such interviews, personal objects, and belongings have come to play leading roles in the ways in which the relationship between people and their homes is understood. Daniel Miller's (2008) life portraits of the inhabitants of a London street, approached through interviews about material objects in people's homes, is one example of what Inge Daniels terms a 'narrative approach'. Similarly, Katie Walsh (2006) uses home interviews in her study of British expatriates in Dubai and builds her argument around transnational homemaking by examining three objects, all chosen for their 'centrality in the interviewees' narratives of belongings and homemaking efforts' (2006: 128).[11]

While providing a valuable methodological approach to studies of the domestic sphere, home interviews pivoting around people's lives and their personal belongings carry with them also a number of problems. In many of these studies, for example, it is unclear how the items around which the conversation with the ethnographer pivots are selected. Does the interlocutor select these items, or is it the interviewer herself? Are the items or possessions that are picked out as important already present in the room where the interview takes place? And what about the things that are not selected to be shown to the ethnographer, considered for example less valuable in the informant's personal mobility narrative? A home consists not only of the things people choose to show to the ethnographer, despite the fact that some possessions may be considered by both the interlocutor and the researcher to play a central role in a life story.

Although home interviews attend to material objects and belongings, anthropologists like Daniels have highlighted how attention remains on people themselves, the result being an 'overemphasis on meaning and the agency of the individual' (Daniels 2010: 20) with less consideration of the materiality and agency of the dwelling and objects itself. Mark Graham (2010) argues on his part that a focus on life stories and objects may be 'a life-story told by someone in control of their narrative using objects as supporters' (ibid: 71). Daniels makes a similar point in her discussion of narrative methodological strategies: 'specific domestic objects are mere props in these human life histories, and one thus loses sight of the fact that all homes are both social and material realities' (Daniels 2010: 20). Thus Graham and Daniels importantly points out that while focussing on material things, home interviews – with the aim of producing a life story – run the risk of approaching material objects mainly to support the recounting of a life narrative. Furthermore, studies of the home in a transnational context, such as Walsh's examination of British homes in Dubai, tend to link domestic materiality and issues of mobility through a narrative account that highlights transnational longing and belonging. While using material objects as a starting point for both conversation and analysis, these life histories are still fundamentally people centred. While material objects feature as nodes in these stories, one could ask whether their materiality actually has been taken seriously enough.

Returning to the caravans at Camping Mares, where movable domestic spheres are homes of people who have downsized to a smaller dwelling, but also migrated across national borders, how to approach the links between materiality and mobility present us with complex methodological issues. How might we, for instance, address not only the mobility of people and their possessions (be it 'objects' or 'things'), but also that of the house or dwelling itself? The following section explores the 'home inventory' as one methodological strategy that allows for a closer examination of what I call the 'material negotiations of mobility' upon which some homes are constituted.

Home Inventories

During my fieldwork in Camping Mares in Benidorm, I examined the spatial layout of the campsite, as well as engaged in home visits and conversations about the caravan with many of the site's British residents. But it was mainly through the method of home inventories that several crucial insights regarding mobility and the caravan home itself became apparent. Compiling an inventory requires making a detailed listing of all the contents of a house, or in this case a caravan, while asking the owners about where and when it was purchased, or received as a gift, and any additional information the interlocutors might have about the object. The inventories I carried out at Camping Mares also involved examining the caravan's interior and exterior structures and constructions, asking about the materials used for building extensions, insulating caravan awnings, and constructing patios.

In an article on loss and material culture, Daniel Miller and Fiona Parrott discuss the ways in which they carried out an inventory of all the objects found in an informant's living room, an inventory that 'on reflection ... turned out to be a résumé of her full life' (2009: 512). Following Miller and Parrott's cue, my sense is that inventories of caravan interiors and exteriors allow for crucial insights into how mobility is materially practised and negotiated. Rather than a pathway to life histories as in Miller and Parrot, however, here the inventory makes visible the unexpected connections between people and their homes.

While in American English the word 'inventory' is often used to refer to the goods that a business holds for resale (or their value), in British English, it commonly refers to a detailed list of all the things in a given place – for example, the contents of a house. In his study of sexuality and its role in people's lives, Graham (2010) notes how inventories can become a useful research tool. Graham notes that the recording of home inventories 'requires a considerable amount of time and generates an enormous amount of material' (2010: 67). But, he importantly adds, the material gained from such inventories needs to be compared with what the same person says and does in other contexts, since the 'narrative through objects is only one version' of a life story. John Bedell (2000) also points to historians' extensive use of probate inventories, lists of people's possessions made just after their death, in studies of material culture of the seventeenth and eighteenth centuries. Such inventories, originally taken for tax purposes, are often detailed lists of a person's possessions, ranging from kitchen utensils to animals, and have been used by historians to study (among other things) standards of living and wealth (Bedell 2000: 223). Inventories have also been used by historians of the early modern period to look at, for instance, spatial organization and room naming (Baker and Hamlett

2010). However, historical researchers have pointed to several problems when using inventories, such as the subjectivity of the person compiling the inventory and the absence of so-called nonvaluable items from the list (ibid: 313; see also Österlund-Pötzsch, this volume, on archive research). By comparing inventories with archaeological data, Bedell (2000) shows that various household goods – most commonly objects considered to have relatively low value, such as sewing equipment and children's toys – are often under-reported in the probate inventories.

It is notable that in home interviews items might be omitted by the informants because of their lack of value for the human life narrative, while in the historical inventories they were often omitted by the researcher because of their lack of economic value (at the time). Reflecting upon historical studies of home furnishing, Robert St. George (2006) notes how these often suffer from an elitist bias. St. George also identifies an additional problem regarding probate inventories; some did cover the contents of each room, but noted that the place in which 'a given chest was actually placed in a bed chamber or where in a kitchen a television might be located, suggests that only ethnographic studies are able to document precisely what things and in what positions a room contained at a given point in time' (2006: 224).

An ethnographer employing inventories as a research method can, in theory at least, avoid some of the challenges, pitfalls, and biases that historical researchers struggle with when using this type of data. Through the ethnographer's presence and own account, the inventory can become an interesting entry point into knowledge about the home dwelling and its materiality, the household and, in this specific case, the transnational mobility that has taken place. The inventories provide a useful tool for revealing factors of mobility, and while challenging a view of home as a stable entity through which mobile subjects and objects pass (Miller 2001), they simultaneously resist one-sided portrayals of biographical narrative and migratory (trans)national belonging. In my discussion below, I show, for example, how caravan kitchens' drawers and their contents, or canned food stored in the top compartments of caravan cupboards, can reveal crucial components of a mobility here deeply intertwined with complex issues of class and nationality – a mobility that stands in stark contrast to that of the relatively affluent individuals normally treated under the umbrella of lifestyle migrants (Benson and O'Reilly 2009).

Below, I explore two cases of materiality of the caravan dwelling that reveal how mobility is negotiated and even materially altered in a context where the temporary mobile dwelling is challenged by housing ideals of permanence and stasis. The discussion is based on inventories carried out in the camping dwellings of two British couples: the caravan of Margaret and Gary, and the motorhome of their friends and neighbours Lucy and

Figure 2.2 Motorhome aesthetics. Photo by the author.

John. Differently from Walsh's (2006) study of British expatriate homes in Dubai, which focuses on objects that play a central role in the narrative of the informants, these two examples feature objects or material forms registered in the inventory but somehow taken for granted: a pink notebook, and tiled flooring. These rather mundane and unimpressive objects, I argue in the sections that follows, can be used as original entrance points for the exploration of the material negotiations of mobility.

A Pink Notebook

Lucy and John's motorhome is parked on the so-called touring area of Camping Mares. The British couple make sure to book the same pitch every year, normally making the drive back to the U.K. in the summer, to visit the family and get the required annual Ministry of Transport test (MOT) on the motorhome.[12] John and Lucy bought what they call 'the van' in the summer of 2007. Lucy retired at sixty-five from her job as a care assistant; half a year later, John retired from truck driving, having spent more than forty years on the road. Staying in Benidorm was the fulfilment, they said, of a lifelong dream of travelling abroad. They had a lump sum from Lucy's pension, and paid £13,000 cash for the 1994 model that is now their fulltime home. Lucy describes how it was love at first sight with the motorhome at their local dealer; she even liked the lightly faded pink textiles of the sofas. Following two years of touring southern Europe, Lucy and John have made Camping Mares their final base. They enjoy the company of the other people there, and the motorhome travelling and touring had simply become too expensive. An annual pitch rent of €4,200 is covered by the rental income they get for the house in the northwest of the U.K., still not sold due to a slow housing market.

On a windy midday in early March 2011, Lucy agrees to let me carry out an inventory of their motorhome. She cannot understand why I find their stored canned food, the numerous paperbacks, and stored-away presents interesting, but is more than willing to talk about them while I move through the caravan making the inventory. In one of the cupboards in the motorhome, we come across a tiny pink notebook, where Lucy has written down with different coloured pens incomes and expenses. Here are to be found the exact amounts and dates of the couple's state pension, together with the small private pensions they have been saving up for, and the monthly expenditures for house insurance, the caravan club, the bankcards, and the road tax. On separate pages Lucy has also listed expenditures of the couples' motorhome travels, registering the price of ferries, of petrol, and campsite fees. When I ask about the numbers, John starts to complain, relating the U.K. expenses to what he sees as the downsides of a house-led life; the gas, electricity, council tax, and phone bills. To him, these numbers present proof of a contrast between what he views as an economically burdensome house-lead reality, and the life a motorhome offers, including the possibility for withdrawing from these same economic constraints. If

John and Lucy manage to finally sell their U.K. house, they plan to 'take the money and enjoy it', they tell me, or invest in one of the 'permanent' caravans at the site.

Lucy's pink notebook, shoved away in one of the motorhome cupboards, offers important insights into the difficult household economics involved in the couple's motorhome mobility. The numbers reflect coexisting and geographically dispersed challenges – dealing with a house in the U.K. that the couple still hasn't been able to sell, while simultaneously managing the day-to-day expenses which motorhome life requires. The notebook's revelatory potential lies partly in its manifestation of income and expenditures, thus serving the researcher a range of hard numbers that through daily talk and interviews are less accessible. But the book also reveals, importantly so, the economic strategies embedded in the fulfilment of John and Lucy's lifestyle choice. These strategies seem to require a considerable degree of risk taking, involving a house in the U.K. that remains stuck in a slow housing market, and the actual high costs associated with a temporary housing offered by the motorhome, based on a rental of plot land on a Spanish campsite.

To Lucy and John however, the numbers written down in the book clearly illustrate something else, namely a manifestation of the affordability of their new life. They see this new reality as a deep contrast to the costs attached to living in a house, costs that John associates with burdening 'sedentary' practices such as taxes and bills. His interpretation of the numbers points to a potential both seem to locate in the mobile dwelling itself. The affordability they associate with the mobile dwelling resonates with other potentials that are embedded in the motorhome's material form. While compiling the inventory of the motorhome, Lucy exclaims that she cannot imagine herself living in a house again. She says the house 'closed me in', though she recognizes that this may sound nonsensical to an outsider, as the house they own (and hope to sell) is considerably more spacious than their motorhome. This latter comment, and the couple's interpretation of the numbers in the notebook, reflects a general portrayal of caravan potentiality informed by ideas of mobility as freedom. Freedom in this context is thus located both in the potential to move constitutive of the materiality of the motorhome, but also – perhaps more surprisingly – in a temporary and spatially limited domestic sphere (that of the motorhome) that nevertheless prevents Lucy and John from feeling 'stuck'. In the section that follows, I consider another example of caravan materiality in order to highlight the ways in which notions of mobility and stasis are renegotiated through material building practices at the campsite. Also in the case that follows, as with the example of Lucy's pink book, we find reference to the potential embedded in the caravan as an alternative domestic form; a home that to its owners seems to constitute a mobile sphere, even when standing still.

Figure 2.3 Caravan awning. Photo by the author.

Tiles

Gary and Margaret, a Welsh couple in their early sixties, own one of the so-called permanent caravans at Camping Mares, located on a pitch along the main asphalted road that traverses the site. Their engagement with caravans stretches years back, since they both used to work as site managers for the U.K.-based Camping and Caravanning Club. After being made redundant and the four years of dire unemployment that followed, they decided to sell their three-bedroom house with garden and leave for Spain. They found a new home at Camping Mares, a site where they had spent some weeks more than twenty years earlier. An elderly lady, eager to return to the U.K., took cash for her caravan and awning, and left it for them fully furnished and with all her belongings still inside. This suited them perfectly, as, for Gary, only a couple of basic requirements were necessary to make a caravan suitable: a 'proper flush toilet' and a 'proper bed'.

On a warm winter day in 2011, Margaret claps her hands enthusiastically when I introduce her to the idea of the inventory. While making a list of the items inside the caravan, the three of us move together from the outdoor patio with the artificial grass 'that we don't have to cut', through the awning with shelves of DVDs, to the photos of the grandchildren (who call them

'Grandma and Grandpa Caravan' to distinguish them from their other set of 'big house' grandparents back in the U.K.) beside the double bed in the inner part of the 1990 German-manufactured caravan. The awning is separated from the outdoor patio with double-glazed sliding doors, and as I continue the inventory, the three of us turn to the light-grey tiled flooring. Gary proudly states that he himself did the tailing, and made sure the tiles were not cemented or nailed to the ground. Although cement would have prevented rain water from coming through, Gary explains that 'the ground rule is that anything permanent is not allowed'.

It slowly emerges that the tiles are just one of many 'nonpermanent' structures in the caravan. Whereas the awning is covered with wooden cladding, this is only screwed on, and easy to dismantle (see Figure 2.3). The awning itself is not concreted to the ground, and neither are the patio sheds. Caravan wheels are concealed behind a plastic skirt, but, by law, cannot be removed. Gary and Margaret explain that all the campsite's buildings and extensions 'revolve around this temporary structure'. Indeed, building checks are occasionally made on behalf of the Valencia Authorities – although generally the campsite manager is able to announce such visits in advance, giving time for caravanners to remove all signs of permanent building structures such as fences or solid sheds.

A set of seemingly inconsequential tiles, then, covering the ground in the caravan awning, can provide entirely new insights into the workings of the mobile home made temporarily 'permanent'. By extending the domestic living space and continuously building to improve the living standard of the caravans, caravanners like Gary and Margaret contribute to a gradual 'physical immobilization' of their mobile dwelling. The caravanners invest considerably into concealing or changing the caravan's mobile features, and making them into material structures that are more associated with 'house-like' Western dwellings. Parts of the interior of Gary and Margaret's caravan have been ripped out and changed, transforming the caravan into, mainly, a bedroom. Other caravanners remove the original caravan door and replace it with a wooden model, while others hide the caravan surface with fabrics attached to the awning. The different material changes are, however, easily reversible (and normally within what is a reasonable economic investment) and thus in constant play with an ideal of what I call 'potential mobility'. The caravanners' relation to this potential mobility obviously has legal implications as it is based in the legal framework that regulates the campsite as a touristic establishment for temporary accommodation – and not for permanent residency. But, I argue, the experienced easiness in changing one's living space furthermore plays into a general idea among caravanners that caravan living implies the possibility of moving, and changing, 'whenever one wants to'.

When compared to the pink notebook discussed above, the tiles take the issue of mobility in a slightly different direction. While the numbers in the notebook give insight into complex financial scenarios, Lucy and John's interpretation of the incomes and expenditures registered in the notebook reflect the caravan's connection to ideas and practices where mobility figures as freedom. Gary and Margaret's tiled flooring, however, shows how mobile features are sometimes actually altered and concealed, in favour of a 'static' house-aesthetics. While conventional housing ideals continue to inform the multiple ways in which caravanners transform their mobile dwellings into permanent housing, the potential for mobility still remains the most important factor for choosing a caravan lifestyle. But the tiles also illuminate how caravans, in the campsite setting, are materially negotiated as specific forms of temporary structures. Both inventory findings reveal how mobility is intimately embedded in specific material domestic forms that are constantly contested and renegotiated. What clearly emerges here, is that to further understand how caravanners come to understand specific practices and infrastructures as 'mobile' and 'static' however, we as ethnographers need to move beyond the predetermined categories these terms seem to evoke in the first place.

Conclusion: Immobilizing the Mobile Home

An engagement with materiality can add considerably to the growing field of mobilities research. But by methodologically focusing on 'narrative objects' (those 'meaningful' objects chosen by informants themselves), studies of home and mobility run the risk of nurturing and feeding an already dominating discourse of transnational belonging approached through life narratives. Further investigating the relationship between mobility and materiality and taking into account polyvalent relations of both class and economy require methodological strategies that partly distance us from this narrative approach. As researchers who often deal with the domestic sphere, particularly in contexts of transnational mobility, we should ask in what ways alternative methodological tools and strategies might raise other emergent issues regarding the ways homes are created in a 'world in flux' (Salazar, Elliot, and Norum, this volume).

In this chapter, I have asked what happens when we turn our gaze to taken-for-granted materiality. Creatively using home inventories as ethnographic method may help us shift our focus towards the ways in which new homes are materially and economically constituted, and embed aspirations for the future. The examples provided in this chapter deal with the formation of alternative homes as part of a mobility pattern that generally involves the move from a house to a caravan, and, in parallel, the move from the U.K. to Spain. As Lucy's pink notebook reveals, relocating in the quest for 'the good life' (Benson and O'Reilly 2009; Fischer 2014; Hoey 2014) is done in difficult negotiation with a tight household economy and other aspects of risk taking, within a framework of European financial crisis and recession. Clearly, then, a central part of the ethnographic fodder obtained through these inventories raises the analytical challenge of dealing with a mobile working class in contemporary Europe, and how imaginaries of mobility are shaped within complex economic and social contexts that enable or constrain mobility, and where the material aspects of this mobility play a crucial role.

An inventory approach in research methodology draws our attention however not only to the small and seemingly more mobile 'things' or 'objects', but also to larger material constructions of building and infrastructure that tell other tales about mobility. Dimitris Dalakoglou's (2009, 2010) work on Albanian migrants' house building in their country of birth, provides an excellent example of how an empirical focus on building processes opens up for a particularly dynamic view of transnational house making. 'The making of these houses has characteristics that potentially bridge the physical distances and the related ambiguities that may emerge in such an age of spatial displacement', Dalakoglou argues (2010: 772). In this chapter, I have shown that British caravan dwellers' home building processes on a campsite can add layers of complexity to our understandings of permanence and temporariness in relation to the home. Indeed, a crucial aspect of making caravan living a fulltime affair involves the very practical processes of physically immobilizing the mobile dwelling. But permanency is fulfilled through a constant interplay with the caravan's mobile character. The possibilities the caravan opens to 'do-it-yourself' projects and the easily reversible material structures it both offers and requires, are part of a caravan's embedded mobile character, one that feeds into the caravanners' perceived possibility of 'being able to move whenever one wants', living in a home that has wheels and can travel. The caravan home thus prevents a sense of 'stuckedness' (Hage 2009) in life – a 'stuckedness' that many caravanners associate with a sedentary, house-led, and economically difficult reality.

The ways in which the material character of the home prevents a social 'stuckedness' brings me to one final issue regarding the study of mobility. At the beginning of this chapter, I suggested that we might need to think in new ways about how people on the move relate to their 'things', as well as of the convergence of theoretical perspectives on mobility with those on material culture this produces in our analysis. Working on the home sphere – even in contexts of transnational homes (what Benson (2011) calls 'situation of relocation') – the data collected as an ethnographer is not necessarily achieved 'on the move', but rather in more stationary positions (D'Andrea, Ciolfi, and Gray 2011). This clearly questions the usefulness of the analytical category 'mobility' itself. In the context of this particular study, we see that it is rather a potential mobility that is rendered visible both in the material practices of home building as well as through emic discourses on the possibility of movement.

The notion of temporariness and the ways in which it is embedded in building practices manifests the importance of potential mobility: the crucial importance of the potential ability to move, both spatially and socially, even when it does not necessarily translate into actual movement. As mobilities research continues to expand, perhaps even more rapidly than the practices it sets out to examine, a careful unpacking of the category of 'mobility' itself becomes vital if we wish to generate the appropriate methodological and theoretical tools to identify its multi-faceted manifestations.

Hege Høyer Leivestad is Postdoctoral Researcher at the Department of Social Anthropology, Stockholm University. Leivestad has done fieldwork in Spain and Sweden, and she is the author of the monograph *Caravans: Lives on Wheels in Contemporary Europe* (Bloomsbury 2018). Leivestad is currently doing research on a European container port, focusing on issues of logistics, mobility and economy.

NOTES

1. I thank my informants at Camping Mares, for their patience and friendship. Mark Graham first introduced me to inventories as a methodological tool, for which I am most grateful. I am indebted to my brother Eirik Høyer Leivestad, for patiently reading and commenting on a range of previous drafts.
2. The past decades have seen an increasing interest within the social sciences in the study of materiality on the move. This preoccupation with the circulation of objects is of course not new to anthropology; we see it described in Bronislaw Malinowski's *Kula* (1920) and in the writings of Marcel Mauss (1967) and Nancy Munn (1977), as well as in Nelson Graburn's (1976) early work on tourist art. What these works share is a consideration of 'mobile objects constituted by, but also constituting people' (Basu and Coleman 2008: 322). Since the 1980s, considerations on a changing, globalizing world imbued with 'transnational flows' necessarily shaped the study of materiality and mobility. In Arjun Appadurai's (1986) edited volume, things acquired 'social lives', and Igor Kopytoff's (1986) view on the biographies of objects has remained important for the study of material culture and the movement of things.
3. The ethnography presented in this chapter is part of my doctoral research on European caravan mobility (Leivestad 2015). In addition to the research on British caravanners in Spain that I present here, the dissertation is based on fieldwork

among seasonal caravanners in Sweden, within the caravanning industry from 2010 to 2011, with subsequent fieldwork from 2012 to 2015. Fieldwork for this project was generously funded by The Swedish Society for Geography and Anthropology (SSAG), Helge Ax:son Johnson's Foundation, and scholarships from Stockholm University.

4. D'Andrea, Ciolfi, and Gray (2011) note a lack of integration between what they call micro and macro components of mobility, and argue that systemic, historical, and geographic research, while setting the tone for the new mobilities research, remain methodologically underdeveloped. Xiang and Toyota (2013) on the other hand, importantly criticize the assigning of empirical observation to micro and macro levels, arguing that one needs to treat 'every movement as simultaneously visceral, bodily, historical, and structural' (2013: 278).

5. Consider for instance the caravan's close attachment to the homemaking practices and mobile lifestyles of gypsies and travellers; see Okely (1986). Note, however, that caravans throughout recent history have been used as dwellings for groups of people whose work has required constant physical mobility – think, for example, of circuses.

6. Numbers offered by the European Federation of Camping Site Organisations and Holiday Parks Associations (EFCO and HPA), 2014.

7. Statistics from the European caravanning industry show a heavy increase in the sales of motorhomes. Industry actors argue that the popularity of motorhomes is linked to their embedded mobility; they are easier to travel with than a conventional car-towed caravan, and thus attract new groups to the world of camping.

8. I have argued elsewhere (Leivestad 2016) that the concept of 'motility', referring to a potential to move, has carried with it Eurocentric visions of mobility and is excessively rooted in the understanding of the individual and active agent.

9. An awning is a tent-like structure with a supporting frame that can be attached to the side of a caravan to provide extra living space.

10. In this sense, the aspirations of mobility and search for community are not unlike those described under the umbrella category of lifestyle migration, where the British in Spain comprise a well-documented group (see Benson and O'Reilly 2009; Casado-Diaz 2009; King, Warnes, and Williams 2000; Oliver 2008; O'Reilly 2000).

11. The literature on home that examines settings of mobility and migration reveal how a dedication to narrative and life history, retold through objects, has tended towards an understanding of home within a conceptual frame of belonging, loss and reinvestment (Cieraad 2010; Fortier 2003; Hecht 2001; Miller 2001, 2008; Savas 2014; Walsh 2006).

12. The Motor Ordinance Test (MOT) is an annual test in Great Britain of most vehicles that are three years or older, and involves testing of safety, roadworthiness and emissions.

REFERENCES

Adey, P. 2006. 'If Mobility is Everything Then it is Nothing: Towards a Relational Politics of (Im)mobilities', *Mobilities* 1(1): 75–94.

Appadurai, A. 1986. *The Social Life of Things*. Cambridge: Cambridge University Press.

Barker, H., and J. Hamlett. 2010. 'Living above the Shop: Home, Business and Family in the "English Industrial Revolution"', *Journal of Family History* 35(4): 311–28.

Basu, P., and S. Coleman. 2008. 'Introduction: Migrant Worlds, Material Cultures', *Mobilities* 3(3): 313–30.

Bedell, J. 2000. 'Archaeology and Probate Inventories in the Study of Eighteenth-century life', *The Journal of Interdisciplinary History* 31(2): 223–45.

Benson, M. 2011. 'The Movement Beyond (Lifestyle) Migration: Mobile Practices and the Constitution of a Better Way of Life', *Mobilities* 6(2): 221–35.

Benson, M., and K. O'Reilly. 2009. 'Migration and the Search for a Better Way of Life: A Critical Exploration of Lifestyle Migration', *The Sociological Review* 57(4): 608–25.

Buchli, V. 2006. 'Architecture and Modernism', in C. Tilley, W. Keane, S, Kuechler, M. Rowlands, and P. Spyer (eds), *Handbook of Material Culture*. London: Sage.

Buchli, V. 1999. *An Archaeology of Socialism*. Oxford: Berg.

Carsten, J., and S. Hugh-Jones. 1995. 'Introduction', in J. Carsten and S. Hugh-Jones (eds), *About the House*. Cambridge: Cambridge University Press.

Casado-Diaz, M.A. 2009. 'Social Capital in the Sun: Bonding and Bridging Social Capital among British Retirees', in M. Benson and K. O' Reilly (eds), *Lifestyle Migration. Expectations, Aspirations and Experiences*. Aldershot: Ashgate.

Cieraad, I. 2010. 'Homes from Home: Memories and Projections', *Home Cultures* 7(1): 85–102.

Daniels, I. 2010. *The Japanese House: Material Culture in the Modern Home*. Oxford: Berg.

Dalakoglou, D. 2009. 'Building and Ordering Transnationalism: The "Greek House" in Albania as a Material Process', in Daniel Miller (ed.), *Anthropology and the Individual: A Material Culture Perspective*. Oxford: Berg.

―――. 2010. 'Migrating-Remitting – "Building" Dwelling: House Making as "Proxy" Presence in Postsocialist Albania', *Journal of the Royal Anthropological Institute* 16: 761–77.

D'Andrea, A., L. Ciolfi, and B. Gray. 2011. 'Methodological Challenges and Innovations in Mobilities Research', *Mobilities* 6(2): 149–60.

Fischer, E.F. 2014. *The Good Life: Aspirations, Dignity and the Anthropology of Wellbeing*. Stanford University Press.

Fortier, A.-M. 2003. 'Making Home: Queer Migrations and Motions of Attachment', in S. Ahmed, C. Castañeda, A.-M. Fortier, and M. Sheller (eds), *Uprootings/ Regroundings. Questions of Home and Migration*. Oxford: Berg.

Graburn, N.H.H. (ed.). 1976. *Ethnic and Tourist Arts: Cultural Expressions from the Fourth World*. Berkeley: University of California Press.

Graham, M. 2010. 'Things in the Field: Ethnographic Research into Objects and Sexuality', *Lamda Nordica* 15(3-4): 65–89.

Hage, G. 2009. 'Waiting Out the Crisis: On Stuckedness and Governmentality', in Ghassan Hage (ed.), *Waiting*. Melbourne: Melbourne University Press.

Hannam K., M. Sheller, and J. Urry. 2006. 'Editorial: Mobilities, Immobilities and Moorings', *Mobilities* 1(1): 1–22.

Hecht, A. 2001. 'Home Sweet Home: Tangible Memories of an Uprooted Childhood', in Daniel Miller (ed.), *Home Possessions: Material Culture Behind Closed Doors*. London: Berg

Henare, A., M. Holbraad, and S. Westell (eds). 2007. *Thinking through Things: Theorising Artefacts Ethnographically*. London: Routledge.

Hoey, B.A. 2014. *Opting for Elsewhere: Lifestyle Migration in the American Middle Class*. Nashville: Vanderbilt University Press.

Hoskins, J. 2006. 'Agency, Biography and Objects', in C. Tilley, W. Keane, S. Kuechler, M. Rowlands, and P. Spyer (eds), *Handbook of Material Culture*. London: Sage.

Kaufmann, V. 2002. *Re-Thinking Mobility: Contemporary Sociology*. Aldershot: Ashgate.

Kellerman, A. 2012. 'Potential Mobilities', *Mobilities* 7(3): 171–83.

King, R., A. Warnes, and A. Williams. 2000. *Sunset Lives: British Retirement to Southern Europe*. Oxford: Berg.

Kopytoff, I. 1986. 'The Cultural Biography of Things: Commoditization as Process', in A. Appaduari (ed), *The Social Life of Things*. Cambridge: Cambridge University Press.

Leivestad, H.H. 2015. 'Lives on Wheels: Caravan Homes in Contemporary Europe', Ph.D. dissertation. Stockholm: University of Stockholm.

_____. 2016. 'Motility', in N. Salazar and K. Jayaram (eds), *The Keywords of Mobility: Critical Engagements*. Oxford: Berghahn.

Löfgren, O. 1999. *On Holiday: A History of Vacationing*. Berkeley/Los Angeles: University of California Press.

Marcoux, J.-S. 2001a. 'The Refurbishment of Memory', in D. Miller (ed.), *Home Possessions: Material Culture Behind Closed Doors*. Oxford: Berg.

_____. 2001b. 'The "Casser Maison" Ritual: Constructing the Self by Emptying the Home', *Journal of Material Culture* 6(2): 213–35.

Merriman, P. 2014. 'Rethinking Mobile Methods', *Mobilities* 9(2): 167–87.

Miller, D. (ed.). 2001. *Home Possessions: Material Culture Behind Closed Doors*. Oxford: Berg.

_____. 2008. *The Comfort of Things*. Cambridge/Malden: Polity Press.

Miller, D., and F. Parrott. 2009. 'Loss and Material Culture in South London', *Journal of the Royal Anthropological Institute* 15: 502–19.

Okely, J. 1983. *The Traveller-Gypsies*. Cambridge: Cambridge University Press.

Oliver, C. 2008. *Retirement Migration: Paradoxes of Ageing*. London: Routledge.

O'Reilly, K. 2000. *The British on the Costa del Sol: Transnational Identities and Local Communities*. London: Routledge.

Salazar, N.B., and A. Smart. 2011. 'Anthropological Takes on (Im)Mobility: Introduction', *Identities: Global Studies in Culture and Power* 18(6): i–ix.

Savas, Ö. 2014. 'Taste Diaspora: The Aesthetic and Material Practice of Belonging', *Journal of Material Culture* 19(2): 185–208.

St. George, R. 2006. 'Home Furnishing and Domestic Interiors', in C. Tilley, W. Keane, S. Kuechler, M. Rowlands, and P. Spyer (eds), *Handbook of Material Culture*. Sage Publications.

Walsh, K. 2006. 'British Expatriate Belongings: Mobile Homes and Transnational Homing', *Home Cultures* 3(2): 123–44.

Xiang, B. 2013. 'Multi-Scalar Ethnography: An Approach for Critical Engagement with Migration and Social Change', *Ethnography* 14(3): 282–99.

Xiang, B., and M. Toyota. 2013. 'Ethnographic Experiments in Transnational Mobility Studies', *Ethnography* 14(3): 277–81.

3

Becoming, There?
In Pursuit of Mobile Methods

Chris Vasantkumar

Mobile Methods after Routes?

The insight that anthropologists and their objects of study are both in motion is hardly a new one. Indeed, the trailblazing works of Appadurai (1989, 1990) Clifford (1988, 1997), Gupta and Ferguson (1997), Malkki (1992), Marcus (1995), Wolf (1982), and others are nearing (or in some cases are well past) their silver anniversaries. Arguably, the signal contribution to anthropology of the long decade separating the publication of *Europe and the People Without History* (Wolf 1982) and *Culture, Power, Place* (Gupta and Ferguson 1997) was to place the mobility of both anthropologists and the world(s) they study at the forefront of the discipline's rhetorical and analytic mixes. Routes have long since taken their place along roots as significant organizing tropes for the process(es) of gathering anthropologically derived knowledge about the world.

Given the historic and continuing importance of this sea change towards an attunement with manifold human mobilities, the question arises as to whether it is actually possible to say anything novel about the articulations of mobility and anthropology. Is there, after both 'traveling cultures' (Clifford 1997) and 'multi-sited ethnography' (Marcus 1995), anything new to say about anthropological research in a context wherein both anthropologists and their objects of study are, inarguably, always already in motion? In this chapter I suggest that, despite initial appearances, there is, but that doing so requires a re-evaluation of the usual ways in which mobility and stasis have tended to be defined against each other, a retuning, in other words, of the distinction between roots and routes upon which much of the classic anthropology of mobility work has traded. This retuning is, I insist, substantially consonant with the emphasis of this volume on supplementing approaches to travelling theories and populations with a renewed attention to mobile methods. Yet, I also contend, a retuning of the sort I intend may also cast some critical light upon received distinctions between mobility and immobility themselves.

This claim will be discussed in due time, but first some attention to a key text in the field will make the stakes of this argument more concrete. It has been over two decades since James Clifford (1997) first elaborated his notions of 'traveling cultures'. The intent of Clifford's intervention was to simultaneously criticize the implicitly sedentary and localizing cast of traditional approaches to anthropological fieldwork and recover what he, following Georges Condominas, termed the 'pretérrain' of the field, 'all those places you have to go through and be in relation with just to get to ... that place of work you will call your field' (1997: 23).

In service of both of these projects, Clifford endeavoured to reverse the relative weight given to the elements of one of twentieth-century anthropology's structuring binaries, that between dwelling and travelling as aspects of anthropological methodology. 'The normative practices' of this anthropology, he argues, '[have] privileged relations of dwelling over relations of travel' to the degree that continuing to 'constr[ue] ethnography as *field-work*' is fraught with conceptual and analytic dangers (1997: 22). Chief among these is the concealment of 'the wider global world of intercultural import–export in which the ethnographic encounter is always already enmeshed' (1997: 23). The solution to this elision of wider connection that has, arguably, characterized classic anthropological accounts, Clifford suggests, is to '[tip] the balance' away from dwelling and 'toward travelling' as an organizing trope for anthropological inquiry (1997: 25).

Clifford's work has been widely influential (and indeed was instrumental in kindling my own early interest in the discipline) and it would be ungenerous not to note its generative resonances. Yet, in this chapter, I contend that the import of theoretical and methodological possibilities opened up by it and other broadly post-structuralist work on the anthropology of mobility writ large, have, ironically, been effectively blunted by lack of critical attention to whether or not the binary between dwelling and travel holds up under close scrutiny.[1]

The Field on the Boil

In what follows, I argue that in the service of thinking through mobile methodologies, the boundary between dwelling and travel itself must be called into question. My aim here is thus not to argue for a rejigging of the relationship between dwelling and travel (or site and preterrain) conceptualized as clearly bounded and easily distinguishable sets of practices. Instead, following Tim Ingold's work on 'lines' (2007) and 'against space' (2010), I ask what an anthropology of (im)mobilities and its methodologies might look like in the absence of a clear boundary between movement and place. I explore possible responses to this question via a reflection on A.C. Haddon's work in the Torres Straits in the late nineteenth century, Tim Ingold's recent deconstructions of the boundary between place and movement, and my own fieldwork on trans-Himalayan Tibet.

In particular, I suggest that anthropological notions of the field have tended to be 'islanded' by the same sorts of 'inversive' logics that Ingold identifies as having deformed our received understandings of linearity, travel, and space. The import of such a reconceptualization is manifold. Without it, the story of the development of anthropology's objects and methods tends to involve an implicit temporal (or narrative) arc from original purities and stases to contemporary complexities and the new confusions of mobility.[2] This story consigns boundedness, practices of dwelling, and 'being there' to the disciplinary past while infusing its present with apparently heroic tropes of 'following [the thing]', multi-sitedness (Marcus 1995) and 'being en route' (Coutin 2005; but see Candea 2007). In this light we can design our mobile methodologies as moral alternatives to the discipline's founding sticks in the mud.

Yet, like the apparently clear division between mobile and immobile, easy demarcations of an immobile anthropological past and a mobile present (at least in methodological terms) are less a reflection of actual reality than the historically contingent and surprisingly fragile outcomes of what the Actor-Network theorists would call the purificatory processes of modernity (see Latour 1993: 10 and *passim*). Moreover, I contend that, as a result of these purifications, the mobility even of early fieldwork methods has been elided. To address this elision, I articulate a re-envisioning of received anthropological concepts of the field that proposes a temporally and geographically unified model of site and preterrain that I term 'coterrain'. Ultimately, I suggest that anthropological research methods in fields so conceptualized are and have always been necessarily mobile. In order to access the mobility of anthropological method, we must first historicize and provincialize the idea of the field as a bounded space. But first some theoretical background is in order.

Islands, Fields, and Other Inversive Logics

Apropos here are Tim Ingold's iconoclastic remarks on lines (2007) and space(s) (2009, 2010) that highlight the lingering effects of what he terms the 'inversions' of modernity on received notions of travel, mapping, textuality and place. For Ingold, the process by which the line 'in the course of its history has gradually been shorn of the movement that gave rise to it' is paradigmatic for the purificatory practices of modernity (2007: 75). Ingold employs a contrast between the line in its entirety as a dynamic temporal trace of gesture, and the line as a static sequence of connected dots to highlight the deforming character of modernity's interventions.

Modernity makes continuous lines into dots. As a result, 'what we see is no longer the *trace of a gesture* but an assembly of *point-to-point connectors*' (Ingold 2007: 75). Once the line has been turned into a series of discrete points, 'to recover the trajectory of [the original movements] that produced the line', Ingold notes, 'one must *join them up*' (ibid.: 74). In place of indeterminate and potentially generative perambulations, this new regime of points always already presumes a final finished form. 'The pattern [the connected dots] eventually form – much as in a child's join-the-dots puzzle – is already given as a virtual object from the outset'(ibid.: 74). The destination, now pregiven, replaces the journey as the focus of movement.[3]

The transmutation of lines as unified gestures into series of discontiguous points, for Ingold, is merely the tip of the inversive iceberg. Running parallel to this pointing of the line are a whole series of roughly analogous deformations that result from theoretical enclosures cutting against the flow of life. The 'logic of inversion', Ingold suggests 'turn[s] the pathways along which life is lived into boundaries within which it is enclosed'. As a result, we imagine the world as being 'filled with existing things rather than [being] woven from the strands of their coming-into-being' (2009: 29). As modernity makes lines into dots, it transforms travel into transport, mapping into route planning, storytelling into precomposed plot and transforms place, from 'a knot tied from multiple and interlaced strands of movement and growth ... into a node in a static network of connections' (2007: 75).

Island(ing) Anthropology

All of the parallel transformations Ingold describes are conditioned by the inversive logic that transforms 'the "way through" of the trail into the containment of the place-in-space' (2009: 32). Anthropology, too, has not been immune from such inversions. In particular, I suggest, the notion of the field(site) as commonly employed in anthropological practice has been subjected to a process by which it 'has been shorn of the movement that gave rise to it', In this inversion, the island (see Baldacchino 2005, Eriksen 1993, Hay 2006) both as an actual site and as a trope has been of central importance.

Kuklick (2011 and 1996) describes, in effect, the processes of inversion, by which classic anthropology's notion of the field came to be rather more place bound than place binding. The notions of field and fieldwork, one will recall, were introduced to anthropology or, as he termed it, 'our Cinderella science', by Alfred Cort Haddon, one of the founding figures of anthropology as a discipline based on empirical field research in the last decades of the nineteenth century. Haddon, whose contributions to the field have often been eclipsed in retrospect by others he brought into it, including Charles Seligman and William Rivers (Kuklick 1996: 613), emerges once more (alongside fellow zoologist turned anthropologist Baldwin Spencer) as a key figure in Kuklick's accounts. Haddon, an erstwhile marine zoologist[4] sought to adapt the Darwinian evolutionary frameworks then current in his original field to the study of human origins and variation. In doing so, he set the stage for both an initial anthropological focus on islands and then, indirectly, for what one might call an unintentional marooning of the discipline with the continued 'islanding' of anthropological research once the field moved from archipelagic to continental objects of study.

In Kuklick's recounting, the early anthropological interest in apparent cultural isolates in island environments was drawn directly from Darwinian 'biogeography'. Haddon's efforts to 'translat[e] biological theory into anthropological precepts' were at the centre of the new 'research paradigm' that emerged in the context of the Torres Straits Expeditions (the first zoological in 1888, the second anthropological in 1898) that laid the foundation for what would later be called the Cambridge School of Anthropology. For Haddon, 'the Darwinian standards he imported into anthropology provided guidelines for determining which cultures would be fragile and where they would be found'(Kuklick 1996: 613). Haddon was interested primarily in salvage, but his reasons for being so diverged in instructive ways from the romanticism of later practice.

Where other, later anthropologists might be at least implicitly concerned with undoing the transition from *gemeinschaft* to *gesellschaft* with their salvage-oriented work, Haddon's concerns were scientific rather than sociological. 'His zoological concern to plot species distribution and variation across geographical space derived from a model that was ... intended to explain change over time ...' (ibid.: 613). This model in turn was 'predicated on ... axioms' that included the notion that 'the geographical isolation necessary to species differentiation in the limiting case of island enclosure resulted in idiosyncratic types unlikely to survive competition with species bred in more competitive continental conditions. If cultural phenomena were analogous to biological ones', Haddon reasoned, islands (whether in the Torres Straits or the far flung fringes of Great Britain) were 'ideal sites for anthropological as well as zoological inquiry' (ibid.: 613).

'Indeed', Kuklick notes, for Haddon and later, at least initially, for Rivers, whose work with the former had transformed him in part from a laboratory to a field scientist, 'insular populations such as those inhabiting the Aran Islands and Torres Straits Islands were *virtual laboratories* for natural experiments in social process' (ibid.: 617). There is a line, in other words, from Darwin's finches in the Galapagos to anthropology's natives in the Trobriands. The processes studied in these virtual laboratories hinged on the differing responses of native forms to integration into the world economy. As such, the ideal informants, Rivers and Haddon both agreed, 'were people who had experienced some culture contact' (ibid.: 617). Strikingly, Rivers was deeply suspicious of the possibility of stripping away, as it were, the accretions of westernization or culture contact 'so as to exhibit [contemporary primitives] as they used to be' (ibid.: 625).

It should be noted, that this was in some respects, an instrumental rather than theoretical ideal – Rivers praised the 'mollifying influence of the official and the missionary' (Kuklick 1996: 617) in rendering informants more willing to speak of 'precontact days'. Yet it is clear that at this moment in the field's history, islands were interesting sites (and metaphors?) not because they were untouched or isolated, but because they presented compelling epitomizations of contact (which Haddon assumed would result in the extinction of geocultural isolates). The island thus came to figure centrally in early anthropology for reasons that were thought at the time to be legitimately scientific – that they were virtual laboratories for understanding change because of their size and that they, moreover, were interesting precisely because of their increasing interconnectedness. Further, Haddon and Rivers were well aware of their specificities as such and of the problems with generalizing island-based methodologies. Rivers, noted for example, that islands, 'afforded "application of the method of difference" rarely appropriate in continental areas' (ibid.: 617).

Yet soon after the successful conclusion of the second Torres Straits Expedition in 1898 there was something of a split between Haddon and Rivers – one with great significance even if it remained relatively implicit and mostly limited to the realm of methodology. To vastly oversimplify Kuklick's nuanced discussion of the subject, as Rivers rose to disciplinary prominence at Haddon's expense, the former's training in laboratory science replaced Haddon's field-science-derived approach as the primary touchstone for new anthropological research projects. Thus, somewhere along the way, islands ceased to be interesting primarily as virtual laboratories for social change and came to be appealing sites for research in so much as they promised an actual 'controlled laboratory' of cultural isolates.

According to Kuklick, Rivers implicitly sought to make islands into laboratories not for the Darwinian study of change but for the study of 'stable, integrated communities engendered by isolation'. By doing so, he rendered Haddon's own approach (and much of nineteenth-century anthropology) 'absurd' (Kuklick 1996: 624). In this transition, the scientific logic for select- ing the island as the locus and implicit model of the field in the first place was lost. In the process, Kuklick notes, memorably, 'the island became cultural rather than physical space' (ibid.: 625). It ceased to be a site and became a metaphor or analogy for anthropology's object of study.

Unlike Haddon (or the early Rivers) who 'found the "insular character of Oceania" of special anthropological interest because it afforded the "preser[vation], often in wonderfully pure form" of archaic social modes, [while] also emphasiz[ing] analysis of contact situations', the later Rivers and those who followed tended to subordinate the latter focus to the former. *Explanandum* became *explanans* in the process. 'Fieldworkers did not select geographically isolated research sites in the expectation that they would probably find societal speciation there, but sought subjects whose idiosyncratic character was the presumed result of social isolation' (Kuklick 1996: 625). In the process, the island as anthropological site *par excellence* became completely unmoored from its 'original coordinates'.

As a result, an insularizing anthropology came to be the primary mode of engaging with the African peoples that comprised the main focus of the British branch discipline from the mid twenties onwards. This is despite the fact that Rivers clearly held that, in Africa, 'the social isolation probable among island peoples was "most exceptional, if it ever occurs"' (Kuklick 1996: 626). In spite of these objections, the island became a sort of port- able prototype, a travelling form for the field. In this form (delinked from particular islands per Eriksen 1993), the fieldsite as island was, in Matei Candea's (2007) words, taken to be 'a "really existing feature of the world out there", a discrete spatial or human entity which was supposed to have its own consistency and meaning – the village, the neighbourhood, the tribe, the kind of entity which could become the subject of an exhaus- tive and comprehensive monograph' (ibid.: 179). The anthropology that emerged alongside the popularization of this inversive notion of the field site was devoted, in turn, to the 'Intensive Study of Limited Areas' (Stocking 1992: 27).

Voting Anthropology off the Island

George Marcus has famously sought to move beyond this insular version of the field by articulating a clarion call for multi-sited ethnographies in and of the world system that 'move from conventional single-site location[s] con- textualized by macro-constructions of a larger social order ... to multiple sites of observation and participation that cross-cut dichotomies such as the "local" and the "global", the "lifeworld" and the "system"' (1995: 95). Yet, according to Matei Candea (2007), even the most traditional of fieldsites are always already 'multi-sited', comprising both 'the many heterogeneous spaces' of their 'physical location[s]', and 'the many historical, institutional, and conceptual spaces in which [accounts]' of the particular site are 'deploy[ed]'(Candea 2007: 177). He thus refuses the exhortations of multi-sited ethnography in a Marcusian vein to 'forgo Crucetta [his field-site] and follow the traces which leave the village, to discover the contours of some wider translocal "cultural formation"' (ibid.: 178). Instead, he turns to an explicitly partial engagement with fieldsites as 'arbitrary locations' – situated 'frameworks for the study [not of some cultural whole that was presumed to inhere therein] but of something else [often a theoretical something else]' (ibid.: 179).

The resonances of Candea's account with Kuklick's description of Haddon's island approach to Darwinian biogeography applied to human societies (rather than Finches) are surprising and instructive. Candea glosses 'arbitrary location' as a heuristic device intended as "the symmetrical inversion of the "ideal type"' (Candea 2007: 179-80). In Candea's formulation, Weber's ideal type has important parallels with the concept of the laboratory – it is, he writes, 'an abstracted notion, nowhere existing and for that very reason easily definable, a notion which served as a "control" for comparative analysis of actually existing instances' (ibid.: 180). By contrast, the arbitrary location 'is the actually existing instance, whose messiness, contingency, and lack of an overarching coherence … serve as a "control" for a broader abstract object of study' (ibid.: 180). Given the parallelism here between laboratory as placeless, artificially standardized space, and ideal type as 'meaning which cuts through space' (ibid.: 180), perhaps it is unsurprising that island as natural laboratory morphed gradually into island as ideal type or even archetype.

Yet this is where Ingold's intervention, I think, proves indispensable. For what if the bound/unbound dichotomy that structures both the multi-sited turn and its recent critique is premised on a false distinction? An Ingoldian emphasis on the mutual constitution of place and movement breaks down any distinction between 'villages' and 'the traces which leave them'. Nor does an Ingoldian approach assume the sort of 'protean' crypto-culturalist holism that Candea sees as underlying and subverting the critical oomph of multi-sited approaches.

Further, per Ingold, this emphasis on binding rather than boundedness does not itself turn on a distinction between an immobile knot at the centre of a network of mobile chords (or 'traces'), where we either stay put (dwell) in one or move (travel) along the other. Rather all elements are themselves on the boil. For Ingold holds that 'lives are not led inside places but through, around, to and from them and to places elsewhere'. In his re-envisioning, 'human existence is not ... place-*bound* ... but place-*binding*. It unfolds not in places but along paths' (Ingold 2007: 33; original emphasis). Ingold terms 'the embodied experiences of this perambulatory movement', central to both movement and place as they are traditionally defined, 'wayfaring'. In the world as he describes it:

> places are like knots, and the threads from which they are tied are lines of wayfaring. A house, for example, is a place where the lines of its residents are tightly knotted together. But these lines are no more contained within the house than are the threads contained within a knot. Rather they trail beyond it, only to become caught up with other lines in other places, as are the threads in other knots (ibid.: 33).

In this reticulate connectivity, which Ingold, following Henri Lefebvre, terms a 'meshwork', places are 'delineated by movement, not by the outer limits to movement' (Ingold 2007: 34).

Thus enframed, Candea's distinction between the village and the traces which leave it is seen to be a false one. A fieldsite is less a geographic locale that exists in what Law and Mol (2001) might call 'volumetric space' than a haecceity, a certain coming together of multiple trajectories of becoming. In this vein, Ingold notes that:

> the lives of things generally extend along not one but multiple lines, knotted together at the centre but trailing innumerable 'loose ends' at the periphery. Thus each should be pictured, as Latour has latterly suggested, in the shape of a star 'with a centre surrounded by many radiating lines, with all sorts of tiny conduits leading to and fro' (Latour 2005: 177). No longer a self-contained object, the thing now appears as an ever-ramifying web of lines of growth. This is the haecceity of Deleuze and Guattari, famously likened by them to a rhizome (Deleuze and Guattari 2004: 290) ... what is crucial is that we start from the fluid character of the life process, wherein boundaries are sustained only thanks to the flow of materials across them. (Ingold 2010: 12)

Approached in such a manner, even the most apparently solid entities start to blur into motion. Even buildings or monuments (not to mention fieldsites) are 'experienced processually in vistas, occlusions and transitions that unfold along the myriad pathways inhabitants take'. In this procession, 'as the life of the inhabitants overflows into gardens and streets, fields and forests, so the world pours into the building'. This give and take between exterior and interior precludes any possibility of a stable line between the two. Indeed, 'it is in these flows and counter-flows, winding through or amidst without beginning or end, and not as connected entities bounded either from within or without, that things are instantiated' (Ingold 2010: 12).

We Have Never Been (Im)mobile

What might anthropological methods (and their corresponding concepts of the field) look like if they were to be conceptualized as similarly unbounded? Approaching things in such a fashion might foreground two sorts of heretofore obscured movement that have been present in fieldwork since the days of Haddon and Rivers: the geographical multiplicity of a fieldsite of co-mobile knots and traces in which travel becomes a kind of dwelling on the one hand, and the quotidian mobilities of fieldwork in which dwelling becomes a kind of travel on the other. In an attempt to illustrate the quotidian mobilities of both ethnographer and field, I turn to my own fieldwork as a restless movement between field and preterrain in order to unwind the boundary between the two.

During my first long stint in the field in 2003–2004, researching the connections between ethnic diversity and economic development in northwest China, I spent much of my time more in orbit than in residence. My field(work) moved in concentric, if eccentric, circuits that took as their centre the small polyglot town of Xiahe/Labrang in the Gannan Tibetan Autonomous Prefecture of Gansu Province in northwest China. But neither my time nor topics were effectively constrained by the span of that terrain. In my research's simplest circuit, I moved back and forth between Xiahe and the provincial capital, Lanzhou, on a tri-weekly basis in order to visit the ATM and to touch base with my academic contacts at Lanzhou University. My tri-weekly circuits within Gansu and Qinghai (Labrang-Lanzhou-Xining-Tongren-Labrang) were supplemented on an erratic basis with more circuitous journeys further afield beyond the bounds of province and region as far as Shenzhen, Beijing and Shanghai. Also, I was able to visit the hometowns of various key informants in the rural areas surrounding Labrang – places such as Sangke, Jianzha and Lintan.

These circuits and the crowded busses, noisy motorcycles and plodding walking tractors that defined them tended to result in an interesting sort of bifocality in which my ethnographic observations in the ethnically mixed uplands were supplemented and critiqued by the perspectives of urban Han academics.[5] Such circuitousness allowed me to keep the profoundly strange juxtapositions of contemporary Chinese society in sharp focus – to hold, in other words, Kendeji (Kentucky Fried Chicken) and the *minzu wenti* (the Ethnic Minorities Question), everyday life in Xiahe and my dialogues with academic (and urban) interlocutors elsewhere (and elsewhen), within a single analytic field. As a result, in my chapter (Vasantkumar 2012) in the volume on *Critical Han Studies*, I was able to highlight the emergence prior to 2008 of multi-ethnic idioms of local community in which local comities (in particular those that saw local Han and Tibetans loosely allied in mutual suspicion of the Hui) could effectively trump the supposedly more fundamental bonds of blood thought to connect local Han or Tibetans with their co-ethnics elsewhere in China.

Moreover, during the course of my fieldwork in 2003–2004 it became increasingly apparent that even 'within' Gannan, 'local' relationships on both individual and collective levels were shaped in important respects by processes that trailed away into other knots of reticulate connection. In particular, I met many Tibetans who had spent time in the exile communities of the Indian subcontinent. The duration of their visits ranged from a few months to upwards of five years. Some detested India from the moment they arrived, some still reminisced fondly about pizza and sang tunes from Bollywood musicals, but all had for various reasons chosen to return to Amdo. While I addressed this population in one chapter of my dissertation, it was also clear that further research – both in and beyond northwest China – would be necessary to begin to contextualize the complex affiliations of these mobile populations.

After completing my dissertation, I conducted additional research into trans-Himalayan Tibetan-ness and constructions of overseas Chinese-ness on both sides of the Himalayas. I returned to Xiahe in 2006, 2007 and 2009. Also, and crucially for my perspective on these matters, I worked with Tibetan migrants from the Amdo region (in which Xiahe is located) in Dharamsala, north India, the epicentre of the exile Tibetan community abroad, in 2006 and 2007. In doing so, I found that Tibetans on both sides of the Himalayas imagined Tibet as a significant but absent elsewhere, conceptualized alternately in territorial or cultural terms (cf. Vasantkumar 2013a). In this research, Tibet itself came to be less the unspoken ground of my study than the focus of its concern – a clutch of trajectories rather than a settled geographical meaning.

The ethnographic descriptions that have resulted from this research are neither precisely nor necessarily about a population linked to one particular place in the crypto-Herderian vein of much anthropological writing but take as their field the intersections of Chinese national development and trans-Himalayan Tibet. In them dwelling and travel coalesce such that ethnographic research itself comes to depend upon the warp and weft of arrivals and departures. Upon this periodicity we build our architectures of apprehension and supposition. The field itself, too, is opened up in both temporal and spatial terms. The latter aspect of this opening up should be clear enough – in moving back and forth from the 'site' to its 'preterrain' the temporal separation between these two collapses. Preterrain becomes 'coterrain', an expanded notion of site that includes both the proximate location of fieldwork and its spatial preconditions and extensities.

Yet coterrain also ramifies temporally. Following Dalsgaard and Nielsen (2013), who note that 'ethnographic fieldwork constitutes a recursive temporal oscillation between different sites that are spatial but also inherently conceptual' (Dalsgaard and Nielsen 2013: 4), mobile methods must address fieldwork not just as multi-sited but as multi-temporal. Echoing distantly an Ingoldian focus on the processual emergence of things, they argue that 'central aspects of doing fieldwork can be [best] accounted for by taking the field to be a processual configuration through which time and space continuously interweave to chart out new analytical terrains' (ibid: 3).

In order to begin to access how the field is opened up in temporal terms, and to understand why such an attunement to multi-temporality necessarily renders preterrain coterrain, a shift in representational form may prove generative. Below, three passages of relatively uncooked 'field' notes highlight the field as a 'processual configuration', an assemblage of absences and presences, entries and exits, beginnings, endings and revisitings.

Coterrains, Temporal and Spatial

What follows are wormhole temporalities – sequential inscriptions of the field and of the ethnographer, as a kind of relativist temporal practice – the inscriptions do not age, yet 'in real life', the field races on and we with it. The cobblers below are gone, the fruit market demolished, the slaughterhouse resacralized, the slow roads erased by expressways.

1. (2003)

> The light this November evening when the cold at once wakens in you a vigilance and does its work on your hands and face, layers of clothes ineffective and forgotten after so many days, dies down to a pale robin's egg blue where the valley narrows off west towards Sangke. The sounds of the street drift up to the third floor deck studded with chimneys. Motorcycle taxis, 'tumbrels' in T's quaint English, sputter and whine as their drivers grind through the gears bumping across the old bridge that divides the monastery from town. Minibuses horn pedestrians out of the way.

Looking out over the monastery, the long tangent of prayer wheels in deep shadow runs rail straight from the ruins of the old slaughterhouse with its boarded up water tower until it dead ends in a fruit market that glows dull orange like Dante's abode of the virtuous heathen. Pigs move and nomads shit in the fields by the prayer wheels. Cobblers by the drainage ditch finish the last jobs of the day.

The view to the east is along the rooftops of Renmin Xidajie (West People's Avenue) a mix of old-style eaves appended to boxy constructions, unadorned boxes, the bulk of the theatre and its discos, clotheslines and white smoke rising from countless stovepipes, chimneys and *bsang* (juniper) fires. It is almost night, but the discourse of the streets continues little abated. It combines with dog bark and the drifting smoke to form the texture of dusk or just after. The burble of a three-wheeler, the odd beast that is the Lanzhou Camel, drifts up from the river. I can look down on the affairs of the cobblers, the card players, the *mahua* (fried dough twirls) salesmen, but this view from above is strictly from my eyes. The mountains, shadow-striped with snow rear above, rife with hidden paths on which sheep are led in the mornings to graze the heights.

I am above and below, on the deck of a seventeen-year-old building on what was once farmland at the edge of a talus fan descending from a valley now dammed, ditched and built up. In November, 2003, having been here for as long as I have, knowing what I know, skewed as only I am skewed. This position of observing, this sundeck with empty clotheslines is as much a construction as this description of it. And we never truly know ourselves so how can we know the man up all night with his wife and young daughter in Hard Seat in the ancient carriages of the Tianjin–Chengde local with dirt under his nails and a peasant's suit and a sun-worn face that marks his place and prospects? Prospect – a view and future.

'*Ren de xin dou yiyang*'. People's hearts are all the same, old Ma, the shopkeeper, says. But how can we know the place by knowing a few people; know the beach by twenty-five grains of sand or two thousand? How particular individuals make place is some component part of the totality of the place that is made. But of what significance? The physical apparatuses of place, its materiality, if you like – mountains, buildings, infrastructure, habitual public habits – all of which appear lasting and even normative, are all in process. They all flow like window glass. Their shifts only occasionally visible: the roads with their oxbows, the different character of the seasons ....

Place, like culture, seems about to vanish. At least like culture in its old holistic evened out form. But it doesn't vanish, it provides the ground and grounding for the workings out of life, love, thought, and enmity. To talk about place is to talk about place in time – meanings, buildings, rivers shift and settle – to freeze a view of place is to freeze culture like a Functionalist. The challenge is to integrate the grounding and ungrounding that result from living somewhere, somewhen under thrall of a somehow (or several conflicting somehows). Placemaking and being made by place. Parting and being partial.

2. (2006)

Historically, we have erased the paths leading to our arrivals, filtered the routine details of passage that set us down at the threshold. Firth is mute on the stevedores and gangplanks of the Southern Cross at the quayside in Rabaul or Lae or Samarai. Malinowski summons us to his tropical beach suddenly like Jinns uncoiling from our lamps; grumpily, halfway through the acrostic. I am inclined to spare you the four loops of town my first Xiahe bus did trawling all the usual places in Linxia for passengers for the slow ride up the valley of the Daxia. [Expressways undreamt of] Journeys and their infrastructure are in flux, in motion, if we can slow our eyes down. The disused loops of the old road filling with reeds up the valley from Wangertan, blooming pot holes nearing Linxia, the new pillars for the viaducts vaulting the valleys one pass away from the tailings of Lanzhou.

At home now in California, I can compare that first bus ride through a territory of unknown names and unfinished roads to all the rest. I can tell you to avoid changing buses in Linxia if at all possible; that the conductors will hustle the unwary or the feeble onto their bus at inflated prices, that a foreign appearance licenses concerted attempts to extract extra fares. I know old Hezhou has its partisans, but I say skip it. Three hours uphill through Shuangcheng where you turn hard left and head up hill. That first day it was memorable only for the open-air butcher's shop; blood on the curb and intestines steaming as the butcher wound them around his forearm like an extension cord, the bus jammed with short-distance travellers. Uphill through the high dry valleys so wan in winter, so green and lovely in new spring with mist filling in the gaps between the peaks. To Wangertan and the junction. The Labrang road so terrible at first and so smooth of late. Hours of slaloming road construction. On that trip I did not count the monasteries or the ruins, nor expect to know people hailing from the blink and you miss 'em villages, old walls at roadside: Damai, Changshitou; Horkajia. I still don't know all the names; I see no point lying about that. But I have walked the last five miles or parts of them with Rinchen and his sister in fitful snow near New Years waiting for his ride to appear.

So rather than begin with a definitive arrival, the baggage carousel, the maglev, the floods in Anhui marooning me in the train station, Dunhuang, my first circuit of the monastery, arrival and departure are the warp and weft I hang this on. A punctuate and finite staying that defeats final knowledge. Necessary to leave every three weeks to go to the automatic teller in Lanzhou; or further to sanity in Beijing, Shanghai, Suzhou. And to return, to have friends in China. Ah, *ni huilai le*. Does one start to belong, or at least to fit, when ones return is acknowledged as such?

These words are now nearly nine years old themselves, another nested inscription. As is this:

3. (2015)

One never steps into the same field twice. As one returns after longer and longer intervals of separation, fieldsites become uncanny terrains, their apparent solidities revealed as matrices of becoming. The temporality of the field-as-a-place is put in bold relief by the ever-widening gap between our particular inscriptions of it and its present reality. This chapter has emerged from an ever-deepening anxiety about the ephemerality of the field as a particular place and time. For me this is not so much the 'empiricist anxiety' described by Feldman as 'express[ing] the contradiction between the ethnographic imperative of "being there" and the obliteration of a place as a bounded methodological construct (Gupta and Ferguson 1997: 4)' (Feldman 2011: 378) as it is a tension between my own situated sense of the field and fieldwork as becoming(s) and the broader anthropological tendency to think the field as a bounded spatial rather than a temporally dynamic location. One way of addressing this gap may be to reconceptualize the field as an assemblage of spatio-temporal distances and proximities, absences and presences, as the whole span of one's thought, writings and movement on a topic. But how might one understand the relationship between mobile methods and such a restless locus of study?

Conclusion: Arbitrary Itinerations

Reflecting back on the iterative process both of 'field' work (with its sequential and concurrent voyages in time and space) and of composing this chapter, I conclude by proposing an alternative to Candea's notion of 'arbitrary locations'. Mobile methods, I suggest would be well served by swapping this vision for one of arbitrary 'itinerations' in which one aims not to 'bound off a site' but, per Ingold, to foreground its bindings (not its boundness but its binded-ness).

How then to approach fieldwork? Justin Armstrong (2011) offers Benjamin's figure of the flâneur[6] as one possible prototype for fieldwork that might reverse modernity's dotting of the line. The resonances between Ingold's call for a return to gestural linearity and Armstrong's description of the motivations behind his work on the ruined landscapes of abandoned farm towns in northern Saskatchewan are apparent:

> I decided to pursue this type of research, because I wanted to reimagine the practice of ethnography as a form of unplanning, an idea that is effectively embodied in the figure of the flâneur. Benjamin, writing on the demise of the force of experience in modernity, stated that '[i]n the place of the force field that is lost to humanity with the devaluation of experience, a new field of force opens up with the form of planning' (Benjamin 2002, p. 801). This 'form of planning' has overtaken almost every aspect of modern life, and rather than only helping to embolden the cult of efficiency that pervades our society, it has penetrated deeply into our subconscious, to the extent that it has become difficult to excise. And while some degree of planning is necessary in the case of ethnographic research (e.g. making arrangements for rental cars, hotels and flights), it is possible to move through ethnographic space without a specifically codified plan of action (Armstrong 2001: 287).

Yet is this in itself novel or merely the acknowledgement of long-standing realities? Even as we acknowledge with new theoretical heft the ways in which our fieldsites slip beyond the apparent bounds of place, have we really departed from what anthropologists have always actually done while being (or, perhaps, becoming) there?

> Soon after I had established myself in Omarakana ... I began to take part, in a way, in the village life, to look forward to the important or festive events, to take personal interest in the gossip and the developments of the small village occurences; to wake up every morning to a day presenting itself to me more or less as it does to the native. I would get out from under my mosquito net, to find around me the village life beginning to stir, or the people well advanced in their working day according to the hour or to the season .... *As I went on my morning walk through the village,* I could see intimate details of family life, of toilet, cooking, taking of meals; I could see the arrangements for the day's work, people starting on their errands, or groups of men and women busy at some manufacturing tasks. Quarrels, jokes, family scenes, events usually trivial, sometimes dramatic but always significant formed the atmosphere of my daily life as well as of theirs. It must be remembered that as the natives saw me constantly everyday they ceased to be interested or alarmed by my presence and I ceased to be a disturbing element in tribal life (Malinowski 1922: 7–8; emphasis added).

Despite the lingering influence of a totalizing rhetoric of fieldsite (perhaps as 'spreading inkstain' (Foster 2008: xvi)) as uniform and neatly bounded geographic space in which anthropologists dwell (a rhetoric that persists at the very least in the stories of what our backward ancestors practised), in actual practice, fields (sited and otherwise) are complex spaces, shot through with splintered (Graham and Marvin 2001) latencies and disconnectivities, leavened with *terrains vagues* (H. Armstrong 2006) of unknowability. Anthropologists must perforce navigate these disjunctive topographies (and, arguably topologies (Law and Mol 2001, Vasantkumar 2013b)), whether by foot, by car, by subway, or by trackpad, and as such, all fieldwork necessarily consists of micro-practices of mobility. Even in their quarters (their hotel rooms, their tents) anthropologists must move in and out, to and fro.

In the field nothing stays still. Perhaps, then, all anthropological methods – even those as immobilizing as Malinowski's (so ready to pin down the world in scientific tables and charts) are mobile methods (just as all sites are multi-; cf. Candea 2007; Mol 2003). Ultimately in lieu of a definitive conclusion, I suggest that in pursuit of mobile methods, anthropologists would be well served by a critical and historical consciousness of the specificity of their own movements through ethnographic space and that in such movements, the journey is, as the old saw would have it, the destination. The line, in other words, may be the whole point.

Chris Vasantkumar is a lecturer in anthropology at Macquarie University in Sydney, Australia. His research interests include the anthropology of mobility, the anthropology of money, standards and standardization, and the history of metrology and measurement. He is currently writing a book on the making of modern money. His work has appeared in *The Journal of Asian Studies*; *Environment and Planning D: Society and Space*; *Ethnos: Journal of Anthropology*; and *Theory, Culture and Society*.

NOTES

1. In this regard, this chapter builds upon insights gleaned from recent critical approaches to concepts of home (e.g. Blunt 2003; Ralph and Staeheli 2011; Tolia-Kelly 2004, cf. Vasantkumar 2013a). As Ralph and Staeheli write in a recent review article on the subject, 'The challenge ... is to conceptualize the simultaneity of home as sedentarist and mobile' (Ralph and Staeheli: 518). They note perspicaciously 'how home is already inflected with mobility and conversely, [how] mobility is inflected with gestures of attachment' (ibid.: 519) with which people 'imbue the notion' (ibid.: 525). Redefining home in such a manner has significant implications for ideas of anthropologists as 'homebodies abroad'.

2. I thus would tend to disagree with certain aspects of the editors' assertion in the Introduction to this volume that because, 'traditional ethnography relied on a rather sedentary approach, with a tendency to privilege face-to-face relationships, permanent residence and fixed boundaries while overlooking mediated interactions,

movements, connections and connectivity (Wittel 2000), ethnographic techniques needed to be adapted to be of use in mobilities research'.

3. Salazar notes that the opposite is the case for contemporary forms of pilgrimage, in which 'many observers [e.g. Coleman and Eade 2004] have noted the opposite movement (whereby the journey becomes more important than the destination' (Noel Salazar, personal communication, 14 November 2014). This may potentially be attributable to the degree to which contemporary forms of pilgrimage may be premised on a consciously anti-modern or amodern approach to mobility.

4. He was an 'enthusias[t]' of sea anemones (Kuklick 2011: 11).

5. Further, the jostling bus rides themselves proved to be surprisingly productive of ethnographically interesting conversations and observation.

6. Kramer and Short (2011) write, 'The original flâneur was an iconic figure apparently wandering at leisure through the passages of rapidly growing, industrializing cities of the nineteenth century. The practice of this urban meander is flânerie. The unhurried gait was deliberately deceptive, however; it was actually a cover for the flâneur's true mission to tap eagerly into urban energies, to absorb readily unforeseen novelties, and to engage playfully (and ruefully) with the mingling of old and new typical of modern cities' (2011: 323). The term of course was seized upon by Baudelaire and later Benjamin as a key trope of urban(e) modernity. See Shaya (2004) for a critical perspective. It is possible that Armstrong's figure of the flâneur as the athlete of the unplanned, as it were, might have more in common with the flâneur's foil – the badaud, or gawker.

REFERENCES

Appadurai, A. 1988. 'Putting Hierarchy in its Place', *Cultural Anthropology* 3: 36–49.
_____. 1990. 'Disjuncture and Difference in the Global Cultural Economy', *Public Culture* 2(2): 1–24.
Armstrong, H. 2006. 'Time, Dereliction and Beauty: An Argument for "Landscapes of Contempt"', The Landscape Architect, *IFLA Conference Papers* pp. 117–27.
Armstrong, J. 2011. 'Everyday Afterlives', *Cultural Studies* 25(3): 273–93.
Baldacchino, G. 2005. 'Editorial: Islands – Objects of Representation', *Geografiska Annaler* 87: 247–51.
Blunt, A. 2003. 'Collective Memory and Productive Nostalgia: Anglo-Indian Homemaking at McCluskieganj', *Environment and Planning D* 21: 717–38
Candea, M. 2007. 'Arbitrary Locations: In Defence of the Bounded Field-Site', *JRAI* 13(1): 167–84.
Clifford, J. 1988. *The Predicament of Culture*. Cambridge: Harvard University Press.
_____. 1997. *Routes*. Cambridge: Harvard University Press.
Coleman, S., and J. Eade (eds). 2004. *Reframing Pilgrimage: Cultures in Motion*. London: Routledge.
Coutin, S.B. 2005. 'Being En Route', *American Anthropologist* 107(2): 195–206.

Dalsgaard, S. and M. Nielsen. 2013. 'Introduction: Time and the Field', *Social Analysis* 57(1): 1–19.

Eriksen, T.H. 1993. 'In Which Sense Do Cultural Islands Exist?' *Social Anthropology* 1(1b): 133–47.

Feldman, G. 2011. 'If Ethnography Is More Than Participant-Observation, then Relations Are More Than Connections: The Case for Nonlocal Ethnography in a World of Apparatuses', *Anthropological Theory* 11(4): 375–95.

Foster, R.J. 2008. *Cocaglobalization.* New York: Palgrave MacMillan.

Graham, S., and S. Marvin. 2001. Splintering Urbanism. New York: Routledge.

Gupta, A., and J. Ferguson (eds). 1997. *Culture, Power, Place.* Durham: Duke University Press.

Hay, P. 2006. 'A Phenomenology of Islands', *Island Studies Journal* 1(1): 19–42.

Ingold, T. 2007. *Lines.* New York: Routledge.

_____. 2009. 'Against Space: Place, Movement, Knowledge', in P. Kirby (ed), *Boundless Worlds: An Anthropological Approach to Movement.* New York: Berghahn, pp. 29–44

_____. 2010. 'Bringing Things to Life: Creative Entanglements in a World of Materials', *Realities.* Working Paper #15. Retrieved September 2013 from www.manchester. ac.uk/realities.

Kramer, K., and J.R. Short. 2011. 'Flânerie and the Globalizing City', *City* (3–4): 322–42.

Kuklick, H. 1996. 'Islands in the Pacific: Darwinian Biogeography and British Anthropology', *American Ethnologist* 23(3): 611–38.

_____. 2011. 'Personal Equations: Reflections on the History of Fieldwork, with Special Reference to Sociocultural Anthropology', *Isis* 102(1): 1–33.

Latour, B. 1993. *We Have Never Been Modern.* Cambridge: Harvard University Press.

Law, J., and A. Mol. 2001. 'Situating Technoscience: An Inquiry into Spatialities', *Environment and Planning D* 19: 609–21.

Malinowski, B. 1922. *Argonauts of the Western Pacific.* New York: Dutton.

Malkki, L. 1992. 'National Geographic: The Rooting of Peoples and the Territorialization of National Identity Among Scholars and Refugees', *Cultural Anthropology* 7(1): 24–44.

Marcus, G. 1995. 'Ethnography in/of the World System: The Emergence of Multi-Sited Ethnography', *Annual Review of Anthropology* 24: 95–117.

Mol, A. 2003. *The Body Multiple.* Durham: Duke University Press.

Ralph, D., and L. Staeheli. 2011. 'Home and Migration: Mobilities, Belongings and Identities', *Geography Compass* 5(7): 517–30.

Shaya, G. 2004. 'The Flaneur, the Badaud and the Making of a Mass Public in France, circa 1860–1910', *The American Historical Review* 109(1): 41–77.

Stocking, G. 1992. *The Ethnographer's Magic and Other Essays in the History of Anthropology.* Madison, WI: University of Wisconsin Press.

Tolia-Kelly, D. 2004. 'Locating Processes of Identification: Studying the Precipitates of Re-memory through Artefacts in the British Asian Home', *Transactions of the Institute of British Geographers* 29(3): 314–29.

Vasantkumar, C. 2012. 'Han at *Minzu's* Edges: What Critical Han Studies Can Learn from China's "Little Tibet"', in T. Mullaney, J. Leibold, S. Gros, and E. Vanden Bussche (eds), *Critical Han Studies*. Berkeley: University of California Press, pp. 234–55.

_____. 2013a. 'Tibetan Peregri-nations: Mobility, Incommensurable Nationalisms and (Un)belonging Athwart the Himalayas', *Journal of Ethnic and Migration Studies* 39(2): 219–36.

_____. 2013b. 'The Scale of Scatter: Rethinking Social Topologies via the Anthropology of "Residual China"', *Environment and Planning D* 31: 918–34.

Wolf, E. 1982. *Europe and the People Without History*. Berkeley: University of California Press.

From Radar Systems to Rickety Boats

Borderline Ethnography in Europe's 'Illegality Industry'

Ruben Andersson

This chapter is concerned with the problems and possibilities that mobility poses for social scientific research, as seen through the lens of my own work on irregular migration from West Africa towards southern Spain. I begin with two contrasting vignettes from Europe's borders that illustrate the paradoxical role of mobility in the continent's escalating 'fight against illegal migration' – as well as the challenges involved in grappling with such mobility ethnographically.

In late May 2013, bus after bus disgorged uniformed border officers at Warsaw's Pepsi arena. They had arrived for the annual European Day for Border Guards, organized by the EU's border agency Frontex, itself headquartered in a skyscraper in the Polish capital. The aim of the event was to share 'best practices' among the disparate European forces working on border security – and, in particular, on keeping irregular migrants from crossing the external borders of the Schengen area of free movement, a task in which Frontex had played a leading role in the decade since its founding. In the registration queues mingled Scandinavian coast guards, Spanish IT contractors, American security experts, and Polish policemen. Some lingered outside, admiring a small surveillance aircraft strategically positioned at the entrance by its manufacturer. Upstairs, defence companies had set up glossy displays showing detection equipment, while border forces offered videos on sea rescues – as did humanitarian organizations a few steps away. Next to them, a Frontex officer showed on a touchscreen how border guards now shared near-real-time information on migrant intercep- tions in the Mediterranean. Here, at the Pepsi arena, it was evident that a motley congregation of sectors and groups were converging around the 'ille- gal migrant' at the EU's external borders: security forces, aid organizations, defence contractors, policymakers, and media and academic visitors such as myself. The material features of this multi-faceted 'illegality industry' (Andersson 2014a; cf. Gammeltoft-Hansen and Sørensen 2013) – from the surveillance aircraft and the information-sharing systems to the buses wait- ing outside – highlighted how Europe's 'fight against illegal migration' relied upon large amounts of mobility for staff, technology, and resources alike.

Spool back to December 2010 and to the capital of Mali, far from the Warsaw showrooms. My fourteen-month period of anthropological field- work on irregular migration was well under way, and I had entered the headquarters of the Malian Gendarmerie to discuss their role as 'subcon- tractors' in Europe's migration controls. The director-general had gathered his top officials in charge of migration for my visit, and all had a word or two to say on the need for more resources from their European partners. 'Until now, the Gendarmerie Nationale has not been equipped', said one of the colonels, comparing his force with the Malian border police, which had new funds, tools, and border posts thanks to the EU and individual member states, principally Spain and France. 'If our thirty-five [border units] are equipped, that will reinforce the control of migratory flows', the officers said, before listing demands that were more specific: computers for their border posts, and solar panels to power them; more vehicles, and petrol for these vehicles. In Mali, the real-time surveillance vision on display in Warsaw was replaced by a much simpler ambition: in one officer's words, to enhance the 'mobility of our units in the field'. It was an aim that their European partners could only partly satisfy, however.

Mobility, in research and in our world at large, is often lent a 'positive valence', implying progress or positive change (Salazar and Smart 2011: ii). Yet one kind of mobility may well be in direct 'conflict' with another. The snapshots above illustrate how multiple mobilities (of money, equipment, personnel) have been 'mobilized' so to speak in order to curtail human movement, while highlighting the stark inequalities in the distribution of such mobility. Ethnographic attention to these dynamics may bring novel perspectives to critical mobilities studies (Glick Schiller and Salazar 2013) while providing a crucial piece in the puzzle of understanding the 'business of bordering Europe'. While I deal with these larger ethnographic tasks in my work as a whole (Andersson 2014a), I will here address the spe- cific methodological problems at the heart of such enquiries into mobile systems. In doing so, I will draw upon existing strands of migration and mobility research to suggest a form of mobile fieldwork across interfaces and disciplines – tentatively glossed as 'borderline ethnography' – that mirrors border workers' own methods while drawing on journalistic practice.

This chapter addresses a key point raised in the Introduction to this volume: how we may fruitfully allow research problems to guide which methods we use, rather than the other way round. In this vein, I will first briefly describe my fieldwork trajectory before embarking on the two substantive themes of my argument. The first part, on design, considers lessons from multi-sited research, the 'extended case method' and actor-network theory (ANT) while drawing up an 'extended fieldsite' concept that allows for an ethnographic exploration of the illegality industry as well as the concrete effects it has on the migrants it targets. The second part, on method, will explore how the 'poaching' of select journalistic techniques may enhance ethnographies of conflictive, secretive, and mobile systems – laying the groundwork for concluding remarks on the pros and cons of 'borderline ethnography' in settings other than Europe's vast and violent borderscapes.[1]

Preamble: From Mobile People to Mobile Systems

So-called 'illegal' or clandestine migration – terms I use here in a folk or 'emic' sense[2] – from Sub-Saharan Africa towards southern Europe has long been a highly mediatized phenomenon despite its relatively minor statistical significance (de Haas 2007). However, the vast majority of this media coverage begins and ends at the EU's external borders. By contrast, most Sub-Saharan Africans, before setting out on their boats, have already completed long, uncertain journeys towards the north, traversing deserts, no man's lands and numerous border checkpoints en route.

As I was preparing for my first fieldwork period in West Africa in early 2010, my aim was to concentrate on this fraught space of movement, which had long remained beyond the scope of both mainstream media attention and scholarly studies. While the newscasts have concentrated on the 'border spectacle' at Europe's edges (De Genova 2012), migration studies have often focused on reasons for leaving, home communities, and the process of arrival and adaptation, leaving unsaid what happens in the process of migration itself, that is, the in-between phase of mobility and enforced immobility (Collyer 2007; cf. Hage 2005). My study, focusing on this phase, would seek to challenge the 'rootedness' and 'sedentary bias' that other writers have criticized in studies of migration, not least in the West African case (van Dijk, Foeken, and van Til 2001). With this theoretical and methodological move, I followed a larger trend, pinpointed also in the Introduction to this volume, of approaching contemporary migrations through a mobilities lens. In studies of irregular migration, such a lens has, for instance, helped cast light on how migrants often conceptualize their journeys beyond simple A-to-B trajectories (Schapendonk 2011), or shown how young men come to experience themselves as 'itinerant bodies', to cite Christian Vium's contribution to this volume. In similar fashion to these authors, my initial plan was to follow migrants on slices of their overland journeys towards Europe, with a phenomenologically informed research question in mind: what it is like to become 'illegal'?[3]

When I arrived in Senegal, in early 2010, to commence my fieldwork, however, I soon faced an unwelcome realization. Sitting in sandswept Dakar courtyards and parrying angry questions about my objectives from Senegalese deportees booted out of Spain after their failed boat migration towards the Canary Islands, I experienced first-hand the deep ethical and epistemological problems raised by research on 'illegal migration' (De Genova 2002). My encounter with Senegal's deportees also revealed a paradox that I would see repeated elsewhere on the clandestine circuit: the 'illegal migrants', stigmatized by their mobility, ironically stayed immobile while their visitors came and went, taking their time and stories away with them.

Following these early fieldwork encounters, I soon changed ethnographic tack. Instead of principally exploring migratory 'being en route' (Coutin 2005), I decided to start with my interlocutors' own analysis of the social situation they faced. Seeing visitors of all kinds descending on their neighbourhoods – from academics to journalists, from politicians and police to NGOs – the deportees offered an acute criticism of the 'business of the borders'. As one leader of a deportee association told me: 'There's lots of money in illegal migration' – not, he specified, for the immobile former boat migrants at the centre of the visitors' manifold attentions, but rather for state officials and border officers, for researchers and reporters churning out studies and documentaries, and for NGOs keen to set up spurious aid projects with the development money that was now pouring into the region.

Following the deportees' criticism, and in a 'grounded theory' vein, I became increasingly interested in the ways in which clandestine migration has been constituted in recent years as a multi-faceted 'business' and as a field of intervention and knowledge gathering. As I discuss elsewhere (Andersson 2014a), the various sectors engaged in these tasks now constitute an industry of sorts, producing novel modalities of migrant illegality even as they seek to curtail it. By using the term 'industry', I have sought to highlight not just the monetary gains of migration controls – significant as these are, as the Senegalese deportees and migrants elsewhere insisted to me – but also the intricate economies of exchange and production that now connect disparate sectors such as the aid world and border police. The term also brings into relief the geographical dispersal of these sectors – a dispersal that crucially involves mobility, as my Malian gendarme contacts implied in the vignette above. The paradox is that Europe's attempts to curb human movement have created vast amounts of corporeal, financial, object, and informational mobility for the illegality industry's workers (Urry 2007). This can be seen, for instance, in the new vehicles provided to Malian police and in European high-speed patrols; in training events and conferences, visited by jet-setting border officials; and in the deployment of aid and policing staff throughout the borderlands. In short, the industry masks the mobility it produces while leaving 'illegal migrants' stigmatized by theirs, even as the latter increasingly finding themselves immobile or moved by police on their journeys north.

The fraught encounter between the illegality industry and former migrants in Dakar would have made a perfectly suitable object of long-term ethnographic research on the industry's localized workings, not least with regards to the uneven distribution of mobility within it. However, such a study would have been an exploration of an emerging system's refraction through a particular setting, rather than of the system itself – and it was the latter that increasingly exerted a pull on my attention.[4] After all, similar aid and policing encounters occurred across all West African countries with which Spain had signed migration agreements in recent years; and these, in turn, were but one aspect of the multi-faceted industry emerging around clandestine routes.

Yet, as I reorganized my research, I faced a twofold dilemma. First, the overarching methodological problem at the heart also of my initial research resurfaced – namely, how to research a mobile system or assemblage, rather than the migrants who found themselves moving or immobilized within it. Second, by researching this system, I risked losing track of its effects on the travellers targeted by controls, thus wholly letting go of my initial research question on the experience of illegality, as well as the attendant ethnographic 'thickness' this implied.

The twin problems of feasibility and scale will certainly be familiar to most qualitative researchers concerned with 'globalized' systems and phenomena, as discussed in the Introduction to this volume. In border and migration studies, for instance, a variety of creative responses to these problems already exists, from following people (as in the work of Schapendonk 2011 mentioned above) to both localized and 'nonlocal' studies of systems-in-the-making (see Mountz 2010 for a compelling example). I will in what follows set out another, somewhat in-between position, forged around the interfaces of the system under study. By 'interface', I principally mean an encounter of some sort, either temporary or perennial – a social point of friction where conflictive groups converge and even clash: a migrant protest or a reception camp, a control room (where migrant boats appear as abstract dots on screens) or a border patrol (where they are physically intercepted). An ethnographic focus on such conflictive interfaces, I argue, allows for crosscutting national or local 'fields' while letting 'target populations' inhabit the same analytical frame as a larger system and its varied actors, including ourselves as researchers. The following section deals with the challenges of such a framing, looking first at the pros and cons of multi-sited research before suggesting a transversal approach to the fieldsite, drawing on the extended case method, interface analysis, and actor-network theory.

Framing Research: The Extended Fieldsite

In a Spanish control room, a border guard catches glimpse of an approaching migrant boat on his radar screen; in the Sahara, an African patrol vehicle intercepts a truckful of overland travellers; and on European shores there await, for those migrants lucky or astute enough to make it, an audience of police officers, reporters and aid workers. The 'illegality industry' is constituted through interactions between such disparate sites and actors. Yet how to frame a study on this complex assemblage or system, stretching from Sahelian border posts to European control rooms, without it being clearly and fully present in any of these places? And how can ethnographers tailor their methods to such framings?

Aware of the challenge of studying processes associated with 'globalization', ethnographers have come to embrace multi-sited methods, as formulated in anthropology by George Marcus (1995) in relation to a longer-standing interest in the discipline with following things, ideas, and people (e.g. Appadurai 1986; see Introduction to this volume). In migration studies in particular, researchers have for many years embarked on 'following' strategies, especially along the U.S.–Mexico border (Alvarez 1995) – much as I did in my initial research plan of accompanying migrants on their journeys. Such multi-sited studies have transcended the ethnographic focus on a 'local community', yet problems remain, as otherwise sympathetic writers have noted. What Nina Glick Schiller and Andreas Wimmer (2003: 598) term 'methodological nationalism' may be subtly reproduced in the 'community focus' of multi-sited, transnational studies, insofar as the nation-state frame remains the unspoken backdrop to the discrete 'sites' explored within each nation. Added to this is the ethical problem identified by Raelene Wilding (2007): while the researcher flits between places, the 'informants' often remain anchored to specific places and identities, whether 'transnational' or not.[5] Ghassan Hage (2005) adds further practical and epistemological problems. For him, multi-sited field-work implies potentially futile (or at the very least physically exhausting) attempts at studying the relation between each instance of a transnational 'community' and its corresponding 'site'. In sum, multi-sited ethnography still seems tied to community and locality even in its promise of abandoning them. Or, as Ulf Hannerz (2003) notes, the anthropological/ethnographic ideal of immersion and 'being there' lives on in the multi-sited world of 'being there ... and there ... and there!' We could ask, along with Bruno Latour (1993:116): 'Is anthropology forever condemned to be reduced to territories, unable to follow networks?'

As multi-sited research is being critically reassessed (Falzon 2009), some ethnographers have returned to the single fieldsite, now reconfigured either as an 'arbitrary location' providing a view onto larger complexities (Candea 2007), or as a 'node' in the world system (Heyman 2004).[6] Another solu-tion among anthropologists concerned with migration and mobility has been to do away with the discipline's lingering 'empiricism' by reconfigur-ing its relationship to locality altogether. This is the approach pursued by Gregory Feldman (2012:184), who argues for a 'nonlocal ethnography' that goes beyond the traditional anthropological privileging of 'evidence obtained through direct sensory contact'. In this, he draws upon the earlier efforts of Xiang Biao (2007), whose study of mobile Indian IT workers made a strong case for a focus on intangible social processes rather than cultural, linguistic and place-bound embeddedness. While it gains ethnographic reach, however, such nonlocal ethnography may lose some of the 'thick description' so cherished in anthropology – something Xiang (2007:117) himself acknowledges in his excellent monograph. One potential corollary is that the ethnographer, instead of 'being there' or 'being there and there', may suddenly be appearing everywhere yet nowhere.

While the approaches outlined above contribute important methodolog-ical innovations and critical ethnographic insight to the problem of mobility and locality, I here wish to add another, complementary, approach, one that explicitly tries to retain some of the 'thickness' of social life in its more or less 'localized' texture and messiness, while not losing sight of broader, more abstract forces and structures. I suggest calling this approach the 'extended fieldsite', in a nod to the extended case method and situational analysis developed by the 'Manchester School' of social anthropology (Burawoy 2000; Van Velsen 1967). Exemplified by Max Gluckman's seminal work, the 'extended case method' brought social groups that previously had been considered as separate – tribesmen and colonizers, for example – into analytical and ethnographic conversation. This approach hinged on giving analytical attention to events in which groups clashed and interacted – for instance, in Gluckman's (2002) famous study, the ceremonial opening of a bridge in Zululand in 1938 by the Chief Native Commissioner.

The 'extended fieldsite' approach I propose here similarly focuses on events and interfaces, yet crucially also 'repeats the process' of interface research across diverse locales. Instead of multiplying sites or sidestepping localities, this approach rather involves a transversal relation to locales in which 'the field' is not conceptualized within narrow geographical boundaries.[7] Put differently, it shifts the focus away from a specific place or community towards a process, tracing its making and unmaking by a large assemblage of actors who work, meet, and clash in a range of conflictive settings and configurations. In this way, the extended fieldsite – understood as 'one site, many locales' – has allowed me to track, trace, and map a complex unit of analysis: the transnational illegality industry, along with the modalities of migranthood it produces.

By talking of an 'extended' fieldsite, I also wish to acknowledge the continuity with earlier anthropological research. Anthropology has always been much more than 'single-sited', as testified not least by Malinowski's explorations of the Pacific 'Kula ring'. The dichotomy between 'single' and 'multi', or between discrete places and studies of systems, is thus largely an artificial concern, to some extent perpetuated through the mythologies of Ph.D. training. Indeed, anthropology has throughout its history sought to connect scales and places – and these attempts keep inspiring mobility and migration studies, as the Introduction to this volume attests. Hage (2005), drawing on Malinowski's work, has in this vein suggested a 'neo-Kulan' approach to ethnographies of migration. Whereas to him, this term highlights connectedness across diasporic communities, I see it as useful in a complementary sense. Much as in the ceremonial exchanges between islanders characteristic of the Kula ring, Europe's 'illegality industry' is concerned with forging direct connections between disparate agencies through the circulation of staff, equipment, money, and ideas – as well as through the circulation of migrants, passed around in chains of expulsions and interactions. Tapping into these circuits at specific points, and then linking these points in a wider circuit of exchange, allows for a simultaneously localized and 'global' view of a system-in-the-making.

Besides building on this specific anthropological trajectory, my approach is also inspired by interface analyses in studies of development (e.g. Long 2001), which have enabled researchers to bring funders, aid workers, brokers, and beneficiaries into one analytical frame. Seeking out such interfaces across an extended fieldsite allows for both exploring 'local' dynamics in social relations and for detecting patterns in these relations. Such transversal research also incorporates 'following' strategies of the kinds mentioned above, thanks to repetition in the systems under study. Indeed, in my case – much as in other large-scale systems – the encounters between the illegality industry and its target population replicate across border towns, enclaves, control rooms, and reception centres in a pattern involving the same or similar actors: European and African security forces, aid workers and journalists, researchers and migrants. In reaching across such repetitive encounters, the aim is however not to 'flatten' the ethnography, nor to essentialize and compartmentalize distinct subject positions, as interface analysis is sometimes alleged to do (Rossi 2006). The purpose is rather to explore how each interface uneasily and imperfectly superimposes a new supra-geographical function on towns, roads, and other locales, and to inquire into the production of new subject positions through the encounter.[8]

In studying mobile systems or assemblages, the question of where to 'cut the network' (Strathern 1996) also arises – that is, of how far we should follow the links between actors organized around a shared problematic. Here, combining a systemic and mobile research outlook with a 'traditional' anthropological approach can again be useful, as I found in my own study. The illegality industry extends far into European territory, through ever-expanding detention facilities, deportation arrangements, policing initiatives, and outsourced migration controls (Rodier 2012). With this dispersal in mind, in designing my own study on the illegality industry I ended up resorting to the 'natives' points of view', to pluralize the old anthropological trope (Geertz 1974). To my informants in the industry (border police, aid workers, and other actors), the 'border' itself, and those who crossed it, was their main field of concern, and their encounters around this border space became the focus of my study.

Defining a fieldsite based on native categories may seem a somewhat risky move, at least when it comes to the highly politicized topic of irregular migration. Was I not simply reproducing the European border of official imaginations, seen as site of enforcement and media spectacle? This risk was certainly real – just as classic anthropological studies of witchcraft, cockfighting or ritual violence risked reinforcing existing conceptual frames of the exotic and the Other. Yet, like in such classical studies, the point here was to encompass and understand, rather than simply repudiate, the fetishized construction of the border and its deep social effects. Moreover, as mobile fieldwork progressed among antagonistic border workers, I came to see how the seemingly straightforward notion of 'the border' diffused into a much larger and more abstract borderscape, allowing for yet another critical 'hold' on the illegality industry.

Thus delineated, my extended fieldsite eventually reached across the whole Spanish section of the Euro-African border and into the border spaces beyond it. Research here was carried out in stops and starts, switching between sites of departure and deportation (Dakar and Bamako, the

Senegal–Mauritania border), ports of entry and reception (the coasts of Andalusia and the Canary Islands), points of blockage en route (Spain's enclaves Ceuta and Melilla in North Africa; Oujda and Tangier in Morocco), and command and control centres (Frontex in Warsaw, Guardia Civil headquarters in Spain). Moving across diverse settings and scales, the aim has been to 'link the phenomenal and the political', as Robert Desjarlais (cited in Willen 2007:12) frames the contemporary ethnographic challenge: from policy and journalistic discourses to the blips on screens in radar control rooms and a policeman's firm grip around the shoulders of a rescued migrant. Put in more general terms, by focusing on the interfaces where a system rubs against specific places, people, and structures – what Anna Tsing (2005) terms 'friction' – we may produce an ethnographic account that spans overarching political logics and those crucial 'grains of dust that jam the machinery' (Agier 2011:7).

Actor-network theory provides a useful theoretical scaffold for doing just this, thanks to its focus on interactions between materialities and people, and as such provides a useful methodological complement to the extended fieldsite.[9] To briefly summarize, actor-network theory (or, rather, the actor-network toolbox) approaches human and nonhuman groups as 'actants' that, in the process of overcoming resistances among them, generate apparently solid systems through what Latour (1993) labels the work of purification and translation. For the purposes of mobility studies, ANT helps sharpening the focus on connections and 'intersections', as Christian Vium terms them in his chapter in this volume, which in turn allows for scaling 'up and out' from discrete settings (see Introduction to this volume). In this way, ANT helps shift away from the two often distinct poles of research on migration in particular – the (political science) perspective that privileges policy and the (ethnographic) insistence on a grounded 'migrants' perspective' – towards the material, virtual and social interfaces (or frictions) in the networks, systems or 'industries' of concern.[10] From this vantage point, the fences, patrol boats, radars, TV cameras, and rescue equipment in Europe's border response can be seen as 'actants' in a network or 'collective' made up of human and nonhuman links. The 'illegal migrants' and their rickety boats here function as connectors or 'tokens' in what I call the illegality industry; their circulation is the language and currency of the network.[11]

The approach briefly sketched here may help bridge the gap between studying a system and its human targets, or between conveying the 'thickness' of locality and abstract linkages beyond it. It may also go some way towards further incorporating mobility concerns into studies of migration and border controls. However, the question of how to actually go about doing this 'mobile ethnography' needs further consideration. One way forward, I will argue here, is to learn from a professional field that has long grappled with mobility and flux: journalism. By selectively adopting or appropriating certain journalistic practices – while avoiding some obvious pitfalls – anthropologists may expand their repertoire for fieldwork on complex and mobile systems, as I will show in the next section.

Doing Research: Journalism and Ethnography

During my research on the illegality industry, I frequently found myself interviewing journalists about their experiences in reporting on the drama of boat arrivals, patrols, and deportations. Such discussions, for all their intriguing detail, were at times uncomfortable. Here was the anthropologist – usually the storehouse of local knowledge, the fully immersed participant in the lives of the weak and voiceless – listening in to the journalist, often accused by academics of simply purveying simplistic snapshots. As I took notes, reporters would discuss their documentaries and books, crafted over months of high-risk engagement with people smugglers, migrants and guards in which they followed deportees back home, sought out bereaved families, joined border patrols or even embarked on clandestine journeys. As I jotted down their reflections, the roles seemed to have reversed: the reporter had turned ethnographer and vice versa.

Even if this role reversal depended upon the extreme levels of media interest in clandestine migration, it was still anything but an anomaly in contemporary fieldwork situations. Journalists and ethnographers increasingly step on each other's toes in both fields of research and expertise, which should come as little surprise since they depend upon some shared concerns and skills (not to mention 'sources'), as Hannerz (2004a) has noted with specific reference to foreign correspondents. Yet despite the obvious overlaps, few academic attempts have so far been made to learn from reporters. In part, this is hardly surprising: researchers after all engage in theory – they do not produce scoops or dig for exposé fodder. In part, however, the lack of engagement might have as much to do with academic fears of being accused of doing 'mere' journalism, without distinguishing sufficiently between long-term, in-depth journalistic work and more superficial versions of the trade.[12] Tackling this reluctance, and drawing on examples from my own research, this section looks at how quality and investigative journalism, of the kind usually given book-length treatment, can help ethnographers expand their methods (rather than their end-products, a separate topic) for investigating mobile and conflictive systems.

As Liisa Malkki (1997) has noted, anthropology in particular has mainly been concerned with durable, culturally transmitted experiences to the detriment of the transitory, dramatic events commonly traded in by journalists. Yet bridging these fields is not easy, as I soon realized in my initial fieldwork in Senegal. First, clandestine migration is largely defined by dramatic events – created and mythologized by the media in collusion with politicians, police, humanitarians, smugglers, and migrants. Second, the resentment among Senegal's deportees towards their international visitors stemmed not least from the working methods of reporters: unequal payments to informants, for instance, or empty promises followed by complete disengagement. A critique of the 'border spectacle', along with the everyday journalistic practices and conflicting perspectives taking shape around it, thus quickly became key to my study in the ethnographic fashion discussed above – that is, as one key aspect of the illegality industry's workings along the Euro-African border.

However, this was not enough. I myself was a participant in the illegality industry, as the deportees made clear to me: indeed, I had entered an overcrowded research arena as I followed in the footsteps of journalists, academic pioneers, NGO workers, government factfinders, and undercover police officers. As my focus on the industry developed across the extended fieldsite discussed in the previous section, my methods similarly needed to follow suit – linking back to the concern, voiced in the Introduction to this volume, of seeking methods relevant to our problems. Mindful of the researchers' role in the illegality industry, I could not simply dismiss or critique the knowledge practices of other actors within it. Rather, the ethnographic challenge became to work in as interdisciplinary a manner as the border professionals themselves, finding inspiration in their mobility and in their methods. That included the journalists traversing borders, notebooks or cameras in hand.

In doing so, I followed Malkki (1997) in using the investigative end of the journalistic spectrum to rethink fieldwork on 'unrepresentative', dramatic, and staged events. Such an exercise is useful, first, since journalistic approaches are attuned to conflictive events and encounters of the kind discussed in the previous section. Second, investigative journalism in particular has long been concerned with movements, linkages, and exchanges across large areas, which ties in with the notion of an 'extended fieldsite' proposed here. To give examples from the field of irregular migration, some investigative journalists have followed migrants on their high-risk journeys (e.g. Gatti 2007), while others have researched tragedies at sea through long-term engagement with migrants and officials both at 'home' and in the anticipated destination countries (e.g. Del Grande 2007; Naranjo 2009). These approaches often surpass what anthropologists can achieve, for instance in their access and attention to 'hidden' aspects of clandestine crossings or border patrols, and a critical engagement with such efforts therefore became a key part of my own research. Fleshing out this approach, the rest of this section will focus on a few key areas where journalistic methods may contribute to 'mobile ethnography': in particular, in their treatment of events, access, contacts, money trails, and scales. These methods, discussed in turn below, may well sound commonsensical to the well-versed researcher – and this is, if you will, precisely the point: what the methods addressed below provide, is simply a 'journalistic tweak' to existing ethnographic skills, a tweak that can prove vital in the context of mobile research on complex systems.

First, journalists track events. They are always thinking one step ahead, looking towards the next election campaign, peace negotiation or street protest – at times, they even seek to create an event themselves, as is sometimes the case with investigative reporters. Such preoccupation with event-seeking is hardly surprising, since this is what defines the journalistic (unlike the academic) endeavour: newsgathering. Besides this difference in focus, journalistic speed is also hard to match for academics for obvious practical reasons (Hannerz 2004a); yet journalistic approaches to events nevertheless hold some useful lessons for ethnographers.[13]

This was certainly the case in my research. In keeping with the 'extended fieldsite' approach, my research hinged upon dramatic events, since it was there – in a migrant protest, a policing conference, a boat arrival, the building or breaching of a border fence – that clashes and interactions between different groups occurred. My research was planned in such a way as to heighten the chances of participation in key events, while also being flexible enough so that I could switch sites at short notice. While in Dakar in early 2010, I factored in authorization for future policing events while readying myself for a shift to North Africa for the 'summer season' of boat departures. Once there, I lingered long enough in the Spanish enclave of Ceuta to follow migrant protests as they broke out, before planning my final stage of research in Mali, involving participation in an activist caravan for the freedom of movement between Bamako and Dakar. While not quite an example of 'parachute anthropology', in Hannerz's sense (2004a, 2004b), my fieldwork across the extended fieldsite unfolded as a semi-improvised journey through a series of interfaces, linked by expected and unexpected events in which the sectors of the illegality industry came face to face with one another.

Besides tracking linked events, one way in which investigative journalists in particular 'go multi-sited' is by following the money – a specific, and more forensic, take on Marcus' (1995) methodological (and theoretical) suggestion to 'follow the thing' through disparate settings. Following money trails can be a useful tool in exploring a system and its interfaces ethnographically. In trying to grasp the workings of the illegality industry, for instance, I soon let my research expand along the money trails that its sectors depended upon. Intrigued by the Senegalese deportees' discussion of illicit gains from their misfortune, I took notes on the tiny payments they had received from visiting journalists and by police during deportation, before exploring their main object of anger – the local associations receiving Spanish largesse for their role in the 'fight against illegal migration'. I followed this funding back to the Spanish NGOs that were providing it, and to Spain's official development agency that funded the NGOs. From there, research branched into the larger humanitarian-security nexus, encompassing the defence sector 'innovations' on display in Warsaw as well as the trickledown of policing gifts to Mali, Mauritania, and Senegal.

A key difference should be noted here between the aims of journalists and ethnographers. While investigative journalists usually engage in such a tracking exercise to inform an exposé of illicit gains, in ethnography it serves rather different purposes. Here it can work heuristically, as a fieldwork tool that may lead research onto new paths, allowing for patterns and relations to emerge among seemingly disparate and conflictive groups. In my case, the money trail highlighted novel connections through which clandestine migration was 'put to work' by a range of agencies spread across ever larger geographical areas – as well as how these connections were understood by migrants and deportees.

Journalists are also masters at sourcing stories. One striking example of this was presented to me during fieldwork by 'Laurent', a TV reporter who himself had organized and filmed a clandestine boat journey from the African coast towards the Canary Islands. To pull off his feat, Laurent had become a master in sourcing and network building as he switched between different roles – aid worker for a fictive NGO, reporter with a falsified correspondent's permit, migrant accomplice, even human smuggler – in order to gain maximum access. Such subterfuge is almost always an ethical no-go zone for researchers (as well as for many journalists) – though it does recall in somewhat 'sinister' ways what Wolcott (2005: 116) has called the 'darker arts' of ethnography. Besides the ethical problems involved, role-shifting to Laurent's extent is also beyond the pale for academic research because of our differing objectives. Indeed, unlike journalists such as Laurent, I had no interest in co-organizing a clandestine passage and thus produce a scoop. My goal was both broader and more modest – to understand the work of those who had made 'illegal migration' their livelihood. To do so, I engaged with antagonistic groups by adopting the empathetic stance inherent to anthropological research to the full without 'discriminating' between kinds of participants, and by deploying subtle shifts in my interaction style and behaviour rather than ethically problematic subterfuge. Crucially, I also embraced mobility to overcome access restrictions and build a thicker book of contacts, conducting 'snowball sampling' across the interlinked agencies of the borderlands (cf. Lucht, this volume). For instance, the Guardia Civil (the law enforcement agency in charge of land and sea patrols in Spain), while limiting access in each location, nevertheless let me visit their installations repeatedly; migrants stuck in southern Spain linked me with their friends in Bamako; and high-level access obtained at policing conferences could be followed up back on African soil.

While collecting contacts, journalists also engage in extensive triangulation between them. Up, sideways, and down: journalists study in all directions, never contenting themselves with one single group. While a certain 'depth' is almost inevitably lost in reaching far and wide for 'sources', it does enable systematic contrasting of research material – something particularly called for in studies of complex systems where access (and thus the use of participative techniques) is limited. Anthropologists also triangulate, of course, yet the frequent ethnographic focus on one discrete group's 'point of view' contrasts with the practice of journalists, who usually have no qualms about challenging their sources' perspectives. Incorporating some of this contrasting work more thoroughly into interview schedules, participant-observation, and the writing of ethnography may provide ethnographers with a broader view of conflictive systems.

In my research, this was certainly the case, for two reasons. First, secrecy was rife; second, the information I jotted down was always incomplete, when not marred by propaganda, half-truths, and lies. Triangulation was thus essential. For instance, the police awe and activist anger towards Europe's new border surveillance systems subsided once aid workers revealed these to be riddled with inefficiencies and migrants were shown to adjust their behaviour by seeking detection during their crossings. Such shifts in perspective did not work 'journalistically' in the news media sense of seeking 'impartiality' or controversy. Rather, they helped produce a plurality of natives' points of view – that is, conflictive yet complementary understandings of Europe's border landscape. In this way, I sought to turn my in-between position into an ethnographic strength, something that was only possible thanks to my mobility across the large field where the agencies of concern worked on clandestine migration.

Triangulation also allows for successful scaling. Journalists are experts at connecting the small and the large, the global and the local. To take an example that encompasses all of the techniques above: journalists position themselves in the 'right' slum just in time for an announcement on development aid disbursements (events), having worked their way through their contacts book to a rubbish-picker (sources) who might see little benefit from the initiative just announced (triangulation) while pointing the finger at local potentates who stand to benefit (money). While this scaling exercise often approaches the formulaic, it is important to note how journalists plan towards such an outcome, unlike in most ethnographic work, where scales tend to be explored mainly at the analytical stage. The contingent research paths of good ethnography – as well as the serendipity that such pathways tends to generate (Rivoal and Salazar 2013) – should be cherished, yet the explicit incorporation of 'scaling' concerns into research design may at least help ethnographers cut to the chase and avoid dead ends. In mobile fieldwork on complex systems, cutting through levels of research is essential for purely practical reasons: it saves time and repetition, as well as costly and tiring journeys. In this sense, scaling techniques – much as the others discussed above – do not necessarily point towards a specific style of doing ethnography, or towards particular results. Rather, all of these methods can be used as an expansion of the research repertoire tailored to our questions, regardless of the ends to which journalists may put them in their work.

Beyond the practicalities of mobile research, techniques such as scaling can also lead to new insights. This is what Xiang (2013) argues in an intriguing recent case for what he calls 'multi-scalar' ethnography, focusing on how migrants' own 'scale-making projects' intersect with state management of scale (see also Introduction to this volume). Scaling is also at work in earlier studies, such as Anna Tsing's (2005) monograph *Friction: An Ethnography of Global Connection,* which compellingly explores friction points between multi-national companies, illicit loggers, environmental groups and villagers. By providing a ground-level grip on complex or nebulous systems, scaling here allows for retaining two key anthropological 'virtues', in the words of Gupta and Ferguson (1997): the focus on the 'thickness' of everyday practices and the perspectives of marginalized people.

Conclusion: 'Borderline' Ethnography?

This chapter has addressed ways of approaching research into a highly mobile industry concerned with the control of human mobility, and has delineated an eclectic approach for this task. This has involved designing an extended fieldsite that focuses on repeat encounters across interfaces, as well as the retooling of ethnographic research at these interfaces through the 'poaching' of select journalistic techniques. In approaching methodology through the particulars of my research, I have sought to highlight how we may fruitfully rethink our methods through our research problems. Beyond my specific field, however, the methods discussed above have a larger purchase too. Indeed, it is hoped that elements of this approach – at the 'borderline' between groups and disciplines – may equally be applied to research on other complex systems (for instance a transnational value chain for producing cheap clothes, or a refugee situation created by an international resource war).

To gloss this eclectic research frame, focused on productive encounters across interfaces, I tentatively suggest the term 'borderline ethnography'. The term acknowledges, somewhat tongue-in-cheek, both my own focus on a 'real' border and the fact that, to some anthropologists, this type of study may not be 'ethnographic' enough in the 'traditional' sense (with all the caveats attached to that problematic label, as discussed above). Above all, however, the term serves to highlight the ethnographic importance and analytical richness of the interface between self and other, industry and migrant, aid worker and border guard, as well as the transformation that people and institutions undergo as they traverse this interface.

This 'borderline' approach has some drawbacks, to be sure. It does not quite address Hage's (2005) practical gripes with the exhausting nature of multi-sited travelling, or indeed the unequal access to mobility noted by Wilding (2007), even if it makes reflexive use of both these dimensions of fieldwork. It also deviates from the traditional fortes of anthropology – 'local' cultural expertise and linguistic skills – and instead relies upon extricating similar levels of complexity from lingua francas and scattered institutional settings. At first blush, it may also appear to fall short on 'immersion', that precious element of successful fieldwork, yet there are 'immersive' gains to be had from this approach, not least as pertains to the topic of international migration. Treating my research area as an extended fieldsite has made me an 'accomplice' of sorts for migrants, reporters, police, and aid workers, who all traverse the same clandestine circuit. As Marcus (1997) notes, such complicity is a treacherous yet thrilling place to be for anthropologists who, trickster-like, specialize in moving with ease between the 'natives' point of view' and their own. Yet one thing needs bearing in mind: the researcher is already 'native' to the illegality industry he writes about. He, like the workers and migrants he encounters, moves through Europe's emerging borderland, and helps create it as he moves (cf. Österlund-Pötzsch, this volume); his personal and professional networks, like theirs, reach from Mali to Madrid and beyond. As he trades anecdotes with migrants or workers about distant contacts, dreary border posts or gruelling overland trips, a shared understanding starts emerging of the Euro-African border, of the industry itself, and of the clandestine journey. This shared understanding, in turn, may inform new theoretical frames on the business of bordering Europe, while skirting the divides between top-down policy perspectives and grounded migrants' views, between the 'local' and 'global', and between mobility and stasis in the borderlands.

Ruben Andersson is an anthropologist and Associate Professor of migration and development at the Department of International Development, University of Oxford, and an associated researcher at the Department of Social Anthropology, Stockholm University. His books *Illegality, Inc.: Clandestine Migration and the Business of Bordering Europe* (2014) and *No Go World: How Fear Is Redrawing Our Maps and Reshaping Our Politics* (2019) are published by the University of California Press.

NOTES

1. The term 'poaching' here is meant to resonate with Kluckhohn's discussion in an earlier period of anthropology's 'intellectual poaching license', cited among others by Malkki in more recent years (2008:162).
2. On the fraught vocabulary of illegality, see Willen (2007) and Andersson (2014b).
3. As noted, all examples mentioned here – including my own – are focused on male overland migrations; the gendered aspects of these mobilities are highly significant, an aspect which certainly calls for further studies.
4. I use 'system' here with trepidation, well aware of its totalizing implications; for this reason, the text intersperses 'system' with 'assemblage', which somewhat better captures the ad hoc nature of Europe's anti-migration efforts.
5. The problem here may be inversed in certain studies of mobility.
6. For one compelling study of irregular migration in this vein, see Pian (2009).
7. In other words, the extended fieldsite as conceptualized here follows the methodological move towards 'shifting locations' suggested by Gupta and Ferguson (1997) without approaching this as a multi-sited proliferation of field spaces or a nonlocal ethnography.
8. Ortner (2010) has similarly suggested 'interface ethnography' as a response to situations of studying 'up' or 'sideways' where, as Gusterson (1997) notes, participant-observation is often difficult to carry out. However, whereas Ortner's interfaces are those where industry insiders meet the larger public, mine are those where different groups of workers mingle with their target population.
9. Arriving from a different angle, Radu (2010) similarly draws on a combination of actor-network theory and the extended case method.
10. Actor-network theory also allows us to move beyond two of the scientific tendencies Latour (1993) warns against: 'sociologization' or studying people-among-themselves and 'discursivization' or the analytical privileging of language and signification.
11. It is important not to lose sight of the complicity of those subject to such circulation and categorization, however: see Andersson (2014a).
12. On this, see contributors to Hannerz (2004b).
13. As Hannerz (2004a) notes, academic funding is often limited and slow to arrive.

REFERENCES

Agier, M. 2011. *Managing the Undesirables: Refugee Camps and Humanitarian Government.* Cambridge: Polity.

Alvarez, RR. 1995. 'The Mexican–US Border: The Making of an Anthropology of Borderlands', *Annual Review of Anthropology* 24: 447–70.

Andersson, R. 2014a. *Illegality, Inc.: Clandestine Migration and the Business of Bordering Europe.* Oakland: University of California Press.

———. 2014b. 'Illegal, Clandestine, Irregular: On Ways of Labelling People', Oxford Border Criminologies blog 8 September 2014. Retrieved from https://www.law. ox.ac.uk/research-subject-groups/centre-criminology/centreborder-criminologies/ blog/2014/09/illegal

Appadurai, A. 1986. *The Social Life of Things: Commodities in Cultural Perspective.* Cambridge: Cambridge University Press.

Burawoy, M. 2000. *Global Ethnography: Forces, Connections, and Imaginations in a Postmodern World.* Berkeley: University of California Press.

Candea, M. 2007. 'Arbitrary Locations: In Defence of the Bounded Field-site', *Journal of the Royal Anthropological Institute* 13: 167–84.

Collyer, M. 2007. 'In-between Places: Trans-Saharan Transit Migrants in Morocco and the Fragmented Journey to Europe', *Antipode* 39: 668–90.

Coutin, S.B. 2005. 'Being En Route', *American Anthropologist* 107: 195–206.

De Genova, N. 2002. 'Migrant Illegality and Deportability in Everyday Life', *Annual Review of Anthropology* 31: 419–47.

———. 2012. 'Border, Scene and Obscene', in H. Donnan and T.M. Wilson (eds), *A Companion to Border Studies.* Oxford: Wiley Blackwell.

de Haas, H. 2007. 'The Myth of Invasion: Irregular Migration from West Africa to the Maghreb and the European Union', IMI research paper. Oxford: Oxford University.

Del Grande, G. 2007. *Mamadou va a morire.* Rome: Infinito.

Falzon, M.-A. 2009. *Multi-Sited Ethnography: Theory, Praxis and Locality in Contemporary Research.* Farnham: Ashgate.

Feldman, G. 2012. *The Migration Apparatus: Security, Labor, and Policymaking in the European Union.* Stanford: Stanford University Press.

Gammeltoft-Hansen, T., and N.N. Sørensen. 2013. *The Migration Industry and the Commercialization of International Migration.* Abingdon: Routledge.

Gatti, F. 2007. *Bilal.* Milan: Rizzoli.

Geertz, C. 1974. '"From the Native's Point of View": On the Nature of Anthropological Understanding', *Bulletin of the American Academy of Arts and Sciences* 28(1): 26–45.

Glick Schiller, N., and N.B. Salazar. 2013. 'Regimes of Mobility across the Globe', *Journal of Ethnic and Migration Studies* 39: 183–200.

Glick Schiller, N., and A. Wimmer. 2003. 'Methodological Nationalism, the Social Sciences and the Study of Migration', *International Migration Review* 37: 576–610.

Gluckman, M. 2002. '"The Bridge": Analysis of a Social Situation in Zululand', in J. Vincent (ed.), *The Anthropology of Politics: A Reader in Ethnography, Theory and Critique.* Malden, MA: Blackwell, pp. 53–58.

Gupta, A., and J. Ferguson. 1997. 'Discipline and Practice: "The Field" as Site, Method and Location in Anthropology', in A. Gupta and J. Ferguson (eds), *Anthropological Locations: Boundaries and Grounds of a Field Science*. Berkeley: University of California Press.

Gusterson, H. 1997. 'Studying Up Revisited', *Political and Legal Anthropology Review* 20: 114–19.

Hage, G. 2005. 'A Not so Multi-Sited Ethnography of a Not so Imagined Community', *Anthropological Theory* 5: 463–75.

Hannerz, U. 2003. 'Being There … and There … and There! Reflections on Multi-Sited Ethnography', *Ethnography* 4: 201–16.

_____. 2004a. *Foreign News: Exploring the World of Foreign Correspondents*. Chicago: University of Chicago Press.

_____. 2004b. *Antropologi/Journalistik: om sätt att beskriva världen*. Lund: Studentlitteratur.

Heyman, J. 2004. 'Ports of Entry as Nodes in the World System', *Identities: Global Studies in Culture and Power* 11: 303–27.

Latour, B. 1993. *We Have Never Been Modern*, trans. C. Porter. Hemel Hempstead: Harvester Wheatsheaf.

Long, N. 2001. *Development Sociology: Actor Perspectives*. London: Routledge.

Malkki, L.H. 1997. 'News and Culture: Transitory Phenomena and the Fieldwork Tradition', in A. Gupta and J. Ferguson (eds), *Anthropological Locations: Boundaries and Grounds of a Field Science*. Berkeley: University of California Press.

_____. 2008. 'Tradition and Improvisation in Ethnographic Field Research', in A. Cerwonka and L. Malkki (eds), *Improvising Theory: Process and Temporality in Ethnographic Fieldwork*. Chicago: University of Chicago Press.

Marcus, G.E. 1995. 'Ethnography in/of the World System', *Annual Review of Anthropology* 24: 95–117.

_____. 1997. 'The Uses of Complicity in the Changing Mise-En-Scène of Anthropological Fieldwork', *Representations* 59: 85–108.

Mountz, A. 2010. *Seeking Asylum: Human Smuggling and Bureaucracy at the Border*. Minneapolis: University of Minnesota Press.

Naranjo, J. 2009. *Los invisibles de Kolda: historias olvidadas de la inmigración clandestina*. Barcelona: Ediciones Península.

Ortner, S.B. 2010. 'Access: Reflections on Studying Up in Hollywood', *Ethnography* 11: 211–33.

Pian, A. 2009. *Aux nouvelles frontières de l'Europe: l'aventure incertaine des Sénégalais au Maroc*. Paris: La Dispute.

Radu, C. 2010. 'Beyond Border-"dwelling": Temporalizing the Border-space through Events', *Anthropological Theory* 10(4): 409–33.

Rivoal, I., and N.B. Salazar. 2013. 'Contemporary Ethnographic Practice and the Value of Serendipity', *Social Anthropology* 21(2): 178–85.

Rodier, C. 2012. *Xénophobie business*. Paris: La Découverte.

Rossi, B. 2006. 'Aid Policies and Recipient Strategies in Niger: Why Donors and Recipients Should Not Be Compartmentalized into Separate "Worlds of Knowledge"', in

D. Lewis and D. Mosse (eds), *Development Brokers and Translators: The Ethnography of Aid and Agencies*. Bloomfield, CT: Kumarian Press, pp. 27–50.

Salazar, N.B., and A. Smart. 2011. 'Anthropological Takes on (Im)mobility', *Identities: Global Studies in Culture and Power* 18(6): i–ix.

Schapendonk, J. 2011. 'Turbulent Trajectories: Sub-Saharan African Migrants Heading North'. Ph.D. thesis. Nijmegen: Radboud University.

Strathern, M. 1996. 'Cutting the Network', *Journal of the Royal Anthropological Institute* 2: 517–35.

Tsing, A. 2005. *Friction: An Ethnography of Global Connection*. Princeton: Princeton University Press.

Urry, John. 2007. *Mobilities*. Cambridge: Polity.

van Dijk, H., D. Foeken, and K. van Til. 2001. 'Population Mobility in Africa: An Overview', in M. de Bruijn, R. van Dijk, and D. Foeken (eds), *Mobile Africa: Changing Patterns of Movement in Africa and Beyond*. Leiden, Boston: Brill.

Van Velsen, J. 1967. 'The Extended-case Method and Situational Analysis', in A.L. Epstein (ed.), *Craft of Social Anthropology*. London: Tavistock Publications, pp. 129–52.

Wilding, R. 2007. 'Transnational Ethnographies and Anthropological Imaginings of Migrancy', *Journal of Ethnic and Migration Studies* 33: 331–48.

Willen, S. 2007. 'Toward a Critical Phenomenology of "Illegality": State Power, Criminalization, and Abjectivity among Undocumented Migrant Workers in Tel Aviv, Israel', *International Migration* 45: 8–38.

Wolcott, H.F. 2005. *The Art of Fieldwork*. Walnut Creek, CA: Altamira Press.

Xiang, B. 2007. *Global 'Body Shopping': An Indian Labor System in the Information Technology Industry*. Princeton, NJ: Princeton University Press.

_____. 2013. 'Multi-scalar Ethnography: An Approach for Critical Engagement with Migration and Social Change', *Ethnography* 14: 282–99.

CHAPTER

5

Idleness as Method
Hairdressers and Chinese Urban Mobility in Tokyo

Jamie Coates

Cope with the ever-changing by sticking to one principle
(*yi bubian, ying wanbian*)

—Chinese proverb

There is a tension at the heart of mobilities studies that relates to whether mobility is an underlying framework for understanding the world, or whether mobility-in-itself is the object of study. A 'metaphysics of flow' (Cresswell 2006: 26) underpins the imaginaries which inform mobility research, making it an ontological as much as an epistemological approach. The perception that we live in a world 'on the move' (Cresswell 2006) has inspired a now well-established critique of 'sedentarist metaphysics' (Malkki 1992), culminating in what has been described as a 'mobilities paradigm' (Sheller and Urry 2006). Mobility has served as a 'concept metaphor' (Moore 2004) allowing once divergent fields such as research on migration, transport, tourism, and communications to speak to each other in new ways. However, as an ontology mobility also poses several methodological challenges to how we capture a world in motion (D'Andrea, Ciolfi, and Gray 2011; Fincham, McGuinness, and Murray 2010; Murray and Upstone 2014), as is demonstrated in the various chapters within this edited volume. Nonetheless, new ontological paradigms do not always necessitate new methods.

Anthropologists and ethnographers more generally have long contended with the vicissitudes of studying a world in flux. As early as the colonial era, anthropological study necessitated attention to how people move. The Manchester School's classic ethnographies are a salient example of this, as Andersson (Chapter 4) and the Introduction to this volume carefully outline. The necessity of dealing with movement grows from the disciplinary commitments of anthropology, which in the interest of understanding the human condition often focuses on the study of people. The twentieth century was an era of massive movements of people due to underlying factors such as colonialism, war, and growing global economic relationships. An ethnographic focus on people necessitated an attention to human movement even when ethnography wasn't imagined in mobile ways.

Research on migration is exemplary in this regard, and has born sustained critiques of the boundedness of culture and nationality that predate the anti-sedentarist turn of the mobilities paradigm (Basch, Glick Schiller, and Szanton Blanc 1994; Glick Schiller, Basch, and Blanc 1995). Migrants are subjects made meaningful to nation-states and border regulators by their lines of movement. They are subject to legal categories that define them by their change in residence, whether historically or currently. This usually takes the form of international movements, but can also be seen in the domestic regulation of movement in places such as the People's Republic of China (Nyiri 2010). Consequently, as a category of people they are often defined by their movement and treated as ready-made examples of mobility-in-itself (Hage 2005). In efforts to subvert the marginalizing subjectivities produced by nation-state definitions of personhood, anthropologists have attempted to develop approaches that avoid 'methodological nationalism' (Wimmer and Glick Schiller 2002) and that recognize the multiple locations that constitute migratory flows of people. More recently, researchers have adopted a mobility lens to afford greater attention to how meaning-laden human movement traces lines across multiple borders and spaces, circulating in a variety of ways. In this sense, mobility, broadly defined as movement ascribed with meaning (Cresswell 2006; see Introduction this volume), has emerged as a useful lens for understanding migrants' lives beyond the nation-states that define them.

In efforts to understand human mobility in a broader sense, researchers have developed innovative approaches to overcome issues of scale and site (see e.g. Andersson, this volume), as well as adopting new patterns of movement as researchers. These narratives echo innovations in ethnography more broadly, where practices of following, 'walking with', flânerie (cf. Ingold and Vergunst 2008; Pink 2008; Jensen 2009; Bairner 2006), 'tandem ethnography' (Molland 2013) and multi-sited fieldwork (Marcus 1995), have been adopted to ameliorate some of the difficulties found in researching people who are often 'on the move' (Cresswell 2006). Broadly speaking, these methodological innovations can be understood as practices of following that are used to understand how people inscribe movement with meaning, which produces mobilities and mobile people.

Under a mobilities paradigm, we live in a world of movement. Things move, meanings move, and alongside people, a range of other beings and entities, from the grand scale of weather systems to the tiny world of ants, move. However, at what point does studying mobilities, such as transport or communication systems, become more about the systems themselves than the people who interact with them? Similarly, when does studying migration as mobility become the study of migration as an example of mobility-in-itself, rather than people who happen to have changed their place of residence? Most importantly, when studying people who move, when does an interest in their movements overtake one's concern for them as people?

How do we contend with the convincing ontological claim of mobility without losing anthropology's powerful focus on people, rather than mobility-in-itself? A continued focus on participant-observation as an *'embodied relational process'* (Davies and Spencer 2010:2, italics in the original) can help us negotiate this tension by positioning the researcher's relationship to other people at the centre of the questions he or she hopes to pursue. In as much as our research questions should inform the decision to move as part of our methodology (see e.g. Introduction), it is the content and quality of the relationships anthropologists form during their fieldwork that often steer research questions and create the serendipitous occurrences that reshape these questions (Rivoal and Salazar 2013). Quantitative approaches to movement are often conducted via data mining and questionnaire surveys that posit the research data as slightly detached, or disembodied, from the researcher. In contrast, ethnographers apply a wide range of methods during fieldwork, but these methods and the data they produce are still predicated on the importance of 'being there' (Borneman and Hammoudi 2009). As Walton states in her discussion of digital ethnographic approaches in studying Iranian photobloggers (see Walton, this volume), 'being there' is not necessarily dependent on location. It is possible to be a 'fully fledged embedded, embodied and everyday ethnographer of the Internet' (page #) so long as one considers the digital as an extension of everyday life. In this sense, her ethnography takes the embodied relational process of digital life seriously, and elicits new understandings of those engaged in digital worlds as an embodied process; a form of 'being there' within a broader understanding of 'being'.

The embodied nature of ethnographic research implies that questions surrounding movement as a methodological decision, the study of mobility, and choice of research location often have little to do with what constitutes an appropriate 'site' or method for research, but rather who or what one is doing research with. As Ghassan Hage has stated in his critique of multi-sited fieldwork, migration research across geographic space is as easily defined as a 'single geographically discontinuous site' as 'multi-sited' (2005: 463). Similarly, Cook, Van Heekeren and Sosamphanh (2009) have argued how an 'un-sited field' can allow researchers to focus more on the ethnographic insights relevant to their theoretical questions, and Andersson (this volume) has shown how sites can be 'extended' to fit questions of scale and movement. In this sense, the flexibility of defining a fieldsite suggests that fieldsites are rarely 'found objects' but rather the product of researchers' decisions (Candea 2007). Candea has argued for greater recognition of how researchers are authors of their own field, adding that creating such 'arbitrary locations' is methodologically useful (2007). An arbitrary location, he writes, 'is "arbitrary" insofar as it bears no necessary relation to the wider object of study' (2007: 180). As such, the study of people within a particular locale can still constitute mobility research, so long as the arbitrary nature of this locale is contextualized within a mobile ontology.

In order to understand migrant experiences, it is not always necessary to move. The dynamics and structures of the relationships formed during fieldwork are two of the biggest influences on how research is made possible and the kinds of understanding research elicits. This is all the more pertinent when urban mobilities affect migrant experiences. Migrants in the city move in ways akin to other urban mobilities that may have less to do with their migrant condition than the vicissitudes of the city. In a related sense, traditional migration studies have often neglected questions beyond cross-border movements and often overlook the urban textures of how migrants move, why they move, and how moving affects their sense of being-in-the-world.

In order to incorporate these various forms of movement however, researchers face the difficult task of disentangling the meshworks of mobilities that constitute the city. Global cities (Sassen 1991) such as Tokyo are particularly vexing in this regard because people live busy, mobile, and often transient lives. Following a single person in a highly mobile context may only tell one so much because the process of following produces particular kinds of relationships with one's interlocutors. In contrast, in a context of research on urban mobility, remaining 'immobile', still, or 'strategically situated' (Marcus 1995) reveals much about the intersections between urban mobility and migrant experiences. With these reflections in mind, this chapter demonstrates how going against the grain of a world in movement by remaining still within wider contexts of mobility allows us to take a mobile ontology seriously, while also focusing on the relational aspects of fieldwork.

Lost in Ethnographic Frustration: Researching Chinese Migrants in Tokyo

In his recent defence of the bounded fieldsite and 'arbitrary locations', Candea (2007) describes how his reinvigorated interest in classic fieldwork imaginaries grew out of the uncertainty and anxiety he experienced during his doctoral research. In attempting to adhere to the unbounded methodologies that became popular in the 1990s and early 2000s, Candea found these new methodologies, which railed against the orthodoxy of fixed, single-sited fieldwork, had become such a common feature of anthropological training that, according to Candea, multi-sited fieldwork almost emerged as an inverted orthodoxy for his generation of anthropologists. My reflections on methodology in this chapter stem from a very similar narrative. I became interested in Chinese migration to Japan while studying in Beijing in 2003 and 2004. Except for a few publications (cf. Liu-Farrer 2007; 2004; Tajima 2003), the lack of research on this migratory flow left me with a creeping sense of the immensity of the topic I'd chosen to research ethnographically. What is more, the dearth of literature on the topic conflicted with my sense that the largest group of resident 'foreigners' (*gaikokujin*) in Japan, the Chinese, would attract the most attention. Originally trained as a China specialist and having only passing knowledge of Japan and Japanese, the spectre of doing fieldwork in Tokyo loomed over my imaginaries of what fieldwork would be like.

My sense was that any form of research resembling classic anthropology would be impossible because I could not determine where an appropriate 'site' for research would be. The existing literature was largely interview based and gave a sense that Chinese migrants in Tokyo were everywhere but nowhere, or in the case of Gracia Liu-Farrer's work, an anonymous dance hall hidden within a global metropolis that I would never possibly find (Liu-Farrer 2004). I looked on enviously at colleagues on my doctoral programme pointing to maps in relation to their village-based research, or listing NGOs as a starting point for urban ethnography. Unable to produce something similar nor imagine my upcoming fieldwork in any sense more fixed than 'Tokyo' writ large, I reassured myself by diving into literature that emphasized deterritorialization, mobility, and networks (Basch, Glick Schiller, and Szanton Blanc 1994; Urry 2007; Cresswell 2006; Latour 2005; Harvey 1989). Many of the arguments made by these authors assuaged my sense of uncertainty by building my faith in mobile ontologies. The vision of a world constantly moving found within this literature, fluctuating and unstable, implied to me that fieldwork was uncertain regardless of where one conducts research. Similarly, a generative 'following' approach such as that found in actor-network theory (Latour 2005) appealed to me, because I could opt to generate the specifics of my research by following the various actants I came across, rather than having to specify exactly where I would conduct my research. Picking Tokyo as the city where I would conduct my fieldwork, my research question was 'how does the experience of moving affect Chinese migrants' sense of self?' I hoped to not only investigate migration narratives as an indication of movement, but also migrants' movement within the city. Consequently, I imagined following migrants across the city as they went about their daily lives, developing a multi-sited approach as I found sites through my interlocutors' movements.

Discovering that a significant proportion of Chinese migrants in Japan initially entered the country on educational visas, I had intended to focus on networks rather than locality, starting from Chinese students I met. I participated in a wide variety of activities, such as attending a private Japanese language school, a government university language-training program, and a small meeting held on weekends in a local park where Japanese people interested in learning Chinese could practise with Chinese students. I also lived in a student dormitory owned by the Japanese government, where 40 percent of the residents were from the People's Republic of China. Through these activities I made many friendships, observed the process of learning Japanese as a Chinese newcomer, and witnessed interesting examples of Chinese student sociality on a few occasions.

The Chinese students I met usually worked more than twenty hours a week and rarely frequented spaces for shared interaction outside of the classroom. They focused on their studies and tried to make up for the economic gap between the support they received from China and the cost of living in Japan. Accommodation in Tokyo for the single, the young, or those on a low salary is notoriously small. Moreover, spaces like cafes, where interaction between friends and classmates might occur, cost money, and there is little public space where people can meet for free. Consequently, outside the classroom there was often little to observe other than the personal, one-to-one interactions between one single interlocutor and myself. The singular and highly personal nature of these interactions was further exacerbated by my desire to move alongside Chinese students as they went about their daily lives. My mobile participant-observation became increasingly about the relationship between an out-of-place Anglo-Celtic Australian who spoke Chinese, and those kind enough to 'hang out' with me. This was not 'deep hanging out' however; I was the 'main attraction' and took up most of the time they would otherwise spend developing relationships with others in their daily life. The limited nature of this kind of ethnography became increasingly apparent to me during the early stages of my fieldwork, and eventually struck home on one occasion when one of my interlocutors, trying to do something more interesting than sitting in his room with me drinking tea, proposed that we go out for the night.

Song was originally from Nanjing in southern China and had never had a night out in Tokyo, having spent most of his time working and studying towards a degree in nutrition studies. As he had little money, I offered to pay for the evening, and so Song selected a club named 'Womb' which was famous for its international DJs and dance spaces. Song and I left our dormitory on our own, none of the other students having enough time or money to come with us, and we awkwardly spent a night together standing at the edge of a dance floor. The space was too noisy to talk and too unfamiliar to Song for him to do anything other than slowly sip a rum and coke while excited Japanese youngsters danced in front of him. Song and I stayed late, hoping to catch the train back home in the morning but the exhaustion and awkwardness of the evening wore thin on this ethnographic encounter. We made our way to a late night noodle shop at 4a.m. where Song fell asleep after apologizing for not being more fun. I waited for him to wake again before we could catch the first train home in the morning.

There was much to learn from this experience. It highlighted the gap between economic circumstances amongst young Chinese students and youth cultures in Japan, while also showing that there were aspects of these cultures that were desirable for Song, if not a little intimidating. Nonetheless, the sleepy train ride home after our evening out left me with a sense that I was responsible for dragging Song out on the town, not so much through coercion but simply because I had pressured him to feel like he should be doing something due to my constant following and questioning. The details about his life that I had come to know were mostly from formal interviews. My following method, however, had provided less of an understanding of how his life related to that of others than I had hoped and, as the evening made clear, my proximity to his everyday life was starting to encourage movements that he might not have chosen himself were I not present.

I tried the same strategy with others, following their lives across Tokyo, but again only managed to cultivate one-to-one relationships. I felt such interactions did not make for great ethnography, my research increasingly feeling like a form of interventionist mobile autobiography. This experience contextualized part of what it meant to live in Tokyo and how the Tokyo environment shapes the possibility for social interaction amongst relatively poor Chinese migrants, but at the same time I craved something with a stronger sense of sociality. In particular, I wanted to find out whether other Chinese migrants lived similarly isolated lives, but had already exhausted the sample of individuals I had been following for six months.

The structure of the relationships I was developing during my research, particularly when following people, seemed to be much less 'social' than I had hoped. Rather, they were closer to Georg Simmel's 'dyad' (Simmel 1950). Theorizing the rudimentary structures of social activity, Simmel argues that two persons whose structural position relies solely on the other constitute a dyad, typified by relationships such as friendships and partnerships.

> Although, for the outsider, the group consisting of two may function as an autonomous, super-individual unit, it usually does not do so for its participants. Rather, each of the two feels himself confronted only by the other, not by a collectivity above him. The social structure here rests immediately on the one and on the other of the two, and the secession of either would destroy the whole. The dyad, therefore, does not attain that super-personal life which the individual feels to be independent of himself. (Simmel 1950: 123)

When applied to the actually lived sociocultural worlds of people, however, such an abstract formulation of social relationships is obviously problematic. We are born into a world already constituted by relationships that extend beyond ourselves with all of the associated meanings and practices that influence who we are and how we interact. However, the assertion that a dyadic relationship differs from wider sociocultural contexts, with all of its associated intimacies and obligations, is worth keeping in mind when forming new relationships as part of a research process. Unlike the dyadic relationship of a key informant whose social capital gives one access to wider networks (see e.g. Lucht, this volume), dyadic relationships with young students who lead relatively isolated lives produce a very different dynamic with significant implications for who else you might meet.

This consideration is even more important when relationships are formed through methodologies of following. Following a person as part of a dyadic relationship differs greatly from following the movements of several interconnected people (cf. Vium, Andersson, this volume). Large urban contexts constituted by a range of mobile people, technologies, and transport add further weight to this concern. Participant-observation still tends to be conducted by a single researcher. The singular researcher, following another person by himself or herself, forms a mobile dyad where the ethnographic encounter can potentially become as much about the researcher as it does about their interlocutor. This dynamic may be desirable at times – Vincent Crapanzano's classic *Tuhami: Portrait of a Moroccan* (1985), for example, explores how biography serves as a vital form of ethnography. However, it also exacerbates the ethical problem ethnographers face in creating relationships of responsibility between the researcher and the researched.

We are not only responsible to those we research. As a Levinasian ethics suggests, our embodied presence to our interlocutors, and their recognition of our own alterity in their presence, produces their own sense of responsibility to us (Benson and O'Neill 2007). Consequently, moving alongside them and the effects this produces, can be a burden on those we research. In designing and starting research in one of the world's 'global' capitals, I had placed too little emphasis on the embodied relational aspects of participant-observation and became carried away by the reassuring and exciting concepts I used to frame my initial research question. I wanted to study people who move, and I assumed that I must move with them. However, to my interlocutors, my constant presence, together with the dyadic relationship emerging from the 'following method', affected the kinds of lives they wished to live in Tokyo. I felt that, after a while, my presence was creating a strong sense of mobile responsibility towards me in my interlocutors.

Following one line of mobility within a dyadic relationship also affected the way I imagined Tokyo as a city. Mobility, according to Cresswell, is meaningful movement, as opposed to movement-in-itself (2006). A process of following often tells us more about that particular line of movement, than it does the way mobilities interact with one another (cf. Ingold 2007). As Johan Lindquist notes, this is akin to riding a train versus watching where trains go from the train station (2008). The former represents a single line of movement, while the latter tells us more about mobilities in the plural. When trying to provide a meaningful depiction of migrant mobility in the city, a 'thick description' as it were (Geertz 1979), attention to the plural mobilities that constitute the textures of urban life allow us to generate contexts from these mobilities. In this sense, relying on dyadic relationships formed through following may indeed reveal less to the researcher about the social and experiential aspects of urban mobility than one may think. Following-based research findings convey a single line, rather than the meshworks of mobility that form our lives (Ingold 2007).

Idleness as Method in a Hair Salon

With these concerns in mind, and although I continued to keep in touch with the students with whom I had spent time during the early stages of my fieldwork, I decided to give them more space. I became less mobile and picked strategic places where I could participate in the intersections of multiple mobilities. As one of my interlocutors quipped, my methodology became one of 'idleness' (*xian*). My use of the term 'idle' within the title of this chapter is a play on my interlocutor's joke. And yet, it speaks in interesting ways to how not moving can be seen as a form of laziness in our current world of accelerated mobility. To remain in one place is associated with doing nothing, while moving is seen as doing something. Contrary to my interlocutor's remark, I was constantly taking notes, photographs, and audio recordings when permitted. I used a smartphone rather than paper and pen, which despite reminders that I was doing research may have given the impression that I was merely 'hanging out'. Nonetheless, my stillness was a privilege that allowed me access to the 'non-events' and 'doing noth-ings' that often constitute daily life (Ehn and Löfgren 2010). I was able to situate myself in 'arbitrary locations' that I saw representative of Chinese life in Tokyo. I started in a tiny, friendly, bustling Chinese hair salon, and was eventually able to sample new spaces in which I could wait, observe, and participate. My 'idle' approach was perhaps more 'old fashioned' as I treated this site and its surrounding neighbourhood as a village of sorts. Nonetheless, I contextualized my approach within an urban mobile ontol-ogy, and found that it revealed more about the relationships between vari-ous forms of mobility than my previous following method had.

I first came across MY Hair Salon (Mingyang Meifa) while scouring a local Chinese newspaper, the *Sunshine City Daily* (*Yangguangcheng Ribao*). The hair salon had placed an advertisement for a spring festival special, in which the three hairdressers stood, fist in palm, making a traditional Chinese greeting gesture. Their hair was asymmetrically cut and tinted in a style common among young fashion-conscious Chinese men at the time. After some difficulty finding the building where the store was located, I finally came across a converted block of apartments with a small letterbox with the characters for the MY Hair Salon written on the front. I headed up the stairs, closing in on the low pulsing of a Chinese pop song I did not recog-nize. As I walked onto the floor on which MY was located, I noticed a cup-board-sized computer repair shop, a hairdresser called JB on my left, and a printing and computer sales shop on my right. Second on my right was the salon I had been looking for. I entered, and said in Chinese that I wanted my hair cut. Faces that had initially registered concern about potential commu-nication problems cleared into smiles, and the usual small talk about how I could speak Chinese. I explained to them that I wanted to research Chinese people living in Tokyo. Aming, the head hairdresser said, 'Well you've come to the right place! Ikebukuro has a lot of Chinese people'.

Having developed a sense of unease around my previous efforts at field-work, and feeling exhausted from my constant movements across the city during my first six months of research, I decided to make Ikebukuro the new 'arbitrary location' for my study. I returned to MY almost every other day, spending most of the day from noon until late into the evening observing the comings and goings of customers and listening to the lively banter of

Aming and his staff. By staying in this one small store, a world of mobilities and relationships opened to me. I was able to meet different people as they came to the store, discovering how their movements flowed through this space. I also saw how these movements were entangled with flows of objects and media. And, because of the convention of chatting within a hairdressing salon, different concerns and lifestyles of Chinese migrants were revealed. Staying put in a single place also had practical effects upon my fieldwork. Not having to constantly move, the quality of my field notes improved dramatically as I was able to sit and take note, experimenting with how I could document this one small space and its many characters. As the clients and staff of MY came to expect my presence, I was eventually allowed to audio record the jokes and turns of phrase thrown around, as well as take photographs.

I strategically stayed in one location to explore the comings and goings of people and things as part of a wider world of mobility by using the ontological claims of the mobilities paradigm to relativize this single space. Moreover, although I developed strong dyadic ties to many of the staff and a few of the customers, these relationships were mostly formed within social settings, which imposed on their singular mobile lives to a lesser degree than my previous following practice. As George Marcus states:

> The strategically situated ethnography attempts to understand something broadly about the system in ethnographic terms as much as it does its local subjects: it is only local circumstantially, thus situating itself in a context or field quite differently than does other single-site ethnography (1995: 111)

In line with this view, my strategically situated and 'idle' fieldwork in the hairdresser shop elicited a range of temporalities, relationships, and mobilities that connected to the wider context of Tokyo.

My idle method gave me access to different groups of people, with their own meaning-laden movements and lifestyles, who would come to the shop throughout the day. Their comings and goings were dictated by time and occupation, giving me a sense of the different lives lived by Chinese migrants in Tokyo and the ways in which movement structured the potential for sociality in the city. Through my initial encounters with these groups, I was able to snowball-sample a wider range of Chinese migrants in Tokyo, and eventually gained access to other spaces where I could conduct participant-observation. Between noon and 3p.m., the majority of customers were business owners and those who worked in Japanese companies, their lunchbreaks dictating when they could have their hair cut. These men and women had on average lived in Tokyo for over five years and had markedly different lives to the students with whom I had spent most

Figure 5.1 Two of the staff of MY hair salon styling the hair of young students. Photo by the author.

of my time in my previous fieldwork. Through chatting with them I came to know about working in a Japanese company as well as what they liked to do when they had spare time. After showing an interest in the snooker competitions many of the local business owners would watch online in the store, I was invited to a weekly competition held in a nearby billiards hall every Wednesday. Through developing relationships from a single setting I was thus able to move to another space to conduct research in Ikebukuro.

After 3p.m., students and shift workers were most common, and their lifestyles and circumstances differed greatly from the business owners and company workers I met over lunchtime. These customers were poorer and shorter on time, and usually went for very quick services. This changed the tempo of the shop, as small groups would come in for a rapid succession of fringe trims, highlights and standard cuts before heading home, leaving the store empty for periods at a time. These small groups were usually new to Japan, on average having lived there for less than three years, and tended to reside in small, privately owned dorms in the cheaper northwestern part of Tokyo. Unlike the students who I had previously followed, these students were on pre-college and vocational study visas, and were far more economically precarious than students studying in universities. Although all the students I met had some form of employment, these younger, less-qualified students were more likely to work in sectors seen as less desirable in the overall job market, such as cleaning and mass food preparation for convenience stores.

The final flow of people passing through the store each day gave me access to another part of Chinese migrant life that I had originally deemed inaccessible. Every evening between 7p.m. and 9p.m., elaborately dressed women would come to have their hair washed and styled before going to work as hostesses in 'cabaret clubs' (*kyabakura*) in the nearby entertainment district. Their hair would be teased and worked into distinct blade-like locks, and bleached before being dyed in other striking colours. They would wear large fake eyelashes, and paint their eyes with heavy mascara to make them seem larger and rounder. Their hands sported ornately decorated nails and in the crook of their arms you would often see handbags with brand names such as Louis Vuitton or Gucci displayed clearly on the side. Their clothes differed, occasionally seeming more like themed costumes than outfits; one day a Gothic Lolita, another day a traditional Japanese *yukata* for the summer festivals.

In adopting a situated form of participant-observation, my embodied relation to fieldwork not only allowed me to observe and develop relations with mobile people, but also with mobile things. Rather than resolving 'to follow the actors themselves' (Latour 2005: 304) as suggested within actor-network theory, I was exposed to the intersections of mobile things flowing into this one store, revealing a multitude of temporalities and experiences. As Basu and Coleman (2008) and Leivestad (this volume) note, despite the proliferation of migration research and material culture research, connections between the two fields are often less developed. My position as an embodied researcher however, meant that it was almost impossible not to see the intersections between these two objects of study.

The atmosphere of the hair salon was as much dependent on meshworks of mobile media and commodities as it was people coming and going. These meaning-bearing mobilities gave the salon a distinct sense of 'Chineseness' and was purposefully encouraged by the owner. On my first entry into MY, besides the repetitive snipping of scissors, the sound of running water as people had their hair washed, and the powerful sound of hairdryers, I was struck by the pumping music, the smell of Chinese 'Zhongnanhai' brand cigarettes, and the noises of a Chinese drama series playing on the small television in the store. At every customer's chair there was a tiny computer that slid out from a tray under the mirror and bench in front. Customers could go online to interact with the vast Chinese-language Internet while waiting for their treatments. An application called PPTV allowed customers to view recent Chinese films and television shows while they were having their hair done, or they could use one of the various social media sites and applications to chat with friends and family. If these devices did not entertain or entice customers, they would text friends, play games on their smart phones, or read the Chinese magazines and newspapers stacked next to each chair.

Because of my previous experience following students in their mobile lives across Tokyo, many of the media technologies found within MY were familiar to me. However, while I had been able to ask each of the students I worked with questions about their media use, by sitting still in the salon for long periods of time, I was able to gain a larger sample of media users as well as developing a greater sense of how media use differed between different customers, and how their media consumption fitted into wider social milieus. For instance, a significant number of young female fans of Korean pop music would ask for feminized versions of their male pop idol's hairstyles, and political discussions were often triggered by businessmen watching news broadcasts.

More broadly, I developed a sense of how the atmosphere created by these various mobilities were an important part of the conviviality of the space – something described by the owners as *renao*. Adam Chau has referred to *renao* as a 'sociothermic affect', a diffuse psychosomatic sense of satisfaction and fulfilment resulting from having partaken in, and co-producing, 'red-hot sociality' (Chau 2008). It features in any lively occasion, such as parties, rituals, and festivals; *renao*'s noisy nature is valued highly as a particularly 'Chinese' form of fun sociality. The first character *re* means heat/ hot, feverish, passionate, and fervent (Chau 2006:149). *Nao*, the second term in the compound, connotes excitement (Chau 2006: 150).

It is used in describing markets, parties, and any space of mischievousness. For example, post-wedding festivities (*naodongfang*) often involve friends and relatives holding a party in honour of the new couple, taunting the bride and groom and playing a series of mischievous games. In many ways, *re* can be seen as an indicator of the number of people and their enthusiasm about a certain thing, whilst *nao* denotes the amount of activity held in that space.

In a formal interview with the owner of the hair salon, he used the idea of *renao* and *kaixin* (happiness, literally 'open heart') to describe the importance of his store.

> In truth our shop is too small. We are all stuffed together in there, but Chinese people like renao environments and it's cheap.
>
> The most important thing in service is to affect the customer's psyche [*xinli*]. We understand that a lot of people feel lonely [*gudan*]. You know, they come in thinking, How did I end up overseas [*guowai*]? ... [He feigns a wistful, longing voice]. Or, they get home and think, Oh, it's just me here. They can often feel like, There's no one who stands with me [*meiyou ren gen wo zhan zai yiqi*]. They perhaps have friends, but friends also have their own lives; they can't be with you every day ... They just work by themselves, make money and go home by themselves. The mental pressure of this migrant lifestyle is too high, and they feel tired. But they can come to our store and be contented that they'll get a good haircut and have some fun while they're here. They can entrust us with their care [*jituo*] and forget that they're overseas ...
>
> However, even if you cut their hair well, they might not feel psychologically relieved [*xinli bu shufu*], so it's the whole atmosphere in our shop. The music ... the banter ... its *renao*. When a customer comes in we try to make it casual and fun. It might not be as good 'service' [*fuwu*] by Japanese standards, but as long as people are happy [*kaixin*] it's enough.

Being 'strategically situated' and carving out an 'arbitrary location' involves limiting the researcher's own movement. By staying 'immobile' as a single researcher in one location, I eventually came to see my fieldwork as an exploration of the mobilities and affects that produce 'plateaus of conviviality' among Chinese migrants in Tokyo. These sites of interaction were produced by a meshwork of urban movements of people and 'stuff' (Miller 2009), while still being informed by the larger context of migration as a subject-producing form of movement. They also facilitated imaginaries that can be themselves understood as a form of mobility. The importance placed on *renao* by the owner of the salon, for example, and the wide variety of transnational media and other objects that produced this atmosphere, suggested that by allowing customers to forget they are overseas, the effects of these various media act as 'technologies of imagination' (Sneath,

Holbraad, and Pedersen 2009), enabling imagined mobilities into 'Chinese' forms of sociality.

Conclusion

'Being there' does not necessarily rely on sedentarist metaphysics. Nor is it a 'sedentarist' method. Rather, it is a careful consideration of the embodied relational process of research. Whether mobile or immobile, 'arbitrary locations' depend on fieldworkers' relationship to those they research. Much like Tim Ingold and Jo Vergunst's (2008) emphasis on place making as the result of movements experienced as both subjective and intersubjective, both fieldwork and the locations it produces are shaped by lines of movement that researchers share with others. As has been demonstrated in several chapters in this volume (e.g. Vium, Andersson, Vasantkumar, Walton), the embodied process of ethnographic research is a useful way to negotiate and follow the various lines of movement that constitute social worlds. As I have shown in this chapter, however, a fluctuating world of mobilities can also be understood from a position of stillness.

As David Bissell and Gillian Fuller have noted, 'a sharpened understanding of stillness *in all its valences* can open up new appreciations of mobile relations' (Bissell and Fuller 2010: 4 italics in original). One 'valence' worth considering within this context is stillness as it relates to researchers themselves. There is great power in the ability of stillness to draw our attention to a mobile world. This has been increasingly acknowledged on an analytical level within mobility studies. For example, contrasts between mobilities and moorings (Hannam, Sheller, and Urry 2006), as well as the popularization of the term '(im)mobility' (Salazar and Smart 2011) are indications of this. With this chapter, I have explored the methodological potential of being strategically situated; idle as it were. While following my interlocutors allowed the development of strong dyadic relationships, it limited my ability to participate in other kinds of mobile sociality. In contrast, being still allowed me to coax different kinds of serendipity out of my fieldwork. While I did eventually move again, being still enabled me to contextualize the highly mobile nature of Chinese migrant lives in Tokyo, and eventually participate in other social activities by making informed decisions about where to move and with whom. With a larger research budget, and more time, it is likely that I would engage in more mobile methods, conducting multi-sited fieldwork and following the sojourning paths of my established interlocutors, who did often return to China. Mobile methods allow for different comparisons and different serendipities but as a Ph.D. student they may not be the best place to start.

Methodologies should be selected based on the disciplinary and episte-mological commitments of the researcher, alongside their object of study. Anthropology and the field of mobility studies, although sharing many methods, differ in this regard. Imagined as a discipline that investigates the human condition in holistic ways, anthropology tends to, and argua-bly should, prioritize methodologies that help them connect with people. Participant-observation is useful in pursuit of this goal, but it also produces relationship-dependent contingencies that should be carefully considered when mobility is also included in one's research question. For those who wish to use participant-observation in cities as the ground onto which they build analyses of people, I would encourage exploring stillness as a method-ological point of departure. Moving alongside groups of people who move together, such as at border crossings (e.g. Lucht, Vium, Andersson, this volume) and with tourists (e.g. Salazar 2012; Graburn 1983) are fruitful methodological approaches but are perhaps best used when one wishes to follow a group who moves, rather than individuals. Here, it is the mobile group itself that becomes a researcher's 'arbitrary location'. Moving along-side interlocutors in the city can be useful too but, as demonstrated in my experiences with Song, such research can often result in tracing a single line of movement rather than meaningful meshworks of mobility. This kind of approach is arguably harder as a starting point for a new ethnographic project. Without the capacity to contextualize individual movements, the dyadic relationships that form between an interlocutor and researcher can make it difficult to generate wider sociocultural meanings. In contrast, once established in a strategically situated space, it is possible to make informed decisions when moving to answer specific questions and find new connections.

It is often repeated that the central role of the ethnographer is 'to make the strange familiar and the familiar strange' (Spiro 1992). In many senses, the challenge of the 'mobility paradigm' (Sheller and Urry 2006) is prem-ised on a monism that sees a world in movement as the foundational ontology for social scientific research. In contrast to the 'sedentarist' and territorialized notions of societies and cultures, mobility research empha-sizes the ways in which movement constitutes the social world. Under such a paradigm, where movement is seen as a constitutive norm, is moving as a researcher the best means of evoking the strange in the familiar? Could we conversely say that going against the flows and movements of this world in flux is a useful way of bringing these mobilities into stark relief? As Candea states:

> The decision to bound off a site for the study of 'something else', with all the blind spots and limitations which this implies, is a productive

form of methodological asceticism. To limit ourselves to arbitrary locations, geographic or otherwise … gives us something to strive against,
a locus whose incompleteness and contingency provide a counterpoint
from which to challenge the imagined totality of 'cultural formations'.
(Candea 2007: 180)

So long as we use mobile ontologies to keep the contingent and arbitrary
nature of locations in ethnographic practice in mind, traditional ethnographic methodologies that often employ staying in one place need not be
criticized or assumed a disposition that some researchers simply cannot
escape. Rather, they can constitute an explicit methodological decision,
one that elicits a 'strange' perspective on mobility distinctly because it goes
against the increasingly familiar grain of a world in flux.

Jamie Coates is Lecturer in East Asian Studies at the University of Sheffield.
He combines visual and digital methods with historical and textual analysis
to explore the relationship between technology, mobility and imagination
in urban Northeast Asia. His current focus is on the political and existential
imaginaries of young Chinese people in Japan.

REFERENCES

Bairner, A. 2006. 'The Flâneur and the City: Reading the "New" Belfast's Leisure Spaces',
    Space and Polity 10(2): 121–34.
Basch, L., N. Glick Schiller, and C. Szanton Blanc. 1994. *Nations Unbound: Transnational
    Projects, Postcolonial Predicaments, and Deterritorialised Nation-States*. New York: Gordon
    and Breach.
Basu, P., and S. Coleman. 2008. 'Introduction: Migrant Worlds, Material Cultures',
    Mobilities 3(3): 313–30.
Benson, P., and K.L. O'Neill. 2007. 'Facing Risk: Levinas, Ethnography, and Ethics',
    Anthropology of Consciousness 18(2): 29–55.
Bissell, D., and G. Fuller (eds). 2010. *Stillness in a Mobile World*. London/New York:
    Routledge.
Borneman, J., and A. Hammoudi (eds). 2009. *Being There: The Fieldwork Encounter and the
    Making of Truth*. Berkeley: University of California Press.
Candea, M. 2007. 'Arbitrary Locations: In Defence of the Bounded Field-Site', *Journal of
    the Royal Anthropological Institute* 13(1): 167–84.
Chau, A.Y. 2006. *Miraculous Response: Doing Popular Religion in Contemporary China*.
    Stanford: Stanford University Press.
_____. 2008. 'The Sensorial Production of the Social', *Ethnos: Journal of Anthropology* 73:
    485–504.
Cook J., Van Heekeren D., and Sosamphanh B. 2009. 'What If There Is No Elephant?
    Towards a Conception of an Un-Sited Field', in M.-A. Falzon (ed.), *Multi-Sited*

Ethnography: Theory, Praxis and Locality in Contemporary Research. Farnham: Ashgate, pp. 47–72.

Crapanzano, V. 1985. *Tuhami: Portrait of a Moroccan*, reprint edition. Chicago: University of Chicago Press.

Cresswell, T. 2002. 'Introduction: Theorizing Place', in G. Verstraet and T. Cresswell, *Mobilizing Place, Placing Mobility* Amsterdam: Rodopi, pp. 11–32.

———. 2006. *On the Move: Mobility in the Modern Western World*, new edn. New York: Routledge.

D'Andrea, A., L. Ciolfi, and B. Gray. 2011. 'Methodological Challenges and Innovations in Mobilities Research', *Mobilities*. 6(2): 149–60.

Davies, J., and D. Spencer. 2010. *Anthropological Fieldwork: A Relational Process.* Newcastle upon Tyne: Cambridge Scholars Publishing.

Ehn, B., and O. Löfgren. 2010. *The Secret World of Doing Nothing.* Berkeley: University of California Press.

Fincham, B., M. McGuinness, and L. Murray. 2010. *Mobile Methodologies.* Basingstoke, Hampshire/New York: Palgrave Scholar.

Geertz, C. 1979. 'Thick Description: Toward an Interpretive Theory of Culture', in *The Interpretation of Cultures: Selected Essays.* New York: Basic Books.

Glick Schiller, N., L. Basch, and C. Szanton Blanc. 1995. 'From Immigrant to Transmigrant: Theorizing Transnational Migration', *Anthropological Quarterly* 68: 48–63.

Graburn, N. 1983. 'The Anthropology of Tourism', *Annals of Tourism Research.* 10(1): 9–33.

Hage, G. 2005. 'A Not so Multi-Sited Ethnography of a Not so Imagined Community', *Anthropological Theory* 5.

Hannam, K., M. Sheller, and J. Urry. 2006. 'Editorial: Mobilities, Immobilities and Moorings', *Mobilities* 1(1): 1–22.

Harvey, D. 1989. *The Condition of Postmodernity.* Oxford: Blackwell.

Ingold, T. 2007. *Lines: A Brief History.* New York: Routledge.

Ingold, T., and J.L. Vergunst. 2008. *Ways of Walking: Ethnography and Practice on Foot.* Hampshire. Ashgate Publishing.

Jensen, O.B. 2009. 'Flows of Meaning, Cultures of Movements – Urban Mobility as Meaningful Everyday Life Practice', *Mobilities* 4(1): 139–58.

Latour, B. 2005. *Reassembling the Social: An Introduction to Actor-Network-Theory.* New York: Oxford University Press.

Lindquist, J.A. 2008. *The Anxieties of Mobility: Migration and Tourism in the Indonesian Borderlands.* Honolulu: University of Hawaii Press.

Liu-Farrer, G. 2004. 'The Chinese Social Dance Party in Tokyo: Identity and Status in an Immigrant Leisure Subculture', *Journal of Contemporary Ethnography* 33.

———. 2007. 'Educationally Channelled Labour Migration: Post-1978 Student Mobility from China to Japan', Ph.D. thesis. Chicago: Chicago University.

Malkki, L. 1992. 'National Geographic: The Rooting of Peoples and the Territorialization of National Identity among Scholars and Refugees', *Cultural Anthropology* 7(1): 24–44.

Marcus, G.E. 1995. 'Ethnography in/of the World System: The Emergence of Multi-Sited Ethnography', *Annual Review of Anthropology* 24(1): 95–117.

Miller, D. 2009. *Stuff*. Cambridge: Polity Press.

Molland, S. 2013. 'Tandem Ethnography: On Researching "Trafficking" and "Anti-Trafficking"', *Ethnography* 14(3): 300–23.

Moore, H.L. 2004. 'Global Anxieties Concept-Metaphors and Pre-Theoretical Commitments in Anthropology', *Anthropological Theory* 4(1): 71–88.

Murray, L., and S. Upstone. 2014. *Researching and Representing Mobilities: Transdisciplinary Encounters*. Basingstoke, Hampshire: Palgrave Macmillan.

Nyiri, P. 2010. *Mobility and Cultural Authority in Contemporary China*. Seattle/London: University of Washington Press.

Pink, S., 2008. 'An Urban Tour: The Sensory Sociality of Ethnographic Place-Making', *Ethnography* 9(2): 175–96.

Rivoal, I., and N.B. Salazar. 2013. 'Contemporary Ethnographic Practice and the Value of Serendipity', *Social Anthropology* 21(2): 178–85.

Salazar, N.B. 2012. *Envisioning Eden: Mobilizing Imaginaries in Tourism and Beyond*, reprint edition. New York: Berghahn Books.

Salazar, N.B., and A. Smart. 2011. 'Anthropological Takes on (Im)Mobility', *Identities: Global Studies in Culture and Power* 18.

Sassen, S. 1991. *The Global City*. Princeton, NJ: Princeton University Press.

Sheller, M., and J. Urry. 2006. 'The New Mobilities Paradigm', *Environment and Planning* 38(2): 207–26.

Simmel, G. 1950. *The Sociology of Georg Simmel*, trans. K. Wolff. Illinois: Free Press.

Sneath, D., M. Holbraad, and M.A. Pedersen. 2009. 'Technologies of the Imagination: An Introduction', *Ethnos* 74(1): 5–30.

Spiro, M.E. 1992. *Anthropological Other or Burmese Brother? Studies in Cultural Analysis*. New Jersey: Transaction Publishers.

Tajima, J. 2003. 'Chinese Newcomers in the Global City Tokyo: Social Networks and Settlement Tendencies', *International Journal of Japanese Sociology* 12.

Urry, J. 2007. *Mobilities*. Cambridge: Polity Press.

Wimmer, A., and N. Glick Schiller. 2002. 'Methodological Nationalism and Beyond: Nation-state Building, Migration and the Social Sciences', *Global Networks* 2(4): 301–34.

Meeting a Friend of a Friend

Snowballing with Mr Hansen in Naples

Hans Lucht

Introduction

This chapter discusses some methodological concerns I have encountered during the writing of a monograph on high-risk undocumented migration from West Africa to Italy via Libya (2011), and again, especially, during fieldwork in Italy in the summer of 2013. My book is based on ethnographic fieldwork in Ghana and in Naples, Italy, and my research on African migration to Europe has since built on this fieldwork and on my relationship with the fishermen from Senya Beraku; I have also been to Niger in 2010 and 2016 to study the migrant desert routes, back to both Ghana and Italy in 2013, have made shorter trips to Athens and northern Italy, and in the spring of 2014 I went to Libya to study one of the major transit points to Europe. In short, in the decade since 2004, I have been engaged in multi-sited fieldwork on this risky and fragmented form of people-movement that extends across regions and continents, and sometimes takes years to accomplish. Indeed it often becomes evident when talking to West African migrants, that their journey is never really accomplished – especially given the current financial crisis in Europe. Every position remains somehow uncertain and intermediate, with the sole exception perhaps of the United States, which is often imagined as the ultimate destination for most young Ghanaian migrants.

Beginning with the period of ethnographic fieldwork in Italy in the summer of 2013, first in Treviso and then in Naples, this chapter explores the ways in which these periods of fieldwork have panned out, drawing from these a series of considerations on methodologies of mobility. I revisit and reconsider certain strengths and weaknesses of my chosen ethnographic research methods, and the results they have so far yielded. My main methodological approach to this mobile and sometimes reluctant field of primarily young Ghanaian men on the move in North Africa and southern Europe has been the snowball sampling technique (see Bernard 2006: 192–94). Reflecting on how 'mobility acquires, and requires, specific forms of methodological thinking and acting' (Salazar, Elliot, and Norum, Introduction to this volume) this chapter explores how snowball sampling became much more than a way of procuring informants but at method in its own right that poses a range of questions.

In its most basic form, this loosely defined approach calls for finding research subjects through one's close connections with key research subjects. Thus, by way of chain referral, the ethnographer acquires the characteristics of an insider who is led from informant to informant, snowballing the field, and in this way works from the ground upwards, and sideways, through unknown social worlds, as opposed to descending on a given field with a master plan. In positivist terms, this form of data collection is classified as 'purposive nonprobability sampling'; that is, as a set of nonrandom and 'biased' data that cannot mathematically represent a 'population' and form the basis of 'accurate and rigorous' social analysis but are, however, accepted as a necessary evil when conducting 'labour-intensive, in-depth studies of a few cases', especially pertaining to sensitive topics and vulnerable subjects, such as undocumented migrants (Bernard 2006: 186). Ethnographers, of course, have always had difficulty with the ideal of separating social science from its object (Hammersley and Atkinson 1983: 3), and have long sought to work creatively with this so-called 'bias' by acknowledging that researchers are part and parcel of the world they study and reflecting on how this may enrich research rather than disqualify it. The snowball sampling method, with its explicit 'exploitation' of social networks, gives rise to certain methodological and epistemological challenges, some more obvious than others, that invites further reflection on how ethnographers may study migrant mobility.

Migrant Reluctance, Time, and Space

Because the field of undocumented migration is characterized by reluctance, one is likely to meet resistance when working with undocumented migrants. It must be said that this is not always the case: many times I have been surprised by the openness and hospitality of migrants who live at the fringes of society. Still, a reasonable amount of reservation is not unusual, which is why snowballing sampling works. The key to unlocking a situation during snowball sampling is often having one insider who can vouch for the ethnographer and create moments of quality engagement; that is, moments of relatively free and uninhibited exchange facilitated by a research assistant. In my own research experience, this method of snowballing through the assistance of an insider who would trigger the process played out thus: Samuel, my original assistant with whom I have conducted fieldwork in Senya Beraku, Ghana, and in Italy and Niger, suggests I bring on a new assistant in Treviso, Peter, and Peter then appoints an assistant in Naples, Mr Hansen. What is interesting about this process is that when a new assistant accepts the work, after having had the details explained by the former research assistant, he or she not only agrees to the work assignment, but also implicitly agrees to make available his social world and vouch for the researcher's integrity. More than specific assistance with the work of research, it is rather the assistant's social capital and the extent of his or her social network that coproduce the data. The data is thus not really 'collected', but rather created in the interactions that the assistant sets up. For example, since many of my Ghanaian informants speak English, many times during my interviews my assistant would stretch his legs and have a look around outside while I would go over the same questions again and again. Here, the assistant becomes a kind of social entrepreneur who creates moments where knowledge can be obtained or co-created. This becomes particularly opportune when one wants to access hidden and hard-to-reach populations or people engaged in illicit activities, such as drug users, sex workers, or pickpockets (Atkinson and Flint 2001; see also Berg 2006; Bernard 2006), but also marginalized people, and, as in my case, undocumented migrants, who often have every reason to avoid attention and detection. One challenge this approach presents is that, at a certain point, the social network of a research assistant becomes saturated, and no new names are generated. This situation leaves it up to the judgment of the ethnographer whether the subject has been exhaustively explored, or whether one may have to start again from a different vantage point with a new research assistant (Bernard 2006: 193) – although with small groups of informants and intermediate locations that may not be possible or even feasible.

Another reason the snowball method remains attractive when studying transnational migration is the fact that time is sometimes a factor when working with undocumented migrants because they are highly mobile and often do not stay long in one place. For instance, during fieldwork in Niger, I spoke with Kelly, a friend of my research assistant Samuel, on the phone several times while he was in Turkey; Samuel believed that Kelly would be a strong candidate to help me out with fieldwork on African migration in the Greek–Turkish borderlands. Kelly and I decided to meet up in Istanbul after my return from Niger, and explore the possibilities of collaborating on a new project on Ghanaian migrants in Turkey and their hazardous journeys to Greece. But when I returned to Denmark a few months later, Kelly had already made the trip to Greece himself, and we ended up conducting a small pilot study in Athens with Ghanaian migrants instead. Throughout our short collaboration, Kelly was constantly making travel plans and constantly having them obliterated by various unforeseen forces. Today, Kelly is living in the Czech Republic, after having spent some hard and unproductive months in Belgium, and he is still working on his plan to find an African wife with an American passport and settle in the United States. My point here being, with reference to Kelly's story, that migrant mobility creates certain spatial and temporal conditions that challenge conventional ethnographic methods. It is not just that time may be limited in each site, but the sites may themselves be ephemeral; their geographic delimitation and short trajectories as lived spaces are often a feature of undocumented migrant worlds, and how migrants see them. In Athens, for instance, we walked the same routes almost every day from Kelly's home to the Internet café, to the square where some Ghanaian migrant friends slept, and then past the mosque, because these were the few places Kelly knew and felt relatively safe moving around in – bad things could happen, and sometimes did, when migrants explored the wider city landscape (Lucht 2013).

Generally, multi-sited fieldwork – for financial and logistical reasons – tends to be shorter and more concentrated in each fieldsite, though this is not universally the case, and one must often hit the ground running. That is, conducting multi-sited fieldwork is sometimes a question of sacrificing time in one site (and the implicit understanding of time as a catalyst for the ethnographic serendipity paradigm) for multiple sites, which makes it even more important to make the most of one's already limited time in the field(s). The snowball method is attractive in that it has the potential to bypass the uncertainty and lack of common ground and direction prevalent in the early stages of single-sited fieldwork – though these of course can be incredibly fruitful – by making arrangements with a research assistant through a previous research assistant. That is to say, through somebody experienced and knowledgeable about the subject and the work require-ments, a researcher can ideally get the snowball rolling with little delay. This situation is naturally a constant worry with respect to the quality and depth of the data and the observations collected, ethnographic depth being so heavily associated with time, and shallowness of research with its lack (Andersson, this volume). Perhaps this is a general challenge for multi-sited ethnography – assuming it is conducted within a tight timeframe. But even if multiple spaces cannot make up for reduced time, they are still generating something else, as Mark-Anthony Falzon argues, in the sense that 'spatial displacement' produces its own insights (see Salazar, Elliot, and Norum, Introduction to this volume), and as a method has a long and founding history in anthropology (Falzon 2009: 8). In my own experience, multi-sited ethnography often entails a kind of ethnographic jetlag in that, while engaging in new fieldwork, one finds oneself still struggling with the impressions and findings of one's previous fieldwork, which may not have yet been explored and organized (Lucht 2011: 189), and which therefore appears as a source of tension or uneasiness that interferes with new insights in an unknown world. But perhaps this juxtaposition of different sites generated by multiple displacements should be explored as more than an embarrassing shallowness, that is, as a different source of insight than one produced by time (or that time is imagined to produce). For instance, with regards to my experience with Kelly in Greece, 'more time' would not necessarily have produced a deeper understanding of Athens or his life there, for the simple reason that he was already moving on, physically and mentally, to other places when I met him, whereas the juxtaposition of this site against other intermediate sites of my research might have actually shed more light on an experience of being on the move or of mobility proper. Or, as Falzon argues: 'if conventional depth is hard to come by in unsettled circumstances, that is probably as things should be, in the sense that it represents the way people *themselves* experience the world' (2009: 9).

This is not to say that time can be completely substituted by space. For instance, in my current research project on African undocumented migration to Europe, my schedule allowed for spending only one month in each village and city I had selected for my interviews. Several of these places constituted entirely new 'sites' for me – here, it was therefore crucial to manage access without too many mistakes or delays. Even though access had been negotiated in advance, this was clearly too little time in the sense that, if the relationship with the research assistant did not work out for one reason or another, there was little time to make new arrangements. And, as we shall see below with the case of Mr Hansen, precisely because of time constraints, the sampling method could even degenerate, at times, into a form of 'convenience or haphazard sampling' – one that basically meant 'grabbing whoever will stand still long enough to answer your questions' (Bernard 2006: 191). In contrast, my long-term and on-going fieldwork in Ghana builds on a well-rehearsed repertoire of ethnographic approaches and a well-known location that I have visited and revisited for more than ten years and where I am integrated into village life and have many contacts and options. And where, crucially, I have time.

Jumping between fieldsites, my sense is that my 'original site', my long-term fieldwork in Ghana, the village of Senya Beraku and my relationship with people there, became the solid ground under my feet; a place and experience shared with the informants, for whom Ghana was the point of departure for their migratory trajectory, to where would return in interviews. In retrospect, I would bring up Senya Beraku not always because it was relevant to the conversation, but to create some kind of viable common ground to work from methodologically, and as a strategy to stress my status as an insider and overcome reluctance. Most definitions of snowball sampling method do not prescribe such a 'master fieldwork' that ethnographer and informants can draw upon – perhaps because it is primarily envisioned to be used for qualitative research 'at home', and they rarely mention engagement with groups that are racially, culturally, and linguistically 'Other'. By contrast, in my own research experience, it is questionable whether access to the Ghanaian migrant lifeworld spread across Europe would have been granted to me without my prior, and ongoing, long-term fieldwork in Ghana. But this sense of a place is not only a method; it entails some form of implicit holism, some recognition that a place experientially has a certain 'soul' and 'charisma' that are 'impervious to falsification by events or experiences that seem to contradict them' (Hansen and Verkaaik 2009: 5). One might add that its inhabitants draw a certain sense of moral and existential substance from belonging to such a particular place.

Multi-sited fieldwork has recently been criticized for implicit holism, both for maintaining the notion of a culturally bounded site, just in multiple forms, and for its search for George Marcus' 'world system' that somehow connects all the sites (Candea 2009). In my work, I am guilty on both accounts, in the sense that I have analyzed the long journey from Senya Beraku to Southern Europe as having certain sociopolitical and historical dimensions with which people engage to surprising effect on a local level. That is to say, the risky journey to Europe across the Mediterranean represents not a dogmatic casual relationship between a 'world system' and its drones, but certainly a chain of interdependence, or 'a figuration', to follow Norbert Elias (1978: 128), that has a particular time, space, logic, and contingency (see also Lucht 2011: 215). Moreover, it is not self-evident to me why there is an intrinsic value in depicting fieldsites as 'arbitrary locations' with no 'meaning or consistency' but composed of a seemingly random group of 'heterogeneous people, things and processes' that are lumped together and whose 'belonging' is some kind of fantasy (Candea 2009: 37; see Coates, Chapter 5 of this volume). As mentioned above, the sense of a place and its boundaries should not be explored because they are analytically consistent or ontological facts, but because they are experiential and existential realities that people live by; home, for instance, is a name we give to a place that has become synonymous with the most intimate inter-subjective events that make up our lives (Jackson 1998: 175). Such places are resistant to contradiction, which easily includes immunity to the analytical effort to deconstruct them. To me, this aporia – that the spaces or sites we inhabit are at the same time hermetic and open-ended, with a constant tension and negotiation at play – represents a much more complex view of the world than assuming beforehand that it is either one or the other. Thus, there is epistemic value in snowballing from fieldsite to fieldsite, the multiple connections between which can hardly be described as 'arbitrary'.

Snowballing Relationships

Some examples from the field – and the problems and possibilities of snow-balling as a method – may shed further light on some of the issues I raise above regarding the methodological and epistemological challenges of studying mobility. I am engaged in a collective research project on undocu-mented migration to Europe and, in this context, I recently wanted to return to Italy to revisit the places where I had conducted fieldwork back in 2005 with Samuel, my long-time field assistant. But, in the meantime, Samuel had been deported back to Ghana. To help me out in my research, Samuel suggested I work with Peter, a friend from his native village in Ghana, who now lived in Italy. A few days after my conversation with Samuel, Peter phoned me, telling me that Samuel had explained the situation and the nature of the work, and expressing his willingness to take over Samuel's role in the project. I wanted to go over the details of the research and his role as research assistant with him, but he reassured me that Samuel had already explained everything and that there was no problem; everything was already understood. And that was it: no job interview, no discussion. I boarded a plane to Venice with only his number in my mobile, and no way of knowing whether our collaboration would work out. Later, I came to think that I was to some extent mimicking how West African migrants arrive in Europe – often on their own with nothing but a phone number.[1]

The fact that Samuel had personally recommended Peter to me, gave me some measure of confidence for the research work to come. Though we had not discussed it explicitly, Samuel knew not only what kind of work I was hoping to do, but also, and more importantly, what kind of person I was looking for. I needed to work with someone with contacts, social skills, and who was respected by his peers – someone who was ready to make his social world available to me and who could make things happen. Peter was precisely that kind of person – maybe a little too much so. Peter was the organizer, the spokesperson, the networker, the optimist, the church leader, the philosopher, the businessperson. He was all of these things and more. He had studied a variant of the ancient Greek understanding of the human soul as consisting of four tempers (sanguine, choleric, melancholic, and phlegmatic). The tempers are believed to be connected to the existence of four types of body fluids, so, the balance of the fluids decides a person's nature. He explained that he was a dominant sanguine person, sociable and likeable, with a little bit of choleric, meaning he also had an ambitious and ruthless streak. 'What am I then?' I asked him once. 'Your temper is melancholic', he responded. 'You like to withdraw from other people and think. You want everybody to do things in a perfect way, the way you do things yourself. But if you don't look out people may see that as being arrogant. Luckily you're also part sanguine'. Indeed, let's not be naïve about observation; it's a two-way street, as the anthropologist and psychoanalyst George Devereux once argued. Maybe Devereaux is right to suggest that analysts as well as anthropologists 'seek to avoid counter-observation because we do not know ourselves and our stimulus value ... and do not wish to know it' (1967: 27) though any serious understanding of the data yielded in the field must surely appraise it.

I met Peter in Venice airport and we drove from there to his home in Treviso, a northern Italian town, and I moved in with him. The idea was for us to discuss our future collaboration in Naples, and then have a look around the Ghanaian community of Treviso while I was there. It soon became evident, however, that Peter would not be able to come with me to Naples, the fieldsite I wanted to return to, as he was too busy with his job. Peter worked as a spray painter in a small factory outside Treviso, and lived on the factory site. Instead of travelling down to southern Italy, as was my initial plan, we ended up snowballing his entire social field in Treviso, in precisely eight days. As soon as he was off work each day, we would drive around the rural landscape in his small beat-up Renault, and would visit friends and contacts from Senya Beraku. This was an extremely exhausting process for both of us, but also a very dynamic and rewarding one, the material created with Peter becoming an important contrast to the material on Ghanaian migrant life in southern Italy I had previously collected for my monograph.

What became obvious about snowball sampling among Ghanaian migrants in Treviso, is the way in which access to knowledge is itself social, in that it activates social networks, and the degree of success of one's research is very closely tied to the temper and social prominence of one's research assistant. This means that the assistant, if a process of snowballing is to be successful, has to be able to put social pressure on potential inform-

ants; he must use his social capital to set up meetings and convince informants to share their private affairs with an anthropologist. Looking back, I
realized that I had been targeting exactly this type of assistant over the years;
those who are somehow, within their social fields, close to power – that is
to say, in migrant terms, close to work, housing, money, or employers – the
type of people the Ghanaians would call 'tycoons'. It is only when one finds
an assistant who has a less prestigious position in the migrant social world
that one realizes how important social standing is for the data that is created. I shall return to this point in my discussion of my fieldwork with Mr
Hansen in Naples.

I do not recall a single person turning us down when I was moving around
with Peter in Treviso. Peter knew, for example, how to approach the elders
of the migrant community, and knew how to get them on board. 'This is
Mr Barnes', he would say. 'He is our big man, our leader; the boss of us all
here' – Mr Barnes would beam with satisfaction, and declare himself ready
to play his part in the research. But Peter also knew how to put pressure on
the younger men of the migrant community, sometimes intimidating them
with his tycoon savoir faire, reminding them of old debts. For instance, he
once opened a meeting by recounting how he had welcomed the informant
into his house when he had first arrived in Italy with empty pockets, and
how he organized a job for him. On other occasions, he appealed to their
sense of duty by stressing the importance of contributing to a book about
Senya, placing the village on the map; a project that the elders in Senya
looked upon with the greatest seriousness. Indeed, it was the Senya elders,
Peter would sometimes suggest to our keen research participants, who had
sent me to Italy to conduct my research, so that the village could reclaim its
rightful position among the important cities of Ghana.

In other words, Peter would stretch the truth from time to time, a practice that always made me slightly uncomfortable. For instance, he realized
instinctively that the tape recorder could be a problem because migrants,
especially undocumented migrants, are nervous about disclosure – and
with good reason (I have written about this ethical challenge elsewhere; see
Lucht 2011: 13). As a result, he usually told our informants the story that
it was he who suggested we 'add' a tape recorder to the session in order to
get the highest quality information about Senya people living abroad. Later,
when I confronted him with this story and said that I felt he was going a
bit too far, he argued that it was part of being a dominant sanguine. 'You
sometimes lie a little bit to make everything flow more easily'.

What my experience with Peter tells us about the snowball method is
that the quality of the data is closely connected to the status of the research
assistant, to his or her social skills and standing. This again points to the
fact that, epistemologically, knowledge is social, in that it grows out of a

relationship between the ethnographer, the assistant, and the informant to the extent that upholding each of these three categories is questionable (Noy 2008: 341) except for what it does for our sense of being real scientists, or perhaps for obtaining funding. But the fact that ethnographic knowledge is social does not pose a problem to ethnographers as long as we do not become 'trapped by scientism' (Tonkin 1984: 221); that is, it is only a problem if one obscures the method and the nature of the data, and the fact that the ethnographer is the medium of the research. Ethnographic knowledge comes from 'individual encounters and include[s] a mass of informal background which cannot be acquired without personal involvement, chance, and all the characteristics which are rejected by the positivists tradition' (ibid: 220). Personal involvement has also been the key catalyst for exploring the world of undocumented migrants in my own work. My research is in many ways the product of my close relationship with Samuel, my first field assistant, with whom I have worked, as mentioned above, on various periods of fieldwork among migrants in Europe and Africa. It is due to the fact that he, and other research assistants appointed by, him not only agreed to work for me, but also vouched for me and never gave up in the demanding tasks of calling, locating, and persuading possible informants – to the extent, in Peter's case, that reluctant informants were intimidated, and the truth was stretched a bit when deemed necessary. Looking back at the past ten years, and the places our inquiries have taken both myself and my research assistants, ethnographic fieldwork has become inseparable from the trajectories of our own lives.[2]

The Awaiting Field

Drawing further on my fieldwork in Naples, some limitations of the snowball sampling method and its implications for the study of migrant mobility may become clearer. When it became apparent that Peter could not accompany me to Naples because of his work situation in Treviso, another assistant, Mr Hansen, also a migrant from Senya, was appointed to me.

Mr Hansen was everything that Peter was not. In terms of ancient tempers, he could probably be labelled as a dominant phlegmatic with a hint of melancholy, and though I came to like him a lot, he was basically a royal disaster as a fieldwork assistant. He had no friends, because he disliked or distrusted most of his colleagues, and the feelings were seemingly mutual. He had no regular work, and he had given up any hope of achieving his goals in Italy. He had instead joined the Jehovah's Witnesses and he seemed confirmed in the belief that everything that went against him or that was wrong with life was a sign of the world coming to a bitter end. Methodologically, the contrast with Peter was clear in the fact that we struggled to get any interviews at all in Naples. People simply did not have time for us – they always had other plans. This is indeed the danger of the snowball sampling method. The snowball was simply not rolling because Mr Hansen could not put any social pressure on the other migrants to share their time and stories with us. In the end, when I was desperate for interviews, being the compulsive interviewer I was, I invited Peter down to Naples, and we did more interviews in two days than Mr Hansen and I had managed to assemble in two weeks.

So, what went wrong? Because of his many duties, Peter had left the job of appointing his successor to Rhino, a mutual friend in Naples who, like his childhood nickname implies, is a big, calm, and friendly person, but not one known for his wits by his friends and fellow migrants. He always mentioned that he had never had the opportunity to study and thus never really learned English, which was why the others were ahead of him, but that he was happy to do manual labour. Rhino appointed Mr Hansen because the latter, unlike Rhino, spoke relatively good English, and had no regular work. As a matter of fact, Mr Hansen was working in a supermarket outside of Naples, but as was common since the 2008 financial crisis, these migrant jobs of handling the trash and packing goods at the counter often went without salary, the only remuneration coming from customers' tips, and they would even have to pay for their own water. So, Mr Hansen was eager to get a job with money, even for a short time: we met outside the Sao Paolo stadium of Naples and decided to give it a go.

But within a week's time, we had exhausted his limited social network, mainly consisting of people from his church, and instead we ended up spending a lot of time together, just waiting; waiting for people to have time for us, but mostly just waiting for the bus to visit people on the far side of town, potential informants who would refuse to give Mr Hansen a specific time. 'When you need help, like we do', Mr Hansen said, 'you always have to wait'. With the bus system in Naples, waiting can acquire tragic undertones, and can really wear one down. There seemingly is no way to predict when or if the bus will come – Mr Hansen and I would just sit in the burning summer heat and stare down the road, watching other people race by. As a method, however, waiting with Mr Hansen offered me very useful insight into the social lives of migrants and the political realities that frame them. It made it plain and clear that being an undocumented migrant is not about living a life of flowing freely around the world, but rather of being stuck and waiting, meeting resistance and restrictions at every turn, and of having one's marginality to 'the world system' travel along everywhere one goes. Or, as Stephen Castles said, 'global linkages' may affect 'every geographical area and every human group' yet only create division and difference; indeed 'global linkages' tend to create inclusion and exclusion at the same time, as 'some become full members in the new global order while others are marginalized' (Castles 1998: 179). In the present age, this tendency appears to be intensifying and hardening.

Mr Hansen would pace up and down the pavement by the bus stop, boiling with frustration, as we had again been waiting for hours, and usually he would direct his anger against the Napolitano drivers. He imagined that they were sitting in a café somewhere, drinking coffee and smoking cigarettes with the simple aim of making black people suffer at the bus stop. 'When there's a game on television', he added angrily, 'you can completely forget about it'. During these long waits we talked about his life; how he had to flee the Liberian civil war as a boy and was caught and molested by the rebels; how his father started a new family in Ghana and disowned him, and how he still struggled with the pain almost every day; how he had lost the people he loved the most in his life – his sister and his mother; how they had been humiliated in Senya, when they came back from the war and nobody wanted to help them, and they had to go around and beg for food, causing him to secretly hate the village and his Senya colleagues; how his 'junior brother' was constantly pestering him with requests from Ghana and insulting him for not being able to send home more money; how they disrespected him in the supermarket; how he had to smile and act happy around the Italian customers in the store in the hope of getting a small tip; how he even had to pet their dogs, though he hated dogs; how the only thing that made him happy was his daydream of one day making it to America. 'In every family there's a person who goes away and never comes back' he would say. 'In my family, I want to be that person'.

So, though I probably did not appreciate it much at the time, and certainly was not receptive to the 'gifts of coincidence' (Leth 2009), the failure of the snowball sampling method in Naples gave me something else. I was gifted many intimate conversations with someone who may otherwise have slipped under the radar simply because he was marginal to his social network and not at all close to migrant power – that is, to jobs, papers, money – but had almost given up on this life. It also demonstrated how the problem of access in itself became a form of knowledge about the internal stratification of the migrant lifeworld. As Elizabeth Tonkin argues, 'Anthropology is characterized methodologically by the researcher's work being the *medium* as well as the recorder and interpreter of his/her research. This means – for instance – that access becomes an end in itself – which has to be interpreted – as well as a means which enables further interpretation' (Tonkin 1984: 221). With Mr Hansen it became suddenly clear that not all doors are inherently open to anthropologists or to migrants – even to a migrant who comes from the same town and shares the same plight as his compatriots – and we were seeing life from a different vantage point. Mr Hansen was one of those informants that one sees in photos taken years before during one's research, an isolated figure standing in the background or on the outer edge of a group, one whose name and story one cannot quite remember anymore.

Waiting with Mr Hansen became a tiresome form of participant-observation in one of the most experientially painful experiences of migrant life, something that is endured on a day-to-day basis: namely the fact that their lives are ironically characterized by immobility. I was already aware of this. But it was useful to be reminded about it again: the full force of negation one feels when one's plans and schedules are constantly obliterated, and the extent to which one feels small and insignificant when one's time is of no importance.

When writing up my research for my monograph (2011), this insight led me to reconsider some of the work on mobility and transnationalism that I had read as an undergraduate student, and had pushed me to search for new approaches that recognized how globalization appears to create both connectedness and disconnectedness at the same time. These were approaches that did not adopt the 'celebratory' perspective of early transnationalism that predicted that migrants, by living trans-nationally, 'could overcome the poverty and powerlessness to which capitalism relegated them' (Levitt and Jaworsky 2007: 131). Rather, these works argued how research on migrant mobility should critically emphasize the ways in which migrants become caught in a global 'order' of peoples and places which do not feel at all interconnected, but rather stratified, 'constituted by what appears as nontraversable strata organized along parameters of colour, race, and social position' (Vigh 2009: 93, see also Ferguson 2006; Castles 1998; 2011; Bauman 1998; 2004). Or, as Knut Graw has argued, to the majority of would-be migrants in Senegal, and probably elsewhere in West Africa too, globalization is predominantly characterized by its failure to materialize – or by the mocking presence of global simulacra such as fake commodities and second-hand clothes – and how locally, 'even rudimentary means of transport' are slipping beyond the reach of the poorest, while it remains a 'virtual impossibility' to obtain safe and legal routes to the U.S. or the EU. 'As a result', Graw continues, 'globalization is by many people primarily experienced in its absence, in the form of nonarrival of change, unfulfilled promises and aspirations, rather than in actual increases of mobility and or flux of goods' (Graw 2012: 32).

Arriving in Italy, the disappointment is substantial when migrants realize that exclusion appears to travel along with them, if in different shapes and forms. Yet, most find ways of coping in this hostile environment; they grit their teeth and endure. Migrant life in Naples is often considered by many to be just a painful prelude to better times ahead, though this painful prelude at times appears to become the permanent state of affairs – that is to say, most young Ghanaian migrants in Naples are so busy keeping their heads above water in the day-to-day struggle for work, food, and housing that this project on its own eventually consumes their time, forcing them to postpone their original plans, and their eventual homecoming.

The long and painful hours of waiting I did with Mr Hansen at the bus stop served as a reminder to me that undocumented migrants sometimes reach breaking points (Jackson 2007: 126); they lose their courage; their lose their footing; they feel they can't go on anymore, that life is pointless, and that they just wish they could disappear and never be heard of again, because the world has nothing good in store for them and it fills them with a deep sense of shame.

So, what was a complete failure in terms of the snowball sampling method – working with Mr Hansen the snowball simply would not roll or gain momentum – became a strong testimony to the breakdown many undocumented migrants experience in Europe today. This experience was accessed not through interviews with Mr Hansen's social network, but through the very fact that his colleagues had turned their back on him. My point here is that the process of creating access, in itself becomes an interesting insight into social context, and the meanings embedded in it. This experience gave me further cause to think about my earlier periods of fieldwork, and the resourceful and dynamic assistants I have been fortunate to have, and how they have shaped my work in ways that I was not well aware of. With Samuel in Ghana and Naples, Peter in Treviso, and Kelly in Greece, I found people whose 'capital' allowed them to get other people to open up and speak. Each of these figures – even the marginalized Mr Hansen in Naples, to an extent – contributed to various co-creations of knowledge that yielded new insights into undocumented migration and into the ways we engage and move with migrant mobility.

Conclusion

This chapter has focused on the possibilities and limitations of the snowball sampling method when studying migrant mobility. This is a method, I argue, which is especially appropriate for conducting shorter, intense studies of a relatively reluctant and mobile group of informants. Yet, the method creates certain forms of disturbance that are not well explored. One source of 'disturbance' in my own work has been the practice of hiring resourceful research assistants who could bring their 'capital' to bear as research assistants while I simultaneously ignored (or failed to consider) less 'prominent' figures such as Mr Hansen. This, to some extent, created a blind spot for my understanding of the internal stratification of the migrant lifeworld. It also blinded me to less celebrated migrant narratives, such as Mr Hansen's negative portrait of Senya Beraku as a community of selfish and heartless people. It is quite possible that Mr Hansen would have been included in the sample with a different research assistant, but it is difficult to imagine that he would have been so candid about his situation and the critique of his colleagues, had we not spend hours simply waiting together on a daily basis. It was 'the constant breakdown' of fieldwork due to Mr Hansen's marginal position, even more than the data that we managed laboriously to 'collect', that spoke to the subject from a new position. Here, to paraphrase Marshall McLuhan, the informant really is the message.

Moreover, the chapter has shed light on how ethnographic fieldwork tends always to be 'biased' in a positivist sense, which is a fact commonly accepted and reflected on by most researchers who undertake ethnographic fieldwork (Hammersley and Atkinson 1983) because we can neither eliminate the effects of our presence, nor become a kind of tabula rasa onto which isolated and pure forms of data can 'appear'. Instead, ethnographers embrace and 'exploit' bias, in the sense that subsequent reflection on the disturbances created becomes a particularly fruitful vessel for discussing the social world in question (ibid: 14–15). Less than being a detached, domesticated, and systematized version of lived reality – though sometimes presented as such for professional and psychological reasons – ethnographic knowledge is the product of 'long-term, organic relationships' with people in the field (Bourgois 1995: 11) and must be explored openly as subjective, situated and limited knowledge and not as a fiction of authority. Ethnographic data, in this sense, relinquishes authority in order to be closer to the social and existential 'truth' about a given field and further from passé notions of objectivity. But the goal of methodological reflexivity is not purely intellectual, though any serious scientific account of how ethnographic work has been done would have to include a rather personal narrative (Whyte 1964: 3–4). Rather, the goal here is to show how managing to live with people for longer periods of time, to find a modus vivendi with people, is perhaps the bedrock of understanding anything about their worlds in the first place (Jackson 1998: 188) – for the simple reason that fieldwork is not so much about 'collecting data' as it is about the experiential teaching of what 'social' means (Tonkin 1984: 219) in a given ethnographic context.

From a writing perspective, methodological introspection on the sometimes painful social education of the ethnographer is often excellent material; it is when you see the human being behind the anthropologist, with all the anxieties and inadequacies that being human entails, and how this has given the ethnographic account its unique flavour and meaning. To me, this is not a weakness in the text; it is a strength – to have the courage (or, indeed, the discipline) to show one's limitations as a fieldworker instead of upholding the traditional positivist attitude that nobody really can believe in. Again, this position is not the conventional rejection of positivism that is part of any ethnographic fieldwork account, or a celebrating of fieldwork, but rather of putting introspection to use in order to shed further light on the subject matter. It is not just the right thing to do methodologically but also produces very strong writing, in part because it is fragile and somehow marginalized from many mainstream accounts – fragile in the sense that submerging into a fieldsite is always about losing control and regaining it through a form of apprenticeship. Ethnography, in this sense, is on the one hand an 'artisanal practice' (Bourgois 2009: 12), and on the other hand a weighing of evidence; a logical and intellectual attempt to do justice to the complexities of lived reality in a given social context. In fact, these two ontologically different approaches – one that basically argues the world is outside our control or grasp, and one that seeks to uncover general social dynamics – or 'social physics', one might say – creates an ever-present tension (Hage 2011: 80).

Concerning the role of 'chance' in fieldwork (Tonkin 1984: 220), it is perhaps difficult to devise a stringent method for anticipating chance except to remain open to the fact that things will invariably happen that are not part of the grand scheme (see Salazar, Elliot, and Norum, Introduction to this volume). Precisely, therefore, these potentially speak from a new and different position, and hold the power to shake conventions. The Danish poet and film director Jørgen Leth has made a method out of embracing things beyond his control to the extent that he does not use screenplays or directorial scripts when making his films. 'I have a contract with coincidence', he writes. 'I keep my door open so that it may enter' (Leth 2009: 15, my translation). To Leth, this method is not so much about insisting on divine or romantic inspirations as it is about redistributing control of the creative effort and making space for 'the gifts of coincidence'. It is about taking seriously the notion that the human lifeworld will not be subjected to our plans or contained by our abstractions but that we must be ready for the unforeseen openings, remain alert to their 'unknown force' and register them in a 'cool and sober' way (Leth 2009: 15, my translation). In the same way, some anthropologists have sought to incorporate the unforeseen, 'the constant breakdown' of fieldwork, as not just an 'annoying incident' but as an integral part of ethnographic inquiry that unsettles any emerging, hard-fought understanding, and reveals new depths and contents (Rabinow 2007: 154).

Upon further introspection, one of my own methodological weaknesses that may taint my research is the fact that I am an almost compulsive interviewer. For my book, my relatively short stay in Senya Beraku (three months) meant that I felt compelled to interview as many people as possible. Looking back now, my time could probably have been used better. At times, it was almost farcical; there were moments when people were queued up outside my room, sleeping in chairs and on the floor, waiting for their scheduled interviews with the anthropologist. Even today, several years on, I have not listened to some of these interviews. It reminded me, again, of Devereux's pioneering work (see also Lucht 2011: 183), in which he reflects on the notion that 'data' should not only include information collected on the subject matter, ignoring or masking any disturbances caused by the observer. Rather, he argues that such data should also include these disturbances in the study, such as: the behaviour of the anthropologist in the field; his or her anxieties; defensive manoeuvres and research strategies that affect the work (Devereux 1967: XIX). Or as Paul Rabinow has argued in his post-fieldwork reflections on his research in Morocco, 'We can pretend that we are natural scientists collecting unambiguous data and that the people we are studying are living amid various unconscious systems of determining forces of which they have no clue and to which we only have the key. But it is only pretence' (2007: 152).

My argument is the following: if we take ethnography seriously as the pre-eminent way of conducting in situ experimental studies of complex social worlds, then we should not only give up mimicking the ideal and the language of contained experiments, but also reorient our focus towards the open-ended lived relationships encountered in the field – beginning with our own. Or, as Devereux radically argues, reflection on 'bias' or the disturbances created by the intervention and the behaviour of the ethnographer, should be the 'basic' source of insight, whereas the actual data becomes of secondary importance or even 'byproducts which, of course, also deserve to be exploited' (Devereux 1967: XIX). The study of migrant mobility and its methods offer particular, subtle sources of disturbance, some of which I have begun to note here.

Hans Lucht is an anthropologist and senior researcher at the Danish Institute for International Studies (DIIS).

NOTES

1. Though, in their case, without a credit card and white skin colour, of course. These differences must not be understated, since money and race are re-emerging as the

main hurdles for people on the move, reserving very sinister and dangerous trajectories that are non-negotiable, yet humanly and ethically problematic.
2. We should, of course, take care not to romanticize our relationships in the field, bearing in mind that subjects are 'very capable of using you, while you are pretending to yourself that you are not really using them' (Tonkin 1984: 221). Michael Jackson, drawing on La Barre, is probably right to suggest that we often exaggerate friendships we have in the field because we are grateful to people for helping us through difficult and testing times – for helping us save face and rescuing our egos in an unknown world (Jackson 1998: 104). These reservations aside, a description of how the insights were generated would have to include some reflexivity on method and social involvement – without falling prey to degenerated 'celebrations of privilege' that, according to Philippe Bourgois, often haunts methodological reflections of fieldwork among the socially and economically marginalized (1995: 14). Rather, introspection must be used to shed light on the field and the method; fieldwork in itself is not an achievement that should be celebrated (Tonkin 1984: 221).

REFERENCES

Atkinson, R., and J. Flint. 2001. 'Accessing Hidden and Hard-to-Reach Populations: Snowball Research Strategies', *Social Research Update*, Department of Sociology. Surrey: University of Surrey.
Bauman, Z. 1998. *Globalization: The Human Consequences*. Cambridge: Polity Press.
_____. 2004. *Wasted Lives: Modernity and Its Outcasts*. Cambridge: Polity Press.
Berg, S. 2006. 'Snowball Sampling–I', *Encyclopedia of Statistical Sciences* 12: 7817–21.
Bernard, H.R. 2006. *Research Methods in Anthropology: Qualitative and Quantitative Approaches*. Oxford: AltaMira Press.
Bourgois, P. 1995. *In Search of Respect: Selling Crack in El Barrio*. Cambridge: Cambridge University Press.
_____. 2009. *Righteous Dopefiend*. Berkeley: University of California Press.
Candea, M. 2009. 'Arbitrary Locations: In Defence of the Bounded Field-site', in M.-A. Falzon and C. Hall (eds), *Multi-Sited Ethnography: Theory, Praxis and Locality in Contemporary Research*. Surrey: Ashgate, pp. 25–45.
Castles, S. 1998. 'Globalization and Migration: Some Pressing Contradictions', in *International Social Science Journal*, 50(156): 179–86.
_____. 2011. 'Migration, Crisis, and the Global Labour Market', in *Globalizations* 8(3): 311–24.
Devereux, G. 1967. *From Anxiety to Method in the Behavioral Sciences*. The Hague: Muton & Co.
Elias, N. 1978. *What is Sociology?* New York: Colombia University Press.
Falzon, M.-A. 2009. 'Introduction', in M.-A. Falzon and C. Hall (eds), *Multi-Sited Ethnography: Theory, Praxis and Locality in Contemporary Research*. Surrey: Ashgate, pp. 1–23.
Ferguson, J. 2006. *Global Shadows: African in the Neo-liberal World Order*. Durham: Duke University Press.

Graw, K. 2012. 'On the Cause of Migration: Being and Nothingness in the African-European Borderzone', in K. Graw and S. Schielke (eds), *The Global Horizon: Expectations of Migration in Africa and the Middle East*. Leuven: Leuven University Press, pp. 23–42.

Hage, G. 2011. 'Social Gravity: Pierre Bourdieu's Phenomenological Social Physics', in G. Hage and E. Kowal (eds), *Force, Movement, Intensity: The Newtonian Imagination in the Social Sciences*. Melbourne: Melbourne University Press, pp. 80–92.

Hammersley, M., and P. Atkinson. 1983. *Ethnography: Principles in Practice*. London: Tavistock Publications.

Hansen, T.B., and O. Verkaaik. 2009. 'Introduction – Urban Charisma. On Everyday Mythologies in the City', *Critique of Anthropology* 29(1): 5–26.

Jackson, M. 1998. *Minima Ethnographica: Intersubjectivity and the Anthropological Project*. Chicago: University of Chicago Press.

_____. 2007. *Excursions*. Durham: Duke University Press.

Leth, J. 2009. *Tilfældets gaver*. Copenhagen: Gyldendal.

Levitt, P., and B.N. Jaworsky. 2007. 'Transnational Migration Studies: Past Developments and Future Trends', *Annual Review of Sociology* 33: 129–56.

Lucht, H. 2011. *Darkness before Daybreak: African Migrants Living on the Margins in Italy Today*. Berkeley: University of California Press.

_____. 2013. 'Necropolis', *Harvard Divinity Bulletin* 41(Summer/Autumn).

Noy, C. 2008. 'The Hermeneutics of Snowball Sampling in Qualitative Research', in *International Journal of Social Research Methodology* 11(4): 327–44.

Rabinow, P. 2007. *Reflections on Fieldwork in Morocco*, 30th anniversary edn. Berkeley: University of California Press.

Tonkin, E. 1984. 'Participant Observation', in R.F. Ellen (ed.), *Ethnographic Research*. London: Academic Press, pp. 216–23.

Vigh, H. 2009. 'Wayward Migration: On Imagined Futures and Technological Voids', *Ethnos* 74(1): 91–109.

Whyte, W.F. 1964. 'The Slum. On the Evolution of Street Corner Society', in A. Vidich and J. Bensman (eds), *Reflections on Community Studies*. New York: Harper Torchbooks, pp. 3–29.

CHAPTER

7

'Being ~~There~~ Where?'
Designing Digital-Visual Methods for Moving With/In Iran

Shireen Walton

Introduction: Anthropological (Im)mobilities

The anthropological notion that 'being there' in a fixed, physical dwelling confers the ability to produce 'authentic' social research has long been debunked by multi-sited approaches in the discipline (Gupta and Ferguson 1992; Marcus 1995; Clifford 1997). However, physical presence in multi-sited fields remains a hallmark virtue of bona fide ethnography (Watson 1999). More recently, technological advances have expanded the anthropologist's capacity for mobility, allowing researcher and participant to be co-present in multi-sited fields (spatial and social) and multi-temporal frameworks, simultaneously. These produce affective and atmospheric feelings of place (Sheller 2010), rely on experiential and sensory qualities (Pink 2011b), and open up new avenues for social enquiry into particularly mobile cultures and/or ways of life. Bronisław Malinowski (1922), the founding father of ethnographic fieldwork, established the view that anthropologists need to be physically present with the peoples they study in order to understand and legitimately represent them. In this regard, fieldwork was posited as an authenticating measure, conceived of as a kind of 'antidote' to the activities of earlier 'armchair anthropologists', who Malinowski and his successors accused of producing imagined, ethnological portraits, and of being physically removed from the peoples and places about which they wrote.[1] Today, however, thanks to the convergence of established and emerging theoretical and methodological trends in the social sciences with developing digital technologies, we are perhaps in a position to reconsider the Malinowskian imperative concerning physical presence. Is 'boots-on-the-ground'[2] presence the necessary basis for proving the 'authenticity' of research, and should it always be the researcher's first prerogative? Moreover, if a particular physical fieldsite is (for political reasons or otherwise) 'besieged', rendering the researcher physically 'immobile', do we modify or abandon our research questions, or should we attempt to approach its various landscapes differently?

In this chapter, I address a central issue raised in the Introduction to this volume concerning how research problems should guide methodological choices rather than the other way around. I explore the potential problems of restricted physical access and presence with regards to my own research in Iran, showing how such 'problems' can inform the development of specific methodological choices and trajectories. Digital and visual methods, I suggest, provide relevant 'solutions' to the quandaries of access and presence. I argue this case through the lens of my ethnographic study with Iranian photobloggers living inside and outside the country, and their online and offline social practices carried out in different geographical settings. I conceptualize my research methodology as a mobile and material ethnographic approach, insofar as it relies on physical and digital movements rooted in the practices, flows, and circulations of Iranian digital photography. To unpack this mobile/material method and its specific affordances, in my discussion I address, along different axes and scales, the varied mobilities I encountered in my work. These include: (1) my own mobility/immobility as a social anthropologist and digital ethnographer of Iran; (2) the various mobilities (physical and digital) of my informants and of their photoblogs (material, digital) in online and offline fields; and (3) the range of mobile methodologies, and methodological mobilities, I employed and designed in order to undertake a digital-ethnographic study largely online, from outside the country. I begin my discussion by introducing two methodological quandaries, deeply rooted in questions of mobility, immobility, and their politics: the issue of restricted access to Iran for some non-'native' researchers, which is perceived to present a 'professional dilemma' (Hegland 2009) for British and American anthropologists in particular, and the mobile challenges posed by Iranian photoblogging as a dynamic field of research. I proceed to link these potential research problems to a 'call to (digital-visual) arms', predicated on the digital mobility afforded by digital-ethnographic research methods. I conclude by suggesting that methodological potentials in digital and visual anthropology in general, and in the development of a digital photography exhibition in particular, offer alternative ways of virtually moving with/in fieldsites and building proximity to subjects from a physically remote or 'immobile' position. I show how these strategies met the specific demands of my study of Iranian photobloggers, but also suggest their more general applicability to studying physically and digitally dispersed, but variously networked, people and objects.

Locating Iran (Online): The Subject of Access and Access to Subjects

Difficult and limited access to Iran for fieldwork-orientated researchers from certain countries presents what Hegland (2009: 53) calls a 'professional dilemma' for many Western/non-native anthropologists.[3] The revolution of 1979 and onset of the Islamic Republic unravelled the close ties with the West existing under the Shah, affecting the ability of foreign researchers from countries such as the U.K. and America to conduct long-term research inside the country.[4] Ideological architects of the new regime argued that cross-cultural associations belonged to the decadence of the former regime, which they claimed was responsible for ushering in a so-called 'plague' of corruptive, Western cultural influence to Iran. Locally known as 'Westoxification' (Al-i Ahmad 1962) and, subsequently, 'occidentosis' (Al-i Ahmad 1984), cultural associations with the west, according to Islamic revolutionary leaders, needed to be purged. The ensuing war with Iraq (1980–1988) and its catastrophic effects on Iranian society only exacerbated the predicament of non-native anthropological research inside the country. In addition to these events, politically saturated national and international 'mediascapes' (Appadurai 2002) in the post-revolutionary era (1979–present) have also crudely presented Iran in binary 'black-and-white' and 'East/West' terms (Dabashi 2008). Amidst this fraught political backdrop, younger generations of foreign researchers have become dissuaded from pursuing research inside the country (Bromberger 2009). Although diplomatic relations with the U.S. and Europe have begun to thaw somewhat following the election of a politically 'moderate' President Hassan Rouhani in August 2013, the Iranian government remains unsympathetic to Western researchers and international journalists being 'on the ground' in Iran. Both categories of knowledge seekers have and continue to be negatively associated with espionage, following a complex history of twentieth-century foreign involvement in Iranian political affairs (Sreberny and Torfeh 2014).

At the beginning of my fieldwork with Iranian photobloggers in October 2012, I was faced with one such 'professional dilemma' which Hegland speaks of. Access to Iran for British citizens had become increasingly more difficult than in previous years, following a violent attack against the British embassy in Tehran on 29 November 2011.[5] Both respective embassies in

Tehran and London were closed as a result, and those requiring a visa to travel to Iran from the U.K. had to do so via alternative consulates, such as ones in Dublin, Paris, or Hamburg. During this period, preference for visa approval was also given to those with Iranian family connections. In the middle of this frenzied climate, understandings about everyday life in Iran 'from below' seemed increasingly part of the 'besieged' knowledge I was aiming to pursue in my research with Iranian photobloggers. Despite the official advice of the British Foreign Office warning against British citizens' travel to Iran at the time, I applied and obtained a tourist visa from the Iranian consulate in Paris, a process no doubt facilitated by my status as a half-Iranian British passport holder. I spent one month in Iran between October and November 2012.[6] Dividing my time between the capital city Tehran and Esfahan (another major city some 200 miles south), I was able to meet with local photographers I had connected with online from the U.K., and undertook some rudimentary fieldwork activities. I conducted interviews, visited emerging gallery spaces and participated on what are popularly known as 'photo tours' (*safarhā-ye 'akkāsi*): social occasions linked to photography, wherein groups of young men and women travel to various provinces of the country in order to develop their craft collectively, including the sharing of technical skills (see Figure 7.1).[7] However, since I was unable as a sole British passport holder to remain in the country for a sustained period of time, physically being in the country clearly could not constitute the substantive component of my fieldwork.

As Hegland (2009) outlines, the solutions to the 'professional dilemma' anthropologists of Iran have sought, have included abandoning research into the country altogether, using research conducted prior to 1979, as well as turning to the study of the Iranian diaspora – in the Internet era in particular, many studies by social scientists have focused on the connections between the diaspora and Iran (Khosravi 2000; McAuliffe 2007; Sreberny and Khiabany 2010; Alinejad 2011; Shakhsari 2011). Following this latter trend, and faced with the 'professional dilemma' of not being able to remain in Iran to conduct long-term fieldwork, I also decided to carry out ethnographic research amongst the Iranian diaspora in the U.K. I studied with Iranian photographers, artists, curators, and journalists based in London, many of whom had either left Iran during or shortly after the revolution of 1979, or belonged to the second and third generation of émigrés born in Europe and America. However, I did not see a turn to diaspora studies as the only possible response to limited physical access to Iran. What I suggest here is another option for (but not limited to) the anthropology of Iran, one that builds on the idea I introduced at the beginning of the chapter: namely, that if we can accept a reconceptualization of 'the field', beyond geographical space/presence, then long-term fieldwork can in fact be conducted with/in a country, community, or society from a location that is physically distant, without compromising ethical and methodological rigour. This assertion is predicated on two key notions explored throughout this chapter: (1) that physical presence is not necessarily a yardstick for defining and/or measuring the 'authenticity' of ethnographic research; and (2) that digital-visual methods can position technologies and imaginaries on an ethico-methodological plane in order to reconceptualize notions of access and presence. I suggest that such methods provide methodological antidotes to cases, such as my own, of what Salazar, Elliot, and Norum call, in the Introduction to this volume, 'involuntary immobility'.

Studying Moving Fields: Iranian Photobloggers' Physical, Digital, and Epistemological (Im)mobilities

It is not just my own physical (im)mobility as an anthropologist of contemporary Iran during a politically fraught climate that reveals peculiar facets of the relationship between mobility and methodology. Themes of (im)mobility and method emerge in crucial ways also by tracing the experience

Figure 7.1 Iranian photobloggers at Kaboudwāl waterfall, near 'Aliābād-e Katul, Golestan province, northeast Iran in November 2009. Courtesy of Amir Sadeghi.

of my Iranian photobloggers' interlocutors themselves. These are physical, digital, and epistemological in nature. In one sense, photobloggers are physically mobile. Those of the diaspora and those in Iran travel to and across the country taking photographs of scenes from everyday life in Iran, with mobile phone and digital SLR cameras (see Figure 7.1). They then exhibit and disseminate their images on photoblogs and social networks such as Facebook, Flickr , and Instagram.

At the same time, photobloggers' practices are also characterized by different forms of 'immobility', confirming how studying mobility invariably requires a critical consideration of 'immobility' (Adey 2006; Salazar and Smart 2011). Some photobloggers, as is the case with young people in Iran more generally, cannot afford to travel outside its borders. International sanctions have impacted upon Iran's domestic economy and have corroded the living standards of many. Photographers I spoke with in Iran had multiple jobs in order to make ends meet. Like many Iranians across the country, they want their country to move beyond economic and diplomatic isolation and become part of global communities and economies. In this sense, many Iranians feel they are being kept 'immobile' by socioeconomic conditions on the ground. This climate of stagnation directly affects how photobloggers see the Internet as affording 'movement' (Salazar and Nilsson 2015). One of my research participants explained this link between physical immobility and visual/epistemological mobility as follows:

> The Internet has changed our world. Without the Internet and the images everyone shares, how can one know or see the world so much, especially if we don't or can't travel? Wait for the new issue of *Time Magazine*?[8]

In light of these offline conditions, the online context takes on heightened social and political salience, as acknowledged by a number of studies on the Internet in Iran (Sreberny and Khiabany 2010; Akhavan 2013). At the same time, official restrictions on communications in Iran aim to maintain a state of 'immobility' as a method of governmentality (Foucault 1991), based on attempts by government hardliners to consciously isolate the nation from global flows and 'scapes' (Appadurai 2002). The Iranian government monitors Internet usage in Iran through the Supreme Council of Cyberspace (SCC) in connection with the regime's efforts to uphold its specific political and cultural values and norms of modesty. Social media sites such as Facebook, Twitter, YouTube, Flickr, and Instagram are officially banned, and connection speeds are notoriously slow. Internet cafés, (or *cafenet* as they are locally known) are periodically raided and shut down and their owners and users have been arrested in recent years for alleged 'moral misbehaviour' (Sreberny and Khiabany 2010:78). These measures

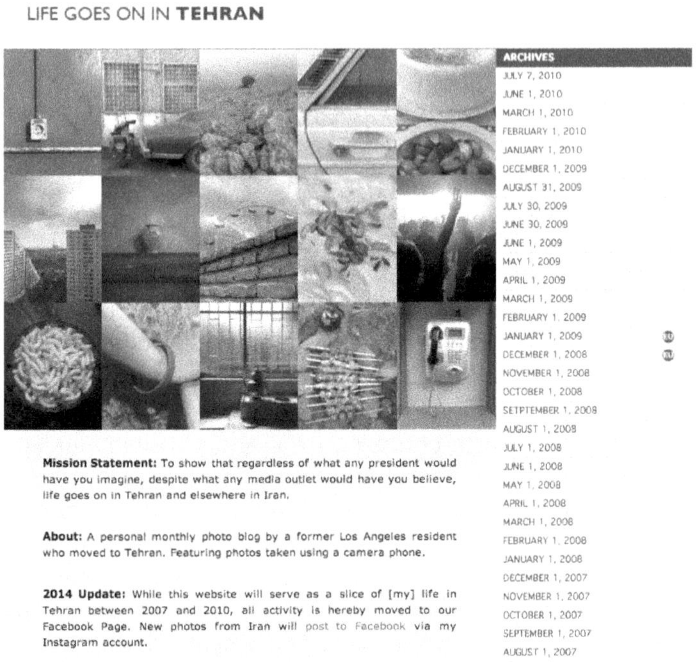

LIFE GOES ON IN **TEHRAN**

Figure 7.2 'Life Goes on in Tehran' photoblog homepage. Source: http://lifegoesonintehran.com, screenshot captured by the author 10 May 2015. Used with permission.

purport to protect a pristine Iranian, Shiite-Islamic cultural identity from what Ayatollah Khamenei, the Supreme Leader of Iran, calls a 'cultural invasion' from 'the West'.[9]

Despite these official conditions, the 30 per cent of the population who use the Internet in Iran effectively do so on their own terms. Comparable, to an extent, with the situation in China, blocks and filters in Iran are routinely circumvented via the use of VPN (Virtual Private Network) connections, which simulate Internet connections from a location outside of the country, as well as 'anonymity networks' such as TOR (The Online Router), a free software programme that conceals users' locations and partially protects them from traffic analysis.[10] Indeed, as I have discussed elsewhere (Walton 2015), photoblogging can be considered part of a flourishing Iranian digital landscape since the early 2000s, more broadly indicative of a salvaged digital mobility 'from below' amongst Internet users in Iran, for many of whom virtual spaces are also places of sociocultural and political expression. Photoblogs also serve as alternative free or low-cost exhibition venues for showcasing Iranian photography, beyond official galleries and public museums inside and outside of Iran, while also enabling photographers to circumvent the Iranian government's various politics, policies, and restrictions to which they would otherwise officially be subject. Figure 7.2 shows an example of one of my research participant's photoblog, entitled 'Life Goes on in Tehran' (LGOIT).

Beyond digital movement, Iranian photobloggers also engage in what could be termed 'epistemological mobility'. This can be seen in the concerted ways in which photoblogs are used to change how Iran is portrayed (and viewed) in national and international mediascapes. As previously mentioned, these mainstream media discourses often present static portraits of Islamic-Iranian identity, conceived of by hardline members of government and various international media discourses alike in socially, culturally, and politically monolithic terms (Varzi 2006). Digital photographs disseminated and displayed on photoblogs are taken and even 'galleried' (Miller 2001) on the photoblog in order to aesthetically posit soft, political points about what has historically been 'left out of the frame' in Iran's international media imaginary: namely, the mundane and the ordinary aspects of lived experience under the Islamic Republic. One example of photobloggers' visual play can be found in how they visually juxtapose photographs of Tehran with images of other cities around the world on their photoblogs ostensibly 'about' Iran (see Figure 7.3). They do this as a way of combatting Iran's political isolation with an aesthetic proposition of cross-cultural similarity that intends to move towards a more inclusive acceptance of the country in international communities. Through these kinds of practices, photobloggers visually articulate a cross-generational desire to renegotiate the image of Iran by constructing digital-visual spaces that 'move' it beyond its dominant narrative-epistemic parameters. One female research participant eloquently summarized this sentiment: 'The media can change views about a whole nation. These new online photo-sharing systems (photoblogs) are the same, but this time, they provide *us* with the opportunity to show who we really are'.[11] As with nonphotography-specific blogging, photoblogging is therefore both a hobby and a visual form of 'politics by other means' (Sreberny and Khiabany 2010). As I proceed to illustrate below, the various (im)mobilities I have briefly sketched here – physical, digital, epistemological, political – directly influenced how and where I studied photobloggers and their practices.

Digital-Visual Ethnography With/In Iran

The principal research participants in my study on Iranian photoblogging were selected from within the network I had entered into. This network had

Figure 7.3 Photographs of Berlin, Vienna and Tehran on the 'Life Goes on in Tehran' photoblog. Source: http://lifegoesonintehran.com/30_September_2009. html, screenshot captured by the author 10 March 2014. Used with permission.

grown out of my initial contact with one of the most prominent Iranian photobloggers (mentioned above), and his photoblog, LGOIT. The eight individuals that eventually comprised my main case studies were some of the most receptive to my research from the start, and were willing to share the most time with me. They were chosen on the basis of the rapport that we had established online. All had been born and grew up in Iran, and then had either stayed or migrated to pursue higher education abroad. At the time of my study, they were based in six countries: Iran, the U.K., the U.S., Australia, Italy, and Germany (see Figure 7.4).[12] In order to access and study Iranian photobloggers, I conducted digital-ethnographic research in physical and digital places. I outline here some of these methods in light of their relationship with on- and offline mobility, before moving to focus, in the latter sections of the chapter, on one specific mobile digital-visual method: the collaborative organization of a digital photography exhibition.

First, a few introductory words on digital/virtual ethnography are due. Digital/virtual ethnography is a cross-disciplinary approach to conducting qualitative enquiry via the Internet.[13] In anthropology, it is the methodological modus operandi of digital anthropology, a nascent 'subfield' (Horst and Miller 2012) in the discipline premised on an 'ethnographic approach' (Miller and Slater 2000) to studying the Internet. For anthropologists, online environments and virtual worlds are seen as generative of ethnographic knowledge through the participatory practices studied and contributed to by the researcher (Boellstorff et al. 2012). This can be carried out purely online, as shown in Boellstorff's (2008) pioneering work on Second Life.[14] Alternatively, as in the case of my own research, digital landscapes can be

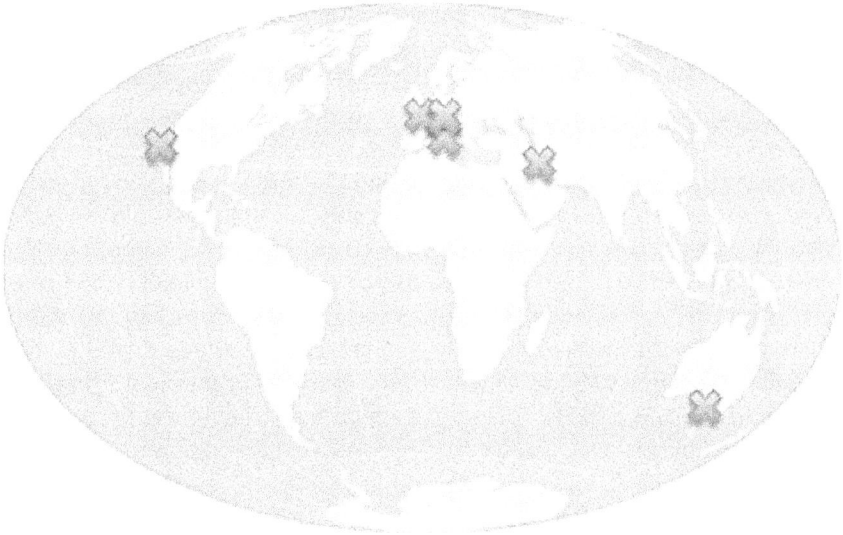

Figure 7.4 Map showing research participants based in six countries. Created by the author.

explored selectively if and when technologically mediated interactions form integral components of participants' lifeworlds (Horst and Miller 2012). Digital ethnography involves tracing networks and flows of communication, or 'communicative travel' (Larsen, Urry, and Axhausen 2006). In this sense, it is a multi-sited methodology insofar as the researcher attends to the 'circulation of cultural meanings, objects, and identities in diffuse time-space' (Marcus 1995: 96). It does this in and across the various physical and social spaces of the Internet. Fieldsites in the digital landscape are therefore both physical (the geographical location where the Internet is being used) and social (the online environments where people form social relationships) places. On this basis, the methodological apparatus of digital ethnography needs to foster ways for the researcher to be mobile virtually and present online in order to study participants' physical and digital movements.

Belonging to an early cohort of fully fledged digital ethnographers when I began my fieldwork in 2012, I relied on emerging digital-ethnographic methods, as well as on my own innovative strategies, developed in direct conversation with my research participants. While I was travelling in Iran, I set up a research photoblog in order to anchor contact with research participants. Once back in the U.K., I had to devise ways to maintain presence and connection with the contacts established in Iran. In order to 'be there' in the Iranian 'photoblogosphere', I carried out online participant-observation of Iranian photoblogging for twelve months, during which I became a 'consequential social actor in online space' (Boellstorff et al. 2012).[15] With permission, I took handwritten notes and recorded video and audio calls on Skype, using a relevant software application. I also printed and physically archived emails, chat correspondence and interview transcripts.[16] Following my decision to trace photobloggers' mobility, and always with their permission, I digitally shadowed a number of my research participants on the move in real time. Invariably, individuals would move discretely between digital platforms, social networks, and mobile devices. The intersection of these different spaces formed part of the overall 'mobility' of my digital fieldsite, wherein I situated myself in what Monterde and Postill (2014) call 'mobile ensembles': the intersection of various digital media, participants, and issues found in certain instances of mobile-technology-facilitated social praxis. This is not dissimilar from the notion of 'personal media assemblages' Day Good (2012) formulated in relation to social networks, conceptualized as a shifting and interactive environment of posted photographs, videos, links, comments, and applications. As with other forms of mobility, I suggest that digital movements to and within these spaces can be equally 'infused with meaning' (Salazar and Smart 2011: ii). However, the complexity and ethnographic salience of Iranian photoblogging led me to search for more specific ways to study the practice. As part of this pursuit, I co-constructed a unique methodological apparatus with my research participants, in direct conversation with my thematic focus and mobile sites of research: a digital photography exhibition.

Designing a Digital Photography Exhibition for Ethnographic Research

After nine months of ethnographic fieldwork researching Iranian popular photographic practices in Iran, the U.K., and online, I discussed with my principal research participants the idea of co-curating a digital photography exhibition of their work (see Figure 7.5). The resulting exhibition presents an example of a site-specific methodology, whereby the form of research (a digital exhibition of digital photographs/photoblogs) is constructed in specific relation to the fieldsite (online environments) (see Figure 7.6).[17] The idea to develop the exhibition stemmed directly from the decidedly digital and visual ways in which I had established relationships with my research participants. Through the setting up of the exhibition, geographically dispersed research participants were introduced to each other, their work and networks, and were able to build a sense of collective identity: they became active and creatively involved participants in the project, rather than just being (or being seen to be) isolated bodies in the

photoblogsiran.com
home / contact

Photoblogs from Iran:
A Digital Exhibition

Methodological component of a PhD research project in Anthropology (2011-2015) conducted at the Institute of Social and Cultural Anthropology, University of Oxford.

ENTER

Figure 7.5 Cover page of the digital exhibition www.photoblogsiran.com

Photoblogs from Iran
A Digital Exhibition

Home   About   Background   Photographer profiles   Contact

Contemporary Iranian Popular Digital Photography

Pages
About
Background
Photographers
— Amir Sadeghi
— Kiana Farhoudi
— 'Life Goes on in Tehran'
— Ehsan Abbasi
— Saleh Ara
— Vahid Rahmanian
— Omid Akhavan
— Nikzad Shahidian

Figure 7.6 Homepage of the digital exhibition. Cover image for the Facebook fan page of the popular photoblog 'Life Goes on in Tehran', http://www.photoblogsiran.com/blog/. Screenshot captured by the author.

digital landscape with whom I conducted research.[18] The concept of the exhibition shares affinity with Varzi's (2006) (offline) ethnographic methodology of the *dowreh* (circle or salon), used in her study of Iranian youth in Tehran, which similarly sought to involve individuals actively in the process of research. While conducting research in Iran, Varzi put together a *dowreh* of college students in the hope of establishing a 'comfortable environment (as opposed to an environment whereby the subject simply answers questions...)' (ibid: 14). This collaborative space aimed to move beyond a focus group governed by her research questions, and towards a more collective project that, as Varzi puts it, 'became their project' of examining their own lives, as they thought about how they consume their public space and public culture (ibid: 14).

The exhibition methodology presented here extends these principles to the digital and transnational Iranian context. Through the exhibition, I was able to generate and extrapolate ethnographic texture by obtaining first-hand experience of what it takes to design, curate, maintain and monitor a photoblog, including 'behind the scenes' details of the process that the presented photoblogs themselves do not share with the general viewing public. Through the exhibition I carried out digital photo elicitation: a digital form of the established visual method of photo elicitation (Collier and Collier 1986), which uses images to elicit discourse with participants and which informs the researcher's analysis. This digitally realizes Pink's (2011a: 96) argument that 'sharing photographs can become a way of doing ethnography', whereby participants help to shape the ethnographic process in an active and participatory manner.

Importantly, the digital exhibition also reconceptualizes notions of travel in ethnographic research. It reconfigures the physical movement of an exhibition as digital travel, whilst modifying the role of the anthropologist from photographer to co-curator. Photographs shown in the digital exhibition were not generated by myself as visual anthropologist (photoethnography), nor by participants for the research process (photovoice). Rather, they pre-existed in primary locations (participants' own photoblogs and related digital places) and moved, as digital copies, to join the digital exhibition without altogether leaving the photoblog from which they came.[19]

One of my main research activities as researcher/co-curator involved sharing online the site's URL to relevant viewing publics, for research purposes. I presented the exhibition to photographers, Iranians in Iran and in the U.K., as well as gallery curators, artists, and journalists in Tehran and London who were contributing to the wider ethnography. This broadened the potential sample base of participating subjects by allowing easier access (virtual and economical) than that traditionally afforded by visiting a physical exhibition. This is particularly salient in relation to Iran, where restricted official economic and cultural support for independent artists and initiatives are seeing the growing popularity and credibility of online environments for exhibiting Iranian art and photography. Digital exhibitions of this kind (and the specific kind of transnational mobility they afford) thus lend themselves to accessing, convening, and studying other groups similarly bound by the confines of wider, offline sociopolitical and economic conditions and/or aesthetic frameworks.

Studying viewership is an important aspect for understanding photoblogging as a dialogical social/media practice of digital photography, rather than merely a one-way, flat or finished representation (Crang 2007; Larsen 2008). Utilizing the digital exhibition as research method allowed me to explore viewer practices and patterns, on- and offline, amongst Iranians and non-Iranians both inside Iran and in the U.K. In my digital research, notions of identity and belonging were similarly explored. I was able to investigate different (but fluid) categories of viewer 'types' based on physical location and individuals' senses of proximity (cultural, political, affective) to Iran, as elicited by acts of viewing digital photographs. I captured these responses at the particular historical juncture in which the digital exhibition was co-constructed and viewed. The exhibition itself fostered novel forms of virtual and imaginative 'travelling' to Iran amongst those I shared it with. Pink (2011b) has suggested that images do not (just) take people back (as in playing 'back' a video), but entail a process of moving forwards within the environments in which they are a part. Indeed, diasporic or exiled Iranian viewers of the exhibition virtually travel (back) to Iran through the site and connect themselves (and their nostalgia) to the forward-moving circumstances of the present. Here, the exhibition becomes, in effect, a contemporary anthropological archive, forming a digital 'cabinet of curiosity' for viewers. The exhibition is made interactive, or what McQuire (2013) terms 'operational', through the social engagement it engenders. And, in turn, this process generates relevant ethnographic material to be critically studied by the researcher.

Methodological Implications for Studies of Mobility and Beyond

The digital exhibition I co-designed during my study of Iranian photobloggers complements studies of mobility by directly addressing three key overall concerns, also outlined in the Introduction to this volume. These involve the researcher's ability to: (1) collaborate; (2) assemble; and (3) explore the lifeworlds of subjects in multi-sited and multi-faceted mobile research environments. First and foremost, collaboration. The exhibition constitutes an interesting form of collaborative digital and visual participatory method, broadly situated in a Participatory Action Research (PAR) framework (Wadsworth 1998). PAR, originally developed in a nondigital context, seeks to establish collaborative relationships in which community actors take an active role in exploring 'local' issues alongside a researcher, developing broader strategies for change (Gubrium and Harper 2013: 30). PAR complements the carrying out of 'glocal ethnography' (Salazar 2010) in a range of digital and nondigital settings by recognizing the beneficial affordances of collaborative and interdisciplinary research methods in complex contemporary fieldwork loci. In the case of the digital exhibition discussed here, this global–local interface is explored digitally and visually by tracing how disparately located individuals collectively negotiate the historically layered image of Iran through socioaesthetic practices of de/reconstruction on the Internet.

Secondly, the issue of assembling. Assembling moving participants is a prominent methodological concern in mobilities research. As Bruner (2008: 228) notes in his studies of tourism and tourist photography, 'a key difficulty in studying tourists is methodological – tourists move so fast through sites that it is hard to keep up with them'. As Christian Vium's chapter in this volume shows, however, photography as an anthropological method of mobility helps us to 'fixate' people and places in 'a vast and intricate web of flows and connections'. Along these same lines, it can be argued that the digital exhibition responds to various methodological challenges precisely by providing a useful 'net' – of and for ethnographic enquiry and carved out from within the broader digital landscape – with which to 'trap'[20] (Miller 2001) and engage moving subjects. This has the effect of creating a 'home space' for the research; a virtual headquarters of consciously constructed digital 'immobility' or stasis, where participants and researcher can convene, explore, reflect upon the research theme within the safe confines of a co-curated platform. In co-constructing a fieldsite for the research to take place with/in, the exhibition demonstrates Clifford's (1997: 8) earlier concept of fieldwork as travel practice, one that involves the movement of the researcher to match the mobility of the objects and subjects of study. Sociotechnological potentials engrained in the digital exhibition further contribute to the researcher's ethnographic perspective by enabling, at once, dual capacities: the experience of 'being there together' online (Schroeder 2010), and the ability to revisit the material after the 'event' of live contact. Here, we may consider the relevance of Urry's (2004: 35) statement about web 2.0 platforms more generally, which enable, he argues, people and networks to 'be connected to, or to be at home with "sites" across the world'. Providing a point of ongoing collaborative contact or 'contact zone' (Clifford 1997), the digital exhibition establishes a suitable basis for nurturing social relations throughout the research process. As I quickly discovered with my own research, this can be a useful way of illuminating latent aspects of the research process, aspects that are more difficult to obtain through more direct strategies of soliciting, or following (physically or digitally), subjects.

Thirdly, there comes the issue of exploration. A digital exhibition such as the one outlined in this chapter can offer a suitably mobile platform to explore dynamic and elusive social fields such as those of identities and imaginaries. Given that my fieldsite pertained as much to social and cultural imaginaries (Taylor 2004; Salazar 2012) as it did to the geographical place of Iran, it seemed, at the outset of my research, even more necessary to explore novel ways of entering Iran's various 'virtual' domains. Salazar (2012: 866) suggests that imaginaries may be studied, anthropologically, by attending to the 'multiple conduits through which they pass and become visible in the form of images and discourses'.

Putting Iran's social imaginaries and digital environments on a methodological plane, my challenge was to co-construct a relevant image/imaginary-based environment of and for the research. Nondigital exhibitions have often been associated with these kinds of explorations of image-based identity politics. Karp (1991: 15) identifies a fundamental relationship between exhibitions and self-representation: 'Exhibitions represent identity, either directly through assertion, or indirectly by implication. They are privileged arenas for presenting images of self and "other"'. Digital exhibitions are not altogether distinct from these observations, and, as I discovered in my own research, can play an equally important role in larger anthropological questions of identity and subjective experience. At the same time, digital exhibitions are not uniform, nor do they necessarily share intentions or outcomes. Exhibitions vary according to the research rubric, researcher, participants, and the social, cultural, and aesthetic frameworks from which the material is drawn and feeds back into. Given the wider indexical conditions in which the making, viewing, and distributing of images from Iran are enmeshed, sharing an ethos of collective visual storytelling with my participants helped us to explore a range of existing and emerging social imaginaries in a distilled, world-recreating environment. The exhibition, as is the case with participants' own photoblogs, is therefore in this sense an explicit site of reconstruction. It asks viewers to reflexively consider ontological, sociopolitical, and cultural questions about, in this case, Iran, and to critically engage with their own situated practices of viewing. Arguably then, this methodological move does make a peculiarly 'local' intervention on the 'global' image of Iran in visual and media imaginaries.

Lastly, a wider point on the ethics and politics of such a 'methodology of mobility'. With the capacity to store and display hundreds or even thousands of digital photographs, the digital exhibition is able to replicate photobloggers' own practices of showing varied image 'types' on their photoblogs. Therefore, given the relevant curatorial ethos, the exhibition has the potential to overcome the representational limits of offline physical exhibitions. Mercer's (2008: 62) reflections on this quandary (posited in relation to the work of Black British artists) provides an important theoretical precursor to the digital exhibition as an anthropological research method, and also points to its broader political implications:

> If, after many years of struggle, you arrive at the threshold of enunciation and are 'given' the right to speak and a limited space in which to tell your story, is it not the case that there will be an overwhelming pressure to try and tell the whole story all at once? (Mercer 2008: 62)

The digital exhibition attends to this potential epistemological predicament by resisting any dominant narrative. Instead, it collates a digital repository of images, cultural experiences, memories, and aspirations that provide a fertile environment for digital-visual cultural storytelling, with viewers as interactive co-narrators. As a befitting model for anthropological research, as well as representation, therefore, the digital exhibition lends itself to other studies of image and imaginary-based mobilities, wherein issues of identity and visual and political representations are intrinsic to social research questions being asked.

Overall, the digital exhibition was, for my own research on Iranian photobloggers, a crucial method through which my research themes emerged, developed, and were communicated to relevant publics. It aided my analytical capacity to construct what Pink (2011a: 96) calls the 'ethnographic place', in which description and theory come together to create a representational rendering of the ethnography. In developing the method, I made use of what Gubrium and Harper (2013: 173) suggest to be the primary goal of placing exhibitions online in the form of online web 2.0 platforms, namely 'to make materials available to a wider public'.[21] The method's public and accessible nature serves as a useful pedagogical tool for disseminating anthropological research within and beyond the academy. Both reflecting and contributing to mobile fieldsites, the digital exhibition thus advances ways in which anthropologists might carry out 'visual interventions' (Pink 2009) with participants in a range of research contexts involving (im)mobilities.

Conclusion: Engaging (with) Digital and Visual Methods of Mobility

In this chapter, I have discussed intersecting layers of ethnographic as well as methodological (im)mobilities, suggesting a direct relationship between the two that offers important insights for studies of mobility in the social sciences. Through the 'double lens' of my digital-ethnographic investigation of Iranian photobloggers, involving a 'frame within a frame' analysis of using methods drawn from the field (digital photography on the Internet) to conduct my study with/in the field, I have discussed one innovative digital-visual method in particular (a digital photography exhibition), and briefly outlined a range of other relevant digital and visual methods of mobility (online participant-observation, shadowing, and interviewing), tracing the types of mobility such methods both capture and afford. I showed how contemporary ethnographers have the possibility of dialogically developing site-specific methods, such as digital exhibitions that allow them to physically and metaphorically 'move' with/in 'intangible' fieldsites such as the Internet, as well as with/in historical and visual-cultural imaginaries. Such methods, I suggest, lend themselves to studies of (im)mobility within and beyond online environments and photography – to research, for example, on migration and tourism, as well as to investigations pursued in/ of places to which the researcher has limited physical access. In presenting these methods, I have argued that these are not a priori strategies, nor are they always applicable, but can be effectively applied, moulded, and developed to complement key social research questions – or even help raise new ones.

In the case of Iran, a largely 'besieged' zone for long-term socioscientific research when it comes to non-native researchers, I have argued how lack or limited physical access for the foreign/nonresident researcher presents less a predicament of 'immobility' than an opportunity for methodological innovation. As I have shown, researchers can, for example, become 'mobile' in a digital sense in an otherwise potential state of 'immobility'. Relevant research strategies, such as the digital photography exhibition, can allow the researcher to legitimately 'be with' participants online, and to participate in this way in the natural ebbs and flows of their everyday lives, in live and nonlive forms. Through mobile methods such as the digital exhibition, I contend that digital anthropology on the one hand and mobility studies on the other can be productively brought to bear on one another and nurture other innovative methodologies of mobility. The digital exhibition specifically illustrates the need to conceive of 'the field' in mobility research as a potentially vast arena of moving images, people, histories, and experiences. I showed how this can be practically realized using the digital and epistemological parameters of an online exhibition space, co-created with geographically dispersed research subjects.

Having conducted my ethnographic research on Iranian photobloggers using digital and visual methods such as the digital exhibition, the overarching issue I raised in the introduction to this chapter, concerning the

Malinowskian fieldwork imperative of physically 'being there', becomes of crucial importance. My contention is that this geospatial imperative need not remain the definitive marker of social scientific 'authenticity'. Such a paradigm can be recast by rethinking two conventional 'virtues' of ethnographic research: physical movement in and out of physical places, and physical co-presence with subjects. Rethinking these virtues, involves recognizing that the contemporary researcher need not be physically extra mobile or hyper nomadic to 'follow the thing' or 'be there' with research participants in relevant fieldsites. Rather, by (re-)emphasizing the mediated basis of social life and research pursuits, I argue that physically remote enquiry is indeed an ethically responsible and methodologically rigorous methodology of mobility in itself, enabling 'travel', co-presence, and connection. I suggest then, that paradigms of social scientific methodology themselves need to be sufficiently mobilized to recognize burgeoning methods of studying mobility.

To conclude, I propose, and not without a grain of irony, that the contemporary ethnographer may in fact, if and when she needs to, return to the proverbial and physical 'armchair' to conduct ethnographic research with/in dynamic research loci.[22] The researcher's capacity for fostering movement in this manner recalls the historical anecdote concerning Xavier de Maistre presented by Salazar, Elliot, and Norum as a befitting Introduction to this volume. Conceiving 'mobility' as 'room travel' allows one to look beyond physical motion and towards imaginative participation in different kinds and forms of journeys. Incidentally, for reasons I have detailed in this chapter, it was in my room that much of my own ethnographic 'travelling' took place. Whilst this need not be considered (and it has not been presented here) as necessarily a 'new way' of doing ethnography, it is my contention that digital and visual approaches, such as digital photography exhibitions, open up a crucial range of methodological avenues and theoretical possibilities for future studies of physically dispersed people, objects, and social imaginaries in flux.

Shireen Walton is a Postdoctoral Researcher on the ERC-funded project *Anthropology of Smart Phones and Smart Ageing* (ASSA) at UCL, currently conducting fieldwork in Italy. Previously, she was a Teaching Fellow in Material, Visual, and Digital Culture at UCL Anthropology. Her research focuses on visual/digital culture in/between the Middle East and Europe. She has published on anthropology and (digital) photography in Iran, and on visual-digital research methods.

NOTES

1. 'Armchair anthropology' is a phrase denoting nineteenth-century ethnology, whereby scholars studied cultural 'others' remotely, through mediated forms such as travelogues and colonial and missionary reports. For a critical discussion of this, see Willerslev (2011).

2. I use this military terminology knowingly in order to infer the ethical implications of instances of critically unexamined 'being there' for research purposes. A notable recent example can be seen in initiatives such as the Human Terrain System (HTS) in Iraq and Afghanistan.

3. For useful genealogies of the social anthropology of Iran, see Nadjmabadi (2009) and Fazeli (2006).

4. I use the complex term 'the West' consciously throughout this chapter since the category is of direct relevance to my Iranian interlocutors. In the national, historical, and rhetorical context of revolutionary and postrevolutionary Iran, 'the West' (mostly pertaining to America and the U.K.) forms one part of a binary held in place by the ideological architects of the Islamic regime between Iran and what it presents as its ultimate other: 'the West'. For further insights see Dabashi (2008).

5. The incident is thought to have been instigated by the paramilitary *Basij* (a volunteer militia established in 1979 by the revolutionary leader Ayatollah Khomeini) in response to U.K.-imposed sanctions on Iran regarding the latter's nuclear programme.

6. Brief research trips to Iran (sometimes on tourist visas) are not uncommon for Iranian and non-Iranian researchers. In these cases, as with my own, the rationale of doing 'quick ethnography' or 'zip in and zip out fieldwork' Hegland (2004) in Iran is a pragmatic antidote to travel injunctions, outweighing ideals of 'being there' for sustained periods of time.

7. 'Photo tours' (*safarhā-ye 'akkāsi*) are an important (offline) aspect of photoblogging as a mobile social practice. These take place via a range of means, from state-funded/associated photography organizations and competitions, which are today also facilitated online, to more informal, independent groups which emerge though online networks and communities.

8. Online interview, 25 January 2013.

9. http://farsi.khamenei.ir/speech-content?id=2627

10. On the history, development, and uses of the Internet in Iran see Sreberny and Khiabany (2010) and Akhavan (2013).

11. Online interview, 27 April 2013.

12. My research sample reflects strongholds of the Iranian diaspora, the largest being in the U.S. (Los Angeles), with sizable communities across various parts of the U.K., Australia, and Germany.

13. The 'digital'/'virtual' distinction reflects disciplines' semantic choices. Whilst anthropologists (Horst and Miller 2012) tend to use the former (since, for them, virtuality implies nonreal and nonmaterial), sociologists such as Hine (2015) comfortably employ the latter.

14. Boellstorff (2008) monograph on Second Life was one of the first to show how ethnography can be conducted exclusively within virtual worlds. This has encouraged anthropologists to take more seriously the prospect of 'cybersociality'. See also ibid. 2012.
15. I coined the term the 'photoblogosphere' in my Ph.D. dissertation. It conceptualizes the multiple spaces, on and offline, in and outside Iran, where photoblogggers and viewers partake in the practice.
16. For a relevant discussion on producing 'live fieldnotes' using digital applications, see Tricia Wang's (2012) report: http://ethnographymatters.net/blog/2012/08/02/writing-live-fieldnotes-towards-a-more-open-ethnography/
17. www.photoblogsiran.com
18. See also my discussion of the digital exhibition on the 'Material World' blog: http://www.materialworldblog.com/2014/12/exploring-digital-visual-anthropological-research-methods-www-photoblogiran-com/
19. For explanation and relevant examples of these visual anthropological terms in digital contexts see Gubrium and Harper (2013).
20. Miller makes the case for 'websites as traps' (borrowing from Gell's (1996) theory of artworks as 'traps') in the digital landscape which draw surfers in to discursive fields of engagement. He shows how this can happen by members of a given culture, as in the case of Trinidadian personal websites.
21. For a relevant discussion on the ethics of making digital research material public, see Gubrium and Harper (2013), pp.45-69.
22. For a similar analogy to the point I make here about 'armchair anthropology', see Willerslev (2011).

REFERENCES

Adey, P. 2006. 'If Mobility is Everything it is Nothing: Towards a Relational Politics of (Im)mobilities' *Mobilities* 1(1): 75–94.
Akhavan, N. 2013. *Electronic Iran: The Cultural Politics of an Online Evolution.* New Brunswick: Rutgers University Press.
Al-i Ahmad, J. 1962. *Gharbzadeghi (Westoxification).* Tehran: Azad.
_____. 1984. *Occidentosis: A Plague from the West.* Berkeley: Mizan Press.
Alinejad, D. 2011. 'Mapping Homelands Through Virtual Spaces: Transnational Embodiment and Iranian Diaspora Blogs', *Global Networks* 11(1): 41–62.
Appadurai, A. 2002. 'Disjuncture and Difference in the Global Cultural Economy', in J.X. Inda and R. Rosaldo (eds), *The Anthropology of Globalization: A Reader.* Oxford: Blackwell.
Boellstorff, T. 2008. *Coming of Age in Second Life.* Princeton: Princeton University Press.
_____. 2012. 'Rethinking Digital Anthropology', in H. Horst and D. Miller (eds), *Digital Anthropology.* London/New York: Berg. 39–60.
Boellstorff, T., B. Nardi, C. Pearce, and T.L. Taylor. 2012. *Ethnography and Virtual Worlds: A Handbook of Method.* Princeton/Oxford: Princeton University Press.

Bromberger, C. 2009. 'Usual Topics: Taboo Themes and New Objects in Iranian Anthropology', in S.R. Nadjmabadi (ed.), *Conceptualizing Iranian Anthropology: Past and Present Perspectives*. New York/Oxford: Berghahn Books. 195–206.

Bruner, E. 2008. *Culture on Tour: Ethnographies of Travel*. Chicago: Univeristy of Illinois Press.

Clifford, J. 1997. 'Travelling Cultures', in J. Clifford (ed.), *Routes: Travel and Translation in the Late Twentieth Century*. Cambridge, MA/London: Harvard University Press. 17–46

Collier, J., and M. Collier. 1986. *Visual Anthropology: Photography as a Research Method*. Mexico City: University of New Mexico Press.

Crang, M. 2007. 'Picturing Practices: Research through the Tourist Gaze', *Progress in Human Geography* 21(3): 359–73.

Dabashi, H. 2008. *Post-Orientalism: Knowledge and Power in Time of Terror*. New Brunswick, NJ: Transaction Publishers.

Day Good, K. 2012. 'From Scrapbook to Facebook: A History of Personal Media Assemblage and Archives' *New Media and Society* 15(4): 557–553.

Fazeli, N. 2006. *Politics of Culture in Iran*. Abingdon: Routledge/BIPS Persian Studies Series.

Foucault, M. 1991. 'Governmentality', in G. Burchell et al. (eds), *The Foucault Effect: Studies in Governmentality*. Chicago: University of Chicago Press, pp. 87–104.

Gell, A. 1996. 'Vogel's Net: Traps as Artworks and Artworks as Traps', *Journal of Material Culture* 1(1): 15–38.

Gubrium, A., and K. Harper. 2013. *Participatory Visual and Digital Methods*. Walnut Creek, CA: Left Coast Press.

Gupta, A., and J. Ferguson. 1992. 'Beyond "Culture": Space, Identity, and the Politics of Difference', *Cultural Anthropology* 7(1): 6–23.

Hegland, M.E. 2004. 'Zip in and Zip out Fieldwork', *Iranian Studies* 37(4): 575–83.

_____. 2009. 'Iranian Anthropology – Crossing Boundaries: Influences of Modernization, Social Transformation and Globalization', in S.R. Nadjmabadi (ed.), *Conceptualizing Iranian Anthropology: Past and Present Perspectives*. New York/Oxford: Berghahn Books. 43–72.

Horst, H., and D. Miller (eds). 2012. *Digital Anthropology*. London/New York: Berg.

Hine, C. (2015). *Ethnography for the Internet: Embedded, Embodied and Everyday*. London: Bloomsbury Academic.

Karp, I. 1991. 'Introductions: Culture and Representation; Other Cultures in Museum Perspective', in I. Karp and S.D. Lavine (eds), *Exhibiting Cultures: The Poetics and Politics of Museum Display*. Washington: Smithsonian Institution Press. 373–385.

Khosravi, S. 2000. 'http://www.iranian.com: An Ethnographic Approach to an Online Diaspora', *ISIM Newsletter* 6.

Larsen, J. 2008. 'Practices and Flows of Digital Photography: An Ethnographic Framework', *Mobilities* 3(1): 141–60.

Larsen, J., J. Urry, and K. Axhausen. 2006. *Mobilities, Networks, Geographies*. Aldershot: Ashgate.

Malinowski, B. 1922. *Argonauts of the Western Pacific: An Account of Native Enterprises and Adventure in the Archipelagoes of Melanesian New Guinea*. London: Routledge.

Marcus, G.E. 1995. 'Ethnography in/of the World System: The Emergence of Multi-Sited Ethnography', *Annual Review of Anthropology* 24: 95–117.

McAuliffe, C. 2007. 'Visible Minorities: Constructing and Deconstructing the "Muslim Iranian" Diaspora', in C. Aitchison et al. (eds), *Geographies of Muslim Identities: Diaspora, Gender and Belonging.* Aldershot: Ashgate Publishing Limited. 29–56.

McQuire, S. 2013. 'Photography's Afterlife: Documentary Images and the Operational Archive', *Journal of Material Culture* 18(3): 223–41.

Mercer, K. 2008. 'Black Art and the Burden of Representation', *Third Text* 4(10): 61–78.

Miller, D. 2001. 'The Fame of Trinis: Websites as Traps', in C. Pinney and N. Thomas (eds), *Beyond Aesthetics: Art and the Technologies of Enchantment.* Oxford/New York: Berg.

Miller, D., and D. Slater. 2000. *The Internet: An Ethnographic Approach.* Oxford: Berg.

Monterde, A., and Postill, J. 2014. 'Mobile Ensembles: The Uses of Mobile Phones for Social Protest by Spain's Indignados', in G. Goggin and L. Hjorth (eds), *Routledge Companion to Mobile Media.* London: Routledge, pp. 429–38.

Nadjmabadi, S.R. (ed.). 2009. *Conceptualizing Iranian Anthropology: Past and Present Perspectives.* New York/Oxford: Berghahn Books.

Pink, S. 2011a. 'Amateur Photographic Practice, Collective Representation and the Constitution of Place', *Visual Studies* 26(2): 92–101.

_____. 2011b. 'Sensory Digital Photography: Re-thinking "Moving" and the Image', *Visual Studies* 26(1): 4–13.

_____. 2009. *Visual Interventions: Applied Visual Anthropology.* Oxford: Berghahn Books.

Salazar, N.B. 2010. 'From Local to Global (and Back): Towards Glocal Ethnographies of Cultural Tourism', in G. Richards and W. Munsters (eds), *Cultural Tourism Research Methods.* Wallingford: CABI. 188–198.

_____. 2012. 'Tourism Imaginaries: A Conceptual Approach', *Annals of Tourism Research* 39(2): 863–82.

Salazar, N.B., and J. Nilsson. 2015. 'Embedded and Re-purposed Technologies: Human Mobility Practices in Maasailand', *Mobilities* 1–17.

Salazar, N.B., and A. Smart. 2011. 'Anthropological Takes on (Im)mobility: Introduction', *Identities: Global Studies in Culture and Power* 18(6): i–ix.

Schroeder, R. 2010. *Being There Together: Social Interaction in Shared Virtual Envionments.* New York/Oxford: Oxford University Press.

Shakhsari, S. 2011. 'Weblogistan Goes to War: Representational Practices, Gendered Soldiers and Entrepreneurship in Diaspora', *Feminist Review* 99: 6–24.

Sheller, M. 2010. 'Foreword', in B. Fincham et al. (eds), *Mobile Methodologies.* New York: Palgrave Macmillan.

Sreberny, A., and G. Khiabany. 2010. *Blogistan: The Internet and Politics in Iran.* London/New York: I.B. Tauris.

Sreberny, A., and M. Torfeh. 2014. *Persian Service: The BBC and British Interests in Iran.* London/New York: I.B. Tauris.

Taylor, C. 2004. *Modern Social Imaginaries.* Durham, NC/London: Duke Univiersity Press.

Urry, J. 2004. 'Connections, Environment and Planning', *Society and Space,* 22(1): 27–37.

Varzi, R. 2006. *Warring Souls: Youth, Media and Martyrdom in Post-Revolution Iran*. Durham/London: Duke University Press.

Wadsworth, Y. 1998. 'What is Participatory Action Research?', *Action Paper International* 2. Retrieved 2 February 2015 from http://www.aral.com.au/ari/p-ywadsworth98.html.

Walton, S. 2015. 'Re-envisioning Iran Online: Photoblogs and the Ethnographic "Digital-Visual Moment"', *Middle East Journal of Culture and Communication* Special issue: Critical Histories of Photography(8): 398–418.

Watson, C.W. 1999. *Being There: Fieldwork in Anthropology*. London: Pluto Press.

Willerslev, R. 2011. 'Frazer Strikes Back from the Armchair: A New Search for the Animist Soul', *Journal of the Royal Anthropological Institute* 17(3): 504–26.

Fixating a Fluid Field
Photography as Anthropology in Migration Research

Christian Vium

This chapter presents two ethnographic cases which illustrate how photography may serve as a privileged methodological and analytical instrument when conducting qualitative research on human mobility. Based on ethnographic research conducted among undocumented migrants in West Africa and Europe between 2006 and 2012, this chapter demonstrates how photographic interventions afford a concrete means of establishing rapport with interlocutors conditioned by distress, disorientation, and uncertainty. These interventions, I argue, afford a dialogical space that invites migrants to perform and narrate their experiences, thus making sense of, and fixating, an otherwise fluid context. From an analytical vantage point, photographs may supplement written field notes and observations, enabling the researcher to elicit detailed and often unexpected information, which might otherwise be overlooked (Mjaaland 2009: 397). Epistemologically, then, the article elaborates on how photography can be used as a medium not only to document, but also to analyse and convey human mobility from an anthropological point of view (MacDougall 2006: 271; Stanczak 2007: 4).

   This chapter engages with material produced during an extended ethnographic research project tracing migrant trajectories from West Africa to Europe via the Sahara desert and the Atlantic Ocean or the Mediterranean (Vium 2007; 2009; 2014).[1] With an emphasis on migrant young men, the project investigates first-hand how they become 'nobody' in their attempts to become 'somebody': how, as the journey unfolds, they are progressively stripped of their human rights, becoming 'bare lives' (Agamben 1998), representatives of what Zygmunt Bauman (2004) calls 'outcasts of modernity'. The drama of their journey is mirrored in a profound psychological and symbolic transformation process, in which the young migrants become suspended in an existential no man's land. Throughout their long and perilous journey, the migrants continually negotiate their marginality and find themselves navigating a form of pro-longed liminality (cf. Turner 1967; 1992). In the process, many of them emerge as a new type of political subject, the 'itinerant body' (cf. Biemann 2008), which is continually departing but seldom reaches 'the' destination. These deterritorialized, itinerant bodies, which defy the boundaries of the modern nation-state (cf. Deleuze and Guattari 2004; Frichot 2008; Papadopoulos and Tsianos 2008), are progressively (re)configured while passing through a complex of nodal points that hold together the clan-destine migration network. I call these points 'intersections', alluding to their connective properties and propensity to direct the multiple heter-ogeneous flows of people, imaginaries, objects, and economies. These intersections – be they border towns in the desert, migrant 'ghettoes' en route, detention centres on the coast, or housing complexes for undocu-mented immigrants in Europe – constitute reflexive spaces for migrants, where the fluidity and uncertainty of their journeys are crystallized. In this sense, migrant intersections may be conceived as a form of thresholds (cf. Diken and Laustsen 2005; Giaccaria and Minca 2011), which transform the undocumented migrant who passes through them, and force her to come to terms with her situation.

Such intersections constitute privileged spaces for research interventions – although far from static in nature, they provide a form of stability in an otherwise highly kinetic space of trajectories (cf. Andersson, this volume; Dalakoglou 2010: 146).[2] In this chapter, I explore the ways in which photography opens unique collaborative spaces in these intersectional contexts. Conducting qualitative fieldwork in these spaces naturally poses a number of challenges for the anthropologist, particularly when cam-eras are an integral part of the research design. Hence, in this chapter, I touch upon issues related to access, ethics, anonymity, and in particular the challenge of, quite literally, focusing on a mobile and fluid popula-tion of itinerant bodies seeking to remain invisible from the authorities. In doing this, I develop three interrelated concepts – 'itinerant bodies', 'interventions' and 'intersections' – which become key for fixating the fluid field of undocumented mobility through photography-based ethno-graphic research.

Figure 8.1 Migrants driving through the Sahara desert on the back of a four-wheel drive pick-up. Northern Mali 2006. Photograph by the author.

Fixating the Figure of 'the Adventurer'

The worn-out four-wheel drive was making its way through the desert in northern Mali, slowly approaching the remote border town In Khalil. The passengers, an exhausted band of young 'adventurers'[3] heading towards Europe on the overland routes through the Sahara desert (see Figure 8.1), would have to change vehicles in In Khalil before attempting to enter Algeria by clandestinely circumnavigating the border patrols. After long hours of uninterrupted driving, the car suddenly came to a halt. One of the Tuareg drivers pointed to a few solitary acacia trees offering protection from the burning midday sun. It was finally time for a break. For two days we had been driving north through incessant heat and dust from the transportation hub of Gao in northeastern Mali, and we were exhausted. Police and military patrols, who extorted money from the migrants, had stopped the car several times along the way and a sense of desperation was beginning to surface among the migrants. Several of them had become acutely aware that they might not have the economic means to pay either for the rest of their journey to Europe or for the possible return fare to their places of departure. Advancing deeper into the vast unknown, they were steadily approaching a point of no return.

The sun was high in the sky, and we quickly found shade under the tree branches. A small fire was made and we prepared a simple dish of over-cooked spaghetti and canned tuna fish, which we shared. Dry bread and warm water with a strong taste of gasoline, due to the recycled plastic containers in which it was transported, constituted a less than favourable, but vital, supplement. A group of the Malian migrants began speaking about the hardship of the journey and their aspirations of making it to Europe. Jokingly, one man explained how, once in Italy, he would marry a white woman. The others laughed heartedly. Here, in the middle of a vast unknown, the small band of adventurers enjoyed a rare moment of rest and shared their visions of the journey, of life, and of their future expectations.

My colleague and travel companion on this particular fieldwork trip, the film director Janus Metz,[4] was filming the conversation, and I photographed moments of rest and talk. As is often the case when I 'make' photographs,[5] I was not talking much, moving about quietly observing and framing spe-cific moments. Once in a while I would intervene, discretely signalling to the migrants and inviting them to 'perform themselves' in various ways. These interventions, as I call them with reference to artistic practice (cf. Bieman et al 2008; Mjaaland 2009; Schneider 1996; 2008), may take a variety of forms in my ethnographic work depending on the context. In this particular case, the intention guiding my photographic 'interventions' was to produce a typological representation of 'the figure of the adventurer', opening a space for migrants to constitute themselves as 'able agents rather than helpless victims' (Mjaaland 2009: 395). I was interested in the notion of a person out of his familiar context travelling through the 'unknown'. Perhaps these images could instil in the viewer a reflection on what was going through the minds of these young adventurers. Certainly, this ques-tion was fuelling my own anthropological research, and by making a space for migrants to perform themselves, I was hoping to find some clues to help me understand this issue. Hence, before once again mounting on the back of the pick-up and continuing the exhausting journey, I asked a few of the migrants I had not yet photographed if I could make portraits of them in the desert with their few belongings.

The portrait of Ishmael,[6] (Figure 8.2), stems from the impromptu por-trait session in the desert I organized in May 2006. It encapsulates a number of methodological and analytical aspects to which I have returned on sev-eral occasions over the years. What I see in this photograph today is a young man performing himself into existence while at the same time projecting himself into the future. Fixing his gaze firmly at the horizon with a noble and stoic posture, he conveys self-esteem and appears convinced that he will succeed in his adventure. He is carrying the possessions he brought along for the journey: a water container wrapped in brown material, a

Figure 8.2 Ishmael. Northern Mali, 2006. Photograph by the author.

small orange bag containing some food (rice, pasta, canned sardines, and tuna), practical footwear and a black plastic bag containing some unknown articles. Most alluring is the laptop case, which he deliberately placed on the front of his torso when preparing for the portrait. The bag does not contain a computer, but along with the pinstriped shirt, his wristwatch and his composure, it conveys the impression of a man who imagines Europe, his destination, in a particular way and who has prepared himself to engage with this 'modern world' beyond the desert and across the sea.[7] With reference to Roland Barthes (2000), these elements may be seen to constitute a 'punctum' in the image: what 'rises from the scene, shoots out of it like an arrow, and pierces me' (Barthes 2000: 26).

As was the case with all portraits made for this series of 'adventurers' en route, I did not direct Ishmael. I deliberately explained that I wanted him to pose the way he wanted. To me, such a 'collaborative' portrait session holds significant qualities as the empirical result of a deliberate methodological approach and as an analytical production. What the portrait session affords is a concrete means of establishing a relationship around the collaborative production of an image, a story, or an argument, as one might conceive of it. In this sense, the motivation is to take people's self-presentations seriously and to apply photography, and 'mediated photographic encounters', as a discursive social process (Mjaaland 2009: 397). My intervention provided men like Ishmael with an invitation and opportunity to testify to their situation and perform themselves – the way they wanted – to the camera and myself, as well as to a larger imagined and global public. The portrait session enabled the 'fixation' of something complex and intangible: for example, Ishmael's embodied experience of the confusing and disorienting act of migrating clandestinely (cf. Collyer 2010; Frichot 2008; Gatti 2008; Lucht 2012; Vium 2014).

Fixation is a key word in photography, and one might say that it encapsulates what photography is all about: fixating a moment in time, a split second in which the flow of time is 'frozen' (cf. Berger 1990; Edwards 2001; Sandbye 2001; Tagg 1988). In photographic language, fixation may refer to a number of things. It may signal the act of fixing one's gaze firmly on a subject – fixing the subject in the frame, so to speak. It also refers to the final process in the development of photographic film and print; the moment when the film or photograph has been developed but needs fixation to become permanent. Technically, this is done by moving the film or print from a bath containing a chemical development liquid (which makes the image appear on the paper) into a bath containing the fixation liquid, which then fixates the image and makes it durable. I believe these aspects are instructive in the case of Ishmael's portrait. He is identified as the central subject; and a space is made for him to fixate himself. Fixating is about creating a form of durable, if not permanent, order in an otherwise ephemeral, fluid, and often chaotic complex of movements and encounters. Fixation is also, quite literally, what enables the image of Ishmael to travel beyond the immediate situation and find an audience further afield.

The portrait session, which resulted from my intervention, constitutes a dialogical space within a fluid and highly mobile context, in which

Ishmael is invited to pause, reflect, and perform – and thus narrate himself. Figuratively speaking, through our technologically mediated collaboration, Ishmael is enacted as an intersection of past, present, and future memories, actions, and imaginaries. In the short moment of the session, Ishmael performs himself, and his image is both exposed and fixated, in this case onto the digital chip of the camera, offering him the opportunity to see himself instances after the picture has been made. This is a very concrete event, but one that holds the potential for more abstract theoretical extrapolation. As Jean Rouch (2003) would have it, the collaboration around the production of the image, and the subsequent reviewing of it in the moment, reflects what he has called 'shared anthropology', that is, a more immersive form of anthropology, in which the 'subject' is encouraged to reflect on and participate in the analysis of his or her actions (Edwards 2001; Mjaaland 2009:409; Fulchignoni 2003; Rouch 2003). The process of fixation, then, affords immediate analytical dialogue in the field.

On the one hand, the portrait session establishes an intimate relationship between ethnographer and interlocutor, which is centred on something concrete and comprehensible (the making of a portrait). On the other hand, it captures and collapses a welter of different elements into a single frame – an image of a person – which becomes an icon of the migratory endeavour at large. In that instant, Ishmael becomes the figure of the adventurer who collapses past, present, and future, appearing as someone who is legible by a global audience. Photography can, as Elizabeth Edwards argues, 'communicate about culture, people's lives, experiences, and beliefs, not at the level of surface description but as a visual metaphor which bridges that space between the visible and the invisible, which communicates not through the realist paradigm, but through a lyrical expressiveness' (Edwards 1997: 58). In the portrait, Ishmael appears not as an exotic figure, but rather challenges the stereotypical image of a desperate migrant from the poor global south seeking his fortune in the affluent global north. He is thus both an individual and a symbol, and when I look at him – or at the image of him – I see the young man departing from the village, the man en route facing the desert, as well as the man in Europe, blending into a new future context. The photograph thus captures and fixates different scales of time, space, and hope, affording a multiplicity of analytical readings.

Interventions: Photography as an Anthropological Method

Intervening with a camera is always an analytical act, and implies the repositioning of both photographer and photographic image in 'an encounter where meanings are mediated between social agents' (Mjaaland 2009:

409). It involves a multitude of choices and decisions, which are constantly adjusted and negotiated in the field according to each situation. Rouch writes the following on the uniqueness of the ethnographer working with cameras in fieldwork: 'instead of elaborating and editing his notes after returning from the field, he must, under penalty of failure, make his synthesis at the exact moment of observation. In other words, he must create his cinematic report, bending it or stopping it, at the time of the event itself' (Rouch 2003: 38).

Considerations concerning whether photographs are made in horizontal or vertical format, whether the camera is hand-held or on tripod, where to point the camera and when to press the shutter, are inherently analytical (Back 2004; Banks 2001; Stanczak 2007). Ideally, and here I adhere to Rouch's approach, intervention becomes a form of 'trance' in which I participate in the situations I photograph by, literally, becoming consumed with the act of photographing (Rouch 2003: 38). Photographing is an immersive and embodied form of immediate sensory engagement within a given environment, in which the photographer must adapt his or her movements and choice of actions to the unfolding events. By intervening, one affects the situation in which one participates, and a dialogue ensues[8] in which both those in front of the camera and the photographer behind it relate to each other and communicate in a form of interactive choreography arising from the moment. To paraphrase Thera Mjaaland, encounters, and their fixation, are together a way of making sense of reality and conceiving of knowledge as emerging 'in' encounters (Mjaaland 2009: 394). Knowledge, then, becomes fundamentally relational.

Photographing, then, is a very concrete and deliberate way of positioning oneself in the field vis-à-vis interlocutors. It affords a means of situating oneself and making oneself identifiable as someone who – among other things – is there to produce images and stories, to be then shown to others. My intentions as an ethnographer and photographer are, to a certain extent, rendered intelligible to the interlocutors. This is particularly important when documenting undocumented migration, where photographing invariably poses a number of ethical questions. For my research, I work with people who desire to remain unseen by the authorities since they are, legally speaking, committing a crime when entering sovereign national territory without the required visas. Hence, taking out the camera, signalling the intention to photograph is a delicate issue that must be evaluated according to each particular situation.

In nearly all cases in the context of this particular research project, I only presented the camera once I had established a relation with the persons I wished to photograph. Ideally, in my work, I want the interlocutors to consider me as a medium through which they can express and communicate themselves. In this case, I sometimes let the interlocutors themselves establish when the moment was right for photographing, and quite a few photographs were made on the request of the migrants themselves. Although the migrants rarely requested anonymity, I chose to apply a photographic aesthetic, which, to a large extent, makes it difficult to identify the people portrayed. While the portrait of Ishmael is in colour, sharp, and readily decidable,[9] the edit of other images from the project, which has been exhibited internationally in various magazines and venues, consists of dark, blurry, black and white photographs, which have been significantly retouched to a point where most of the people appearing in the images would be only recognizable to their family and friends. This is a deliberate choice, which is both analytically and ethically motivated, in the sense that I find this aesthetic mirrors my analytical arguments and the themes I identified in the ethnographic fieldworks I conducted (see Vium 2014).

Photography, in its very constitution, is about framing, focusing, exposing, and fixating the object or field under scrutiny. In the case of undocumented migration from Africa into Europe, this becomes a crucial method of research, as it is a vast, complex theme, which associates a bewildering amount of dynamic elements and people across borders and in multiple interconnected spaces, both real and imaginary (Appadurai 1996; Lado 2005; Sheller and Urry 2006; Vigh 2009). Migration invariably entails movement, and, in this particular case, many fragmented movements (Chavez 1996; Collyer 2007; 2010; Coutin 2005; Gatti 2008; Vium 2014), often over long periods of time, interspersed with more or less involuntary immobility (Carling 2002; Lubkeman 2008) of varying duration (Figures 8.3 and 8.4). Due to the duration (often several years) and fragmentation of the undocumented migrant's journey, it is next to impossible to follow one single migration journey. In the context of this long-term project, photography becomes a means of identifying, delineating, describing, and analysing a number of significant spaces of migration, which I conceive of as migratory nodal points that associate a welter of itinerant bodies. I call these 'intersections', referring to the multiple flows they accommodate and their connective properties, as well as their function in directing these flows. The analytical concepts of the 'itinerant body' and the 'intersection' have major implications – both for my research design and for the ways I have come to understand my work within the field of migration and mobility studies in general. Hence, before proceeding with the empirical cases, I briefly turn to these two analytical concepts.

Intersections: Transformative Thresholds

In order to analyse the migration network and the nature of intersections, it may be helpful, as Ruben Andersson also proposes in this volume, to

Figures 8.3 and 8.4 Migrants stuck in the border town. In Khalil in northern Mali, 2006. Photographs by the author.

engage in a brief discussion of actor-network theory (ANT), since it proposes to analyse social life as being made up of dynamic and heterogeneous assemblages of actors (Latour 2005; Murdoch 1995). At the core of ANT lies a relational approach, which favours connections as opposed to fixed entities or structures. In this chapter, I describe a number of intersections in the migration network, in the hope of demonstrating how these bind different actors together in a complex system. In my research project on human mobility, I have tried to 'trace a network' (Latour 2005: 128), a network I understand as inherently plural in the sense that it is composed of a multiplicity of actor networks that are juxtaposed (Callon 1987: 93-94), thus forming an assemblage (Delanda 2006; Marcus and Saka 2006). The migration network is plastic and fluid, it has structure and presence, but not in a singular sense. It is enacted in 'intersections or interferences between different spaces including regions, networks, and fluid' (Law 2004 102). This ANT-inspired approach directly relates to the 'new mobilities paradigm' (Introduction, this volume) in that it gives attention to both notions of boundedness and fluidity, while prioritizing the connections that sustain the migration network: the intersections, and the actors constituting these.

In addition to sustaining the migration network, the intersections act in particular ways on the migrants. They may be conceived of as a form of thresholds or threshold spaces, where the potential for transformation is intensified. One cannot, I argue, pass through these intersections without becoming somehow transformed. Furthermore, my ethnographic material leads me to tentatively propose that as the migrant moves through a succession of these threshold spaces, he or she (un)becomes proportionally, sometimes to the extent that he or she is reduced to a form of 'bare life' (Agamben 1998). Hence, there is a sense of accumulated, potentially negative transformation inherent in the continued transgression of thresholds.

Itinerant Bodies: Departures without Arrivals

In order to comprehend (im)migration, one must understand that it first of all entails emigration – a departure from somewhere familiar (Sayad 1999). An emigrant becomes an immigrant only through a perilous process that often takes years of fragmented journeying and is governed by tremendous uncertainty, particularly when a valid visa or other required documentation are not available. The intermediary period between departure and the aspired arrival is often prolonged indefinitely. Whilst in this liminal state (cf. Van Gennep 1960 [1908]; Turner 1967; 1992), the migrant is often uncertain about when his situation will change (Lucht 2012; Schuster 2005), and does not know when and how he will be able to proceed onwards on his journey (Figures 8.3 and 8.4). The migrant does not just jump from the village into the metropolis; rather, he is suspended in existential liminality throughout the journey, and often finds himself stuck in various intersections along the way (Collyer 2010).

While migration scholars have tended to overlook the actual migration journey itself, I believe it provides an optimal vantage point from which to explore the quintessential question of (social) becoming, which constitutes a key aspect of the migratory endeavour (Frichot 2008; Lucht 2012; Pandolfo 2007; Papadopoulos and Tsianos 2008; Vigh 2009). The journey of undocumented migrants is composed of a continuum of departures, which, I argue, accumulate and gain momentum with each step the migrant takes into the unknown that extends before him. The French have a saying – *Partir c'est mourir un peu* (to leave is to die a little) – that is particularly instructive in the case of undocumented migration. Analytically, I regard these departures also as a process of both literally and figuratively becoming 'a departed' (i.e. dead in the etymological sense of the expression). This paradoxical process of (un)becoming – or 'inverted becoming' – is, as I have argued elsewhere (Vium 2014), paramount to comprehending undocumented migration in the context I have been working in.

In the following case from fieldwork in the city of Nouadhibou on the Atlantic coast of Mauritania, I discuss how I intervene in one particular intersection in the migratory network, and how photographing becomes a way of fixating the 'itinerant body', analytically honing in on these transformatory thresholds.

Nouadhibou: A Utopian Antechamber

Due to its strategic position on the frontier between Mauritania and Morocco, and its relative vicinity to the Canary Islands, the coastal city of Nouadhibou in northern Mauritania has become an important intersection on the migration route between West Africa and Europe over the last decade. Thousands of Sub-Saharan Africans transit through this city every year, hoping to find a means of embarking on small boats to the Canary Islands. Cheikh Oumar Ba and Armelle Choplin (2005:4) have defined Nouadhibou as an 'antechamber' of Europe, which nevertheless offers more or less utopic possibilities of passage: a place of 'broken dreams', as it were (ibid.:6).

Many prospective migrants spend years in Nouadhibou, trying to earn money to pay the expensive and dangerous maritime crossing into Europe. Some work on large international fishing vessels in the rich maritime waters off the coast, while others find jobs in the artisanal fishing industry. The city is dotted with migrant communities, and many migrants inhabit so-called 'ghettos', where they pay to sleep in crowded rooms often organized according to nationality. Here, migrants find themselves 'stranded' in a situation of involuntarily immobility, constantly waiting to leave (Ba and Choplin 2005: 7; Carling 2002; Collyer 2010).

In 2006, when I first conducted research with prospective migrants in Nouadhibou, an estimated 33,000 migrants arrived in the Canary Islands, many having embarked in boats from the beaches near Nouadhibou, and further north, near the Moroccan interior cities of Dakhla, Layoune, and Tarfaya (Choplin and Lombard 2008). Offshore patrolling along the Atlantic coast of northwestern Africa, largely supervised by the Spanish coast guard as well as the EU border agency FRONTEX (Andersson, this volume), had been intensified (Choplin and Lombard 2008: 153). Boatloads of aspiring migrants were regularly intercepted off the coast of Nouadhibou and subsequently transferred to overcrowded detention centres in the city, where migrants waited to be sent back to their countries of origin. In May 2006, the International Red Cross, which was overseeing these premises, granted me access to one such detention centre.

'Guantanamito': The Epitome of a Migration Intersection

Established in what was previously a primary school, and now supplemented by a number of large canvas tents pitched in the courtyard behind a high wall with barbwire fences, the centre I visited was known popularly as 'Guantanamito' (Little Guantanamo). At the time of my arrival, migrants who had been intercepted offshore by the coast guard were detained in three different rooms on the premises. With dirty, torn clothes, bloodshot eyes, and dry skin from exposure to saltwater, the exhausted men waited in silence with little but their thoughts to occupy them (Figures 8.5 and 8.6). Because of our cameras, the men readily identified my companion Janus and myself as journalists as soon as we entered 'Guantanamito', and a collective performance soon began taking place. A group of men came forward and began recounting their experiences, describing how they had been drifting for days at sea, how they were now stuck, waiting to be released or deported to their countries of origin, without knowing when that would happen. Others soon joined the men, and a choir of lamentations emerged.

'They don't even allow us to call our families!' one young man exclaimed, while others nodded insistently. 'The journey is hard, very hard', another man confided, demonstratively drinking water from a plastic bottle. With the camera as a technological mediator, a conversation ensued. The men addressed themselves directly to the camera, looking firmly into it, explicitly speaking to a larger imaginary audience, whom they anticipated would be watching their emotional 'testimony'. It was hardly necessary to pose questions, as the men readily proclaimed to us and the camera that they were 'honest men just hoping to make a living for our families', that 'poverty drove us to migrate', and that they saw no choice but to continue in their attempt to reach Europe in spite of the dangers involved. 'Right now, it is Europe or death!' one man stated dramatically while looking insistently into the lens of the camera – as if he felt invited by the camera itself to pronounce himself and act out his frustrations. Several men stressed the hardships of the ocean crossing, and voiced discontent with the amoral middlemen and corrupt police officers they had encountered. Beyond these discontents, a more substantial undercurrent of critique was directed towards a global system of inequality, in which they found themselves involuntarily embedded (cf. Lucht 2012; Vigh 2009).

As so often before when working with a camera as an analytical instrument in anthropological research, I was impressed by the migrants' capacity to distil complex issues into coherent and concise statements, 'one-liners', which, when combined with their gestures, seemed to fixate vast, complex problems into moments of remarkable clarity. Our presence, and the presence of the camera, seemed to activate a virtual stage upon which the men performed an improvised choreography.

When reviewing the videos and photographs made that day, and while cutting up the material and reassembling it in a new narrative montage (cf. Deleuze 2005; Eisenstein 1988; Suhr and Willerslev 2013), it became apparent to me that the men identified us and the cameras as mediums for the expression of a deeply personal and critical discourse – or more poignantly, a testimonial – on the inequality and dehumanization characterizing their situation. Contrary to the spectacular (cf. De Genova 2013) but numbing images (Broomberg and Chanarin 2008) of desperate African men arriving in hordes at the shores of Europe, intersected by coast guards or at the border fences of the Spanish enclaves Ceuta and Melilla, this particular situation invited the migrants to contextualise and communicate their endeavours. They did so by evoking 'universal' aspects such as love, family, and children, thus allowing an imagined 'Western' or European audience to identify with them and their frustrations. In this specific case, one important aspect, as already stressed, was the way in which the migrants projected themselves, through the camera, towards an audience and a future not physically present at the time of the encounter with the researcher. I am inclined to believe that this acknowledgement of a larger audience, combined with the migrants' awareness that their physical appearance and bodily gesticulations are registered, significantly alters the way interlocutors perform their 'narrative argument'. By intervening in interlocutors' lives with the camera, a space for dialogue is opened up where researcher and interlocutors together produce, or perform, a largely improvised collaborative narrative addressed at a third party. Hence, I argue that the camera brings to the fore novel potentials for qualitative social science research. Let me move to another example to develop this argument.

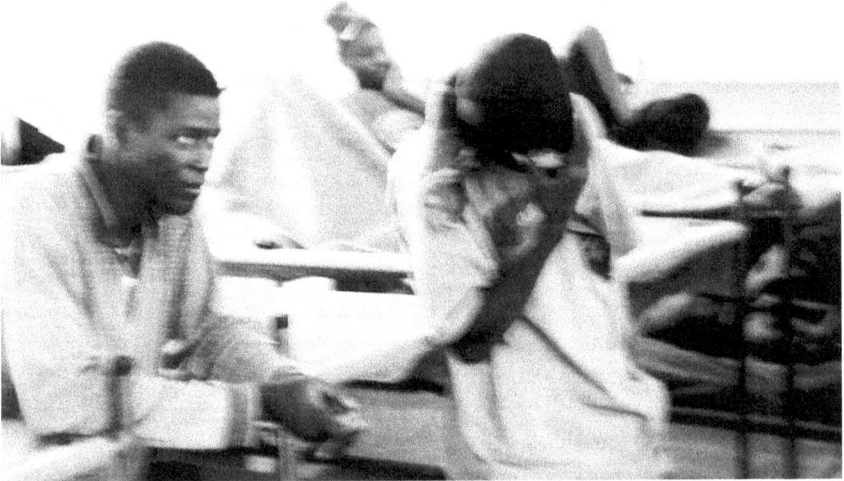

Figure 8.5 Detained migrants in Nouadhibou, Mauritania, 2006. Photograph by the author.

Upon arriving in one of the communal 'cells' in the Guantanamito detention centre, I made a brief tour, introducing myself to the approximately thirty men in the room, explaining that I was there to speak with them, listen to their stories and make (as opposed to 'take') photographs (Vium 2014: 19). I made it clear that if they did not wish to be included in the photographs, they should either signal this to me, or simply move out of the frame of the camera. I then moved to the back of the room, where a man was doing his ablutions, in preparation for prayer. I signalled my intentions of photographing him during prayer by establishing eye contact and smiling as I gently lifted my camera upwards and pointed it towards him. The man accepted my request silently by returning my gaze, and continued his activities. My presence was now established and acknowledged, not only with the man in front of me, but potentially vis-à-vis all the men in the room, who could see what I was doing. A few minutes later, as the man finished his prayer, I nodded at him appreciatively whilst smiling, and moved slowly away.

I continued photographing the cell – I photographed some men gazing dreamingly out of the window, and a man half asleep in a bed who, however, indicated he did not want to be photographed by turning away his face and covering himself with a blanket. In the adjacent bed, a young man wearing a dirty long-sleeved T-shirt caught my attention. As I approached him, he pulled forward his upper body from his lying position with a dramatic gesture, and looked straight at me. I introduced myself and he told me his name was Seydou and that he was from neighbouring Senegal. He proceeded to explain that this was the third time he had attempted, and failed, to reach the Canary Islands. He told me that migrating was his best – if not only – chance of providing for his wife and two small children, whom he had not seen since he left for Nouadhibou nearly two years earlier. He then began telling me the story of his latest failed attempt to cross the ocean and reach the Canary Islands. They were about seventy people in a *pirogue* (artisanal fisherman's boat) that capsized in the open sea. Half of the passengers, many of whom could not swim, drowned, but Seydou managed to cling to a piece of the boat along with some others. To their luck, the strong currents took them back towards the African coast, and they were eventually detained by the Mauritanian coast guard.[10]

Towards the end of his story, I began photographing Seydou. His reaction was immediate, as if he had been waiting for this all along. He began striking a variety of poses, seemingly experimenting with different ways of presenting himself: as someone who was suffering, as someone who had gone through terrible ordeals. While at the beginning of the photography session he appeared relaxed and smiling, he soon looked increasingly exhausted and troubled. I link this directly to the presence of the camera.

My intervention with the camera became, as I understand it, a way for Seydou to order his experience and give it concrete form. My sense is that he had had time to rest and come to terms with his migratory experience and, far from a voiceless 'victim', he now was a man with a firm conviction, strong opinions and a desire to make himself heard and understood. The camera played a central role in this. As was the case with Ishmael's portrait in the desert described earlier, our meeting presented Seydou with the possibility of exposing and fixating his sentiments, while at the same time relaying his experience to a wider audience. The latter became acutely evident to me when, having finished photographing Seydou and having made a few snapshots of the bottom of the room, I turned round and found Seydou standing at the opposite end of the 'cell', at the exit leading to the courtyard. His face was illuminated by the external daylight, and on the blackboard behind him he had written a message in chalk, knowing that I would be likely to photograph it when I saw it. It read '*Laissez nous retourner au pays domicile*'.[11] His posture next to the blackboard was by no means a coincidence. On the contrary, he was extremely aware of the kind of argument he was making by placing himself by the cell's exit, gazing into the daylight. Through his deliberate actions, he was performing a message to me and, because of the camera I was holding, potentially also to a much wider audience. I followed his invitation and made the photo.

Figure 8.6 Seydou. Detention. Nouadhibou, Mauritania, 2006. Photograph by the author.

The image (Figure 8.6) I later selected and retouched by various means, exposes Seydou's performance of 'suffering' and fatigue, as well as his existential message and his conscious reflection of his state of being at that point in time.

Photography: Dialogue and Collaborative Knowledge-Making

I have always considered photography, and indeed anthropology, as essentially being about meeting people, about making a space for dialogue and exchange. For such an exchange to occur, a mutual interest must be established. Photography is, first and foremost, about collaborating with the person in front of the camera, establishing a relationship that enables dialogue. Such a dialogical relationship must be generated. The photographer must, in a sense, seduce the person whom he or she wishes to photograph. For my part, I need, or indeed desire, something from the interlocutor: an opinion, a point of view, and or his or her image. I depend on him or her to provide me with an openness, willingness, vulnerability, or opinion. The interlocutor is aware of this. And by showing that I am aware of my dependence on him or her, he or she is automatically empowered: the interlocutor has the power to grant or deny me my wish. In my experience, an honest interest in people and an expressed desire to know and learn from a person is most often met with a positive response. I believe most people are pleased when subject to attention, and even more so when put in a position where they can help one understand and fulfil genuine desire. The seemingly simple act of pointing the camera at somebody is, in fact, a very strong signal: it is a fundamental, human recognition of the other. It is a way of saying: 'I see you'. Many photographs are taken as opposed to made collaboratively and with consent, but, ideally, photography should always be a collaborative endeavour – particularly when used as a research tool.

Working with photography as an integral part of my research design and implementation was decisive in my identification and application of the analytical concepts of 'itinerant bodies', 'interventions', and 'intersections' discussed in this chapter. Not only did the act of intervening with a camera enable me to establish dialogical relationships with my interlocutors; it also provided me with the opportunity to invite them to (re)present themselves and engage in a form of collaborative storytelling mediated through the camera.

More fundamentally, I have argued that this collaborative storytelling might serve to literally 'fixate' the person in front of the camera, inviting him or her to reflect on his or her situation and thus make sense of the often disorienting experience of migrating clandestinely. Hence, photographing can become an analytical process of making sense and order not only for the photographer/researcher, but also for the person in front of the lens. Photography becomes a concrete tool for making ethnography together with one's interlocutors, inviting them into the analytical process and thus granting them the opportunity to express themselves, not just verbally, but also performatively. This, I believe, is the great potential of using photography in social science research. Within the field of mobility studies, the inter-related notions of fixation and collaboration attain particular importance as part of a knowledge-making process that enables a more nuanced and qualitative insight into both practical and imaginary aspects of moving or being mobile.

The main challenge that remains for anyone doing photography research is to do away with the misconceived but widespread idea that photographs are more manipulated (understood in the negative sense) than, say, textual ethnography. Photography remains largely stigmatised within anthropology – and this means anthropology risks missing out on a powerful methodological and theoretical tool, which may be used to identify and address key aspects and dimensions of social life. This becomes particularly evident when conducting research on human mobility. As I have shown in this chapter, the act of photographing itself may facilitate an immersive and concrete form of collaborative knowledge making that opens up the field of study and invites new, nuanced insights. As with any other social scientific method, critical reflection is fundamental when working with photography. One crucial benefit of working with cameras is that one is constantly compelled to critically reflect, as people react in specific ways to the camera and to the person operating it.

In the wider context of mobility research, photography helps to identify, situate, and fixate people and places in a vast and intricate web of flows and connections. It becomes a way of seeing and framing, delineating and ordering social life in a context that is nebulous, fluid, and often intangible. Photography, when applied critically, – is a methodological and analytical tool that enables focusing on and isolating dimensions of an otherwise cacophonic assemblage of images, imaginaries, itineraries, and encounters. Photography enables, quite literally, the fixation of a fluid field.

Christian Vium (PhD) is Associate Professor in Anthropology at Aarhus University and an award-winning photographer and filmmaker whose research focuses on the intersection between the social sciences and the visual arts. He was awarded the Prix HSBC Pour la Photographie 2016 and published his first monograph, *Ville Nomade,* in July 2016.

NOTES

1. Fieldwork was carried out in West Africa in 2006, 2009–2010, and 2011, as well as in Paris, France, between 2006 and 2012, with one or two short trips each year.
2. Hannam, Sheller, and Urry (2006) use the term 'moorings' to designate such nodes, which serve to anchor or tie together multiple mobilities in what Brenner (2004: 66) labels as 'complex, polymorphic, and multiscalar regulatory geographies' (see also Biao 2013).
3. In West Africa, migration is commonly known as an 'adventure', and those who undertake it are called 'adventurers', alluding to the fact that they venture into the unknown, face numerous challenges, and grow as human beings as a result of the acquired experience, knowledge and recognition which the dangerous endeavour entails.
4. On this particular five-week research journey during the spring of 2006, I was travelling with Janus Metz, who was preparing a feature documentary on migration from Africa to Europe. The empirical material was used for my master thesis in Human Rights and Democratization (Vium 2007) and also edited into a short TV documentary, which aired on Danish National TV in early 2007.
5. I use the term 'make' as opposed to 'take' in relation to my work process, pointing to its fundamentally collaboratory nature, as I describe later in this chapter.
6. All names have been changed.
7. Imaginaries, needless to say, play a pivotal role in the migration endeavour (see, e.g. Appadurai 1996; Barrère and Martuccelli 2005; Gaonkar 2002; Lado 2005; Salazar 2011; Strauss 2006; and Vigh 2009).

8. This dialogue can be both verbal and nonverbal.
9. Ishmael wanted to be seen, to project himself to the audience as an icon or epitome of 'the adventurer', i.e. migrant en route to Europe. This came across clearly in both our dialogue and in his manner of performing himself in front of the camera.
10. I have elaborated on my meeting with Seydou elsewhere (Vium 2014: 228–30); here I limit my analysis to a discussion of the analytical importance of editing and sequencing.
11. 'Let us return to our home country'.

REFERENCES

Agamben, G. 1998. *Homo Sacer: Sovereign Power and Bare Life*. Stanford: Stanford University Press.

Appadurai, A. 1996. *Modernity at Large: Cultural Dimensions of Globalization*. Minneapolis: University of Minnesota Press.

Ba, C.O., and A. Choplin. 2005. 'Tenter l'aventure par la Mauritanie: migrations trans-sahariennes et recompositions urbaines', *Autrepart* 36: 21–42.

Back, L. 2004. 'Listening with our Eyes: Portraiture as Urban Encounter', in C. Knowles and P. Sweetman (eds), *Picturing the Social Landscape. Visual Methods and the Sociological Imagination*. London: Routledge, pp. 132–46.

Banks, M. 2001. 'Making Images', in M. Banks, *Visual Methods in Social Research*. London: Sage Publications. pp. 111–37.

Barrère, A., and D. Martuccelli. 2005. 'La modernité et l'imaginaire de la mobilité: inflexion contemporaine', *Cahiers internationaux de sociologie* 118: 55–79.

Barthes, R. 2000. *Camera Lucida*, trans. R. Howard. London: Vintage.

Bauman, Z. 2004. *Wasted Lives: Modernity and its Outcasts*. Cambridge: Polity Press.

Berger, J. 1990. *Ways of Seeing*. London: Penguin.

Biao, X. 2013. 'Multi-Scalar Ethnography: An Approach for Critical Engagement with Migration and Social Change', *Ethnography* 14(3): 282–99.

Biao, X., and Toyota, M. 2013. 'Ethnographic Experiments in Transnational Mobility Studies', *Ethnography* 14(3). 277–81.

Biemann, U. 2008. *Mission Reports: Artistic practice in the field*. Manchester: Cornerhouse Publications.

Brenner, N. 2004. *New State Spaces: Urban Governance and the Rescaling of Statehood*. Oxford: Oxford University Press.

Broomberg, D., and O. Chanarin. 2008. 'Unconcerned but Not Indifferent', www.foto8.com, 4 March 2008.

Büscher, M., and J. Urry. 2009. 'Mobile Methods and the Empirical', *European Journal of Social Theory* 12(1): 99–116.

Callon, M. 1987. 'Society in the Making; The Study of Technology as a Tool for Sociological Analysis', in W. Bieker (ed.), *The Social Construction of Technological Systems: New Directions in the Sociology and History of Technology*. London: MIT Press, pp. 83–103.

Candea, M. 2007. 'Arbitrary Locations: In Defence of the Bounded Field-Site', *Journal of the Royal Anthropological Institute* 13(1): 167–84.

Carling, J. 2002. 'Migration in the Age of Involuntary Immobility: Theoretical Reflections and Cape Verdean Experiences', *Journal of Ethnic and Migration Studies* 28(1): 5–42.

Chavez, L.R. 1996. *Shadowed Lives: Undocumented Immigrants in American Society.* New York: Harcourt Brace Publishers.

Choplin, A. and J. Lombard. 2008. 'Migrations et recompositions en Mauritanie. "Nouadhibou du Monde". Ville de transit... et après?', *Afrique Contemporaine* 228(4): 151-170.

Collyer, M. 2007. 'In-between Places: Trans-Saharan Transit Migrants in Morocco and the Fragmented Journey to Europe', *Antipode* 39(4): 668–90.

_____. 2010. 'Stranded Migrants and the Fragmented Journey', *Journal of Refugee Studies* 23(3): 273–93

Coutin, S.B. 2005. 'Being en Route', *American Anthropologist* 107(2): 195–206.

D'Andrea, A., L. Ciolfi, and B.Gray. 2011. 'Methodological Challenges and Innovations in Mobilities Research', *Mobilities* 6(2): 149–60.

Dalakoglou, D. 2010. 'The Road: An Ethnography of the Albanian–Greek Cross-Border Motorway', *American Ethnologist* 37(1): 132–49.

De Genova, N. 2002. 'Migrant "Illegality" and Deportability in Everyday Life', *Annual Review of Anthropology* 31: 419–47.

_____. 2013. 'Spectacles of Migrant "Illegality": The Scene of Exclusion, the Obscene of Inclusion', *Ethnic and Racial Studies* 36(7): 1–20.

Delanda, M. 2006. *A New Philosophy of Society. Assemblage Theory and Social Complexity.* New York: Continuum.

Deleuze, G. 2005. *Cinema 1: The Movement-Image.* London: Continuum.

Deleuze, G., and F. Guattari. 2004. *A Thousand Plateaus.* London: Continuum.

Diken, B., and S. Laustsen. 2005. *The Culture of Exception: Sociology Facing the Camp.* London: Routledge.

Edwards, E. (ed.). 1992. *Anthropology and Photography 1860–1920.* New Haven, CT: Yale University Press.

_____. 1997. 'Beyond the Boundary: A Consideration of the Expressive in Photography and Anthropology', in M. Banks and H. Morphy (eds), *Rethinking Visual Anthropology.* New Haven, CT: Yale University Press, pp. 53–80.

_____. 2001. *Raw Histories.* Oxford: Berg.

Eisenstein, S. 1988. 'Be´la Forgets the Scissors', in R. Taylor and I. Christie (eds), *The Film Factory: Russian and Soviet Cinema in Documents, 1896–1939.* London: Routledge, pp. 145–49.

Foucault, M. 1984 [1967]. 'Des espaces autres', *Architecture, Mouvement, Continuité* 5: 46-49.

Frichot, H. 2008. 'Holey Space and the Smooth and Striated Body of the Refugee', in A. Hickey-Moody and P. Malins (eds), *Deleuzian Encounters,* New York: Palgrave Macmillam, pp. 169–80.

Fulchignoni, E. 2003. 'Cine-Anthropology: Interview with Jean Rouch', in S. Feld (ed.) *Cine-Ethnography.* Minnesota: University of Minnesota Press, pp. 147-187.

Gaonkar, D.P. 2002. 'Toward New Imaginaries: An Introduction', *Public Culture* 14(1): 1–19.

Gatti, F. 2008. *Bilal sur la route des clandestins*. Paris: Éditions Liana Levi.

Giaccaria, P., and C. Minca. 2011. 'Topographies/topologies of the Camp: Auschwitz as a Spatial Threshold', *Political Geography* 30: 3–12.

Hage, G. 2005. 'A Not so Multi-Sited Ethnography of a Not so Imagined Community', *Anthropological Theory* 5(4): 463–75

Hannam, K., M. Sheller, and J. Urry. 2006. 'Editorial: Mobilities, Immobilities and Moorings', *Moorings* 1(1): 1–22.

Lado, L. 2005 'L'imagination africaine de l'Occident: Entre ressentiment et séduction', *Études* 7(403): 17–27.

Latour, B. 2005. *Reassembling the Social: An Introduction to Actor-Network-Theory*. New York: Oxford University Press.

Laurier, E. 2002. 'The Region as a Socio-Technical Accomplishment of Mobile Workers', in B. Brown, N. Green, and R. Harper (eds), *Wireless Worlds*. London: Springer, pp. 46–60.

Law, J. 2004. *After Method. Mess in Social Science Research*. New York: Routledge.

Lorimer, J. 2010. 'Moving Image Methodologies for More-Than-Human Geographies', *Cultural Geographies* 17(2): 237–58.

Lubkeman, S.C. 2008. 'Involuntary Immobility: On a Theoretical Invisibility of Forced Migration Studies', *Journal of Refugee Studies* 21(4): 454–75.

Lucht, H. 2012. *Darkness before Daybreak: African Migrants Living on the Margins in Southern Italy Today*. Berkeley: University of California Press.

MacDougall, D. 2006. *The Corporeal Image: Film, Ethnography, and the Senses*. Princeton: Princeton University Press.

Marcus, G. 1995. 'Ethnography in/of the World System: The Emergence of Multi-Sited Ethnography', *Annual Review of Anthropology* 24: 95–117.

Marcus, G., and E. Saka. 2006. 'Assemblage', *Theory, Culture & Society* 23(2–3): 101–9.

Mjaaland, T. 2009. 'Evocative Encounters: An Exploration of Artistic Practice as a Visual Research Method', *Visual Anthropology* 22: 393–411.

Morphy, H., M. and Banks (eds). 1997. *Rethinking Visual Anthropology*. New Haven, CT: Yale University Press.

Murdoch, J. 1995. 'Actor-Networks and the Evolution of Economic Forms: Combining Description and Explanation in Theories of Regulation, Flexible Specialization, and Networks', *Environment and Planning A* 27: 731–57.

Olwig, K.F., and K. Hastrup (eds). 1997. *Siting Culture: The Shifting Anthropological Object*. London: Routledge.

Pandolfo, S. 2007. 'The Burning: Finitude and the Politico-Theological Imagination of Illegal Migration', *Anthropological Theory* 2007(7): 329–63.

Papadopoulos, D., and V. Tsianos. 2008. 'The Autonomy of Migration: The Animals of Undocumented Mobility', in A. Hickey-Moody and P. Malins (eds), *Deleuzian Encounters: Studies in Contemporary Social Issues*. London: Palgrave Macmillan, pp. 223–34.

Pink, S. 2013. *Doing Visual Ethnography*. Thousand Oaks: Sage Publications.

Pinney, C. 2011. *Photography and Anthropology*. London: Reaktion Books.

Rouch, J. 2003. 'The Camera and Man', in P. Hockings (ed), *Principles of Visual Anthropology*. New York: de Gruyter, pp. 79-98.

Salazar, N.B. 2011. 'Tanzanian Migration Imaginaries', in R. Cohen and G. Jónsson (eds), *Migration and Culture*. Cheltenham: Edward Elgar, pp. 673–87.

_____. 2013. 'Anthropology', in P. Adey, D. Bissell, K. Hannam, P. Merriman, and M. Sheller (eds), *The Routledge Handbook of Mobilities*. London: Routledge, pp. 53–63.

Salazar, N.B., and A. Smart. 2011. 'Anthropological Takes on (Im)mobility: Introduction', *Identities: Global Studies in Culture and Power* 18(6): i–ix.

Sandbye, M. 2001. *Mindesmærker: Tid og erindring i fotografiet*. Copenhagen: Rævens Sorte Bibliotek.

Sayad, A. 1999. *La double absence: Des illusions de l'émigré aux souffrances de l'immigré*. Paris: Seuil.

Schneider, A. 1996. 'Uneasy Relationships: Contemporary Artists and Anthropology', *Journal of Material Culture* 1(2): 183–210.

_____. 2008. 'Three Modes of Experimentation with Art and Ethnography', *Journal of the Royal Anthropological Institute* 14: 171–94.

Schuster, L. 2005. 'The Continuing Mobility of Migrants in Italy: Shifting between Places and Statuses', *Journal of Ethnic and Migration Studies* 31(4): 757–74.

Sheller, M., and J. Urry. 2006. 'The New Mobilities Paradigm', *Environment and Planning A* 38: 207–26

Stanczak, G. 2007. *Visual Research Methods. Image, Society, and Reproduction*. London: Sage.

Strauss, V. 2006. 'The Imaginary', *Anthropological Theory* 6(3): 322–44.

Tagg, J. 1988. *The Burden of Representation: Essays on Photography and Histories*. London: Macmillan.

Turner, V. 1967. *The Forest of Symbols – Aspects of Ndembu Ritual*. New York: Cornell University Press.

_____. 1992. *Blazing the Trail – Way Marks in the Exploration of Symbols*. Tucson: The University of Arizona Press.

Van Gennep, A. 1960 [1908]. *The Rites of Passage*, trans. M.B. Vizedom and G.L. Caffee. Chicago: The University of Chicago Press.

Vigh, H. 2009. 'Wayward Migration: On Imagined Futures and Technological Voids', *Ethnos* 74(1): 91–109.

Vium, C. 2007. 'Clandestine: An Ethnographic Account of Undocumented Migration from West Africa to Europe', MA thesis. Venice: EIUC.

_____. 2009. 'Eventyrerne: Et billedessay om udokumenteret migration fra Vestafrika mod Europa', *Jordens Folk* (4).

_____. 2014. 'Icons of Becoming: Documenting Undocumented Migration from West Africa to Europe', *Cahiers d'Études africaines* LIV, 1–2 (213–14): 217–40.

Willerslev, R. and C. Suhr. 2013. 'Introduction: Montage as an Amplifier of Invisibility', in Willerslev, R. and C. Suhr (eds.) *Transcultural Montage*. New York: Berghahn, pp. 1–16.

Im/mobile Method/ologies

Simone Abram

The emphasis on mobility in the social sciences (and in anthropology in particular) arose in response to an imbalance: a perceived overemphasis on stasis and an analytical repertoire with more to say about people and things in places rather than in motion. As such, it was a welcome corrective to a potentially ossifying tendency to fix ideas and categories in time and space, one that severely restricted the available approaches to complex and fluid issues including migration, travel, and tourism. The notion of mobility, encompassing movement and travel (see the Introduction to this volume) at all scales, brings with it some curious effects, though. While drawing attention to the static approaches in previous analyses, it has a similarly all-encompassing effect, flattening very diverse and sometimes incommensurable forms of motion and movement and integrating them into one conceptual arena. In doing so, it may be subject to the same type of criticism it posed to premobility research – as a blanket approach that prioritises mobility over stasis, rather than vice versa, which is implicit in the tendency to refer to a mobilities 'paradigm' or a 'turn'. One of the challenges of this volume is to pick through the various aspects of mobility research that pose methodological challenges, while retaining awareness of stasis as more than the absence of mobility. In this brief afterword, I reflect on some of the implications, possibilities, and limitations of the concept of mobility.

What Does Mobility Do?

What does it mean to say that a 'mobilities approach' offers the potential to integrate different kinds of movement into one conceptual arena? On the one hand, using a concept as broad as mobility allows us to step back from judgments and distinctions between different kinds of movement, and suspend our preformed categorizations. In other words, it allows for a nonjudgemental approach to human movement that offers an escape route from politically and socially loaded terms such as migration, tourism, commuting, and travelling. It also enables us to draw comparisons across both time and space, between species, and between material and immaterial forms. Mobility is a term that has relevance not only for human movement but also for the movement of other beings, material, and ideas. Nor is mobility scale-specific, and since almost everything in the universe moves at some scale, mobility can be explored at the scale of the atom and that of the universe and more or less everything in between. Yet mobility at the intimate scale is quite different conceptually and materially from mass migration. What value does a concept have that covers everything from walking round a room to intercontinental migration, even as it relativizes them (Adey 2006)?

In this volume, the emphasis is on human movement and all the material and immaterial movement that supports moving humans. Packed into the term mobility, however, there are confusions. Several terms tend to comingle: movement and mobility interlink with kindred terms such as travel or distance (Cresswell 2006). As the introduction highlights, movement can be purely in the mind and the potential for movement can be as significant as any actual movement, certainly in relation to the perception of human freedom, for example. Motility – the potential to be mobile – is important to all of the people represented in the chapters here, albeit in different ways. Leivestad draws out the significance of the wheels remaining on the caravans and mobile homes of the British residents at Camping Mares. Even though they may be disguised behind panels, their existence is important not only to satisfy the rules of the campsite, but also to emphasize the motility of the inhabitants in a paradoxical state of temporary permanence. British mobile-home dwellers are not participating in the nomadism of nonsettled people, but imagine themselves in a permanent state of revolt or resistance to a state, while clinging to the ideology of nationalism; dreaming of being free Englishmen while fleeing the benefits the state wishes to endow, for which it demands the participation of its citizens. Anderson, Vium, and Lucht emphasize in different ways how the difference in the travel trajectories between the would-be migrant adventurers, police, border guards, and participants in what Anderson calls the 'illegality industry' lie in their level of potential freedom to travel and the ways in which different kinds of restrictions delineate the limits to their mobility. These cases also highlight the European ambivalence towards nomadism, both a romantic fiction and a feared instability.

They key ambivalence in the volume lies in the methodological responses to the recognition of mobility and motility. The folklore of ethnographic individualism lives on despite its mythical footings, which several contributors allude to, Anderson noting the unfortunate tendency of anthropology departments to reproduce the single-ethnographer myth through doctoral training and reminding us again that even the great mythologizer Malinowski conducted multi-sited fieldwork. The British and American traditions also pay less attention to the great French ethnologists, such as Georges Henri Rivière, whose commitment to European ethnography and museology saw multi-disciplinary teams of researchers embark on collecting exercises (see Chiva 1985), with its apotheosis in the Aubrac studies in the 1960s (CNRS 1970–1982) and their subsequent associated migration studies (see Chodkiewicz 2014). Comparison between such projects and their precursors in folkloric collection practices might be drawn with the Swedish-Finnish nation-building folklorism that Österlund-Pötzsch describes in such wonderful detail. As she points out, the enthusiastic mobility of the young collectors overemphasized the immobility of the folk visited, reinforcing the notion of a link between land and nation that made a Swedish-speaking nation a political force in Finland on the back of the romantic nature-nationalism that swept across Europe in the latter part of the nineteenth century. It is fascinating to contemplate the variable scales of mobility at play in the enterprise described by Österlund-Pötzsch, as collectors adopted walking-and-talking methods only relatively recently identified as a 'method' per se (e.g. Ingold and Vergunst 2008; Powell and Rishbeth 2012).

What is newer to ethnographic research, on the other hand, is the potential for digital participant-observation, a co-presence that Walton describes as physicality that is mediated through online media, specifically images, so that the co-presence is as much image-to-image as face-to-face, using photoblogging, geolocating and image sharing. Digital ethnography and 'netnography' are now widespread methodological approaches (see Murthy 2008; O'Reilly 2012; Hsu 2013; Postill 2015) and Walton shows how mobility can be considered within and through digital methods, particularly in the context of difficult-to-access fields. The digital exhibition she co-curated with her interlocutors is an elegant concept, since visitors can come and go at a digital exhibition as they can at a physical gallery, and perhaps the emotional, conceptual, and communicative distance and proximity with the curators is equivalent in virtual terms.

The co-curating, on the other hand, is of a different order, requiring intense preparation and negotiation, a co-production for a new ethnography that is public, applied and theoretical (Pink and Abram 2015). Photography is another methodological theme that emerges in this volume, not least in Vium's discussion of his use of the camera as a tool to generate dialogue as much as to create images. Vium's concern here is with the dialogical relation that the camera facilitates between himself as photographer and the clandestine migrants that he is documenting, but through his photography he is also generating dialogues with viewers of the images, another pertinent methodological direction. Indeed, although much of this volume is taken up with the field methods of ethnography, we can also turn our attention to the mobile methodology that is the creation of the ethnographic work and its circulation among different audiences and interlocutors. So often these are treated as separate domains, yet the current climate of preoccupation with the 'impact' of research actually reinforces those approaches that see them as contiguous, such as Walton's. In this approach, ethnographic research 'with' (in Ingold's 2008 sense) is interwoven in an ongoing dialogue, the fields of research and dissemination blending into a shared journey. Research projects do have beginnings and ends, proposals, actions, and outcomes, but for ethnographers these often blur into longer commitments to people and ideas, and seep into the everyday life of the researcher as well as the researched (see Smart, Hockey, and James 2014).

Mobile Methods

The implications of mobility for methodology can be summarized under two headings. First, as suggested above, the shift to mobility in the social sciences has been a pendulum swing from roots to routes, from static to mobile social sciences. Österlund-Pötzsch highlights the historical ambivalence intrinsic to this swing by reminding us that mobile methods themselves are not new, illustrating how the distribution of mobility and stasis between researcher and researched have shifted. Still, either of the two poles – mobility or stasis – can eclipse the other, and the gradual shift of the pendulum should take us forward to a new resting place, where methods acknowledge both the mobile and the immobile. From this new starting point, mobility and immobility need not be set in opposition to one another creating yet another dichotomy to be overcome, but can be combined with an awareness of the unequal distribution of mobility and immobility as in the chapters here that focus on migration and the illegality industry. The freedom of Vium and Lucht to travel is also their freedom to leave and to return, in contrast to their co-travellers. The new methods proposed in this volume recognize that the world is in motion, without reifying movement over stasis. The challenge here is to acknowledge mobility without prioritizing it, to see im/mobility as complementary, rather than 'shadow' concepts (see Strathern 2011).

Second, bringing all kinds of movement into the same conceptual terrain under the rubric of 'mobility', while potentially flattening (as I indicated above), also creates spaces for rewarding comparative critique. It can reveal the commonalities between movements, and separates the movement from the meanings attached. Migration need not be seen as a categorical directional trajectory, since it encompasses partial, repetitive, forced, and voluntary movements. Drawing comparisons between the migration of West African farmers and Polish enforcement officers raises a whole range of urgent political and sociological questions. Just as tourism anthropologists long ago critiqued the binary distinction between hosts and guests (see Abram, Waldren, and Macleod 1997) that veiled our view of family visitors, settled visitors, migrant tourism workers, and so on, mobility encompasses all sorts of tourism and leisure-related travel without fixing analysis in particular relations of hospitality. It enables us to broaden the focus to include not only the movement but the structures and material means by which movement is made possible. Movement, the state of being in movement (mobility), and the potential to be mobile (motility) are performative moments and their potential. Just as being a tourist is less an identity than a set of ideas and relational positions, people can be migrants at home, and be at home as a migrant. The movement that Vium describes from 'somebody' to 'nobody' and back is one that migrants perform within their journeys, which are full of intersections, hiatuses, uncertainty, and danger. Lifting the label of 'migrant' (one rarely applied to the multi-homed international wealthy) enables us to see the persons moving. Mobility requires methods with nuance, and analytical angles that can tease out the axes for comparison, as indicated in this volume.

It is very clear from the contributions to this volume that a focus on mobility paves the way for innovative and integrative approaches, and that the requirement to conceptualize mobility generates new research questions and theoretical reflections for further development. Shifting the ground on which stereotypes of migration are founded is an essential tool in the armoury against racism, xenophobia, and prejudice. Hence, the methods outlined in this book should be seen as crucial political moves, increasingly needed in a troubled world.

Simone Abram is Professor of Anthropology at Durham University, where she is also co-director of the Durham Energy Institute. Recent books include

Culture and Planning (2011 Ashgate) and co-edited volumes: *Green Ice: Tourism Ecologies in the European High North* (2016 Palgrave), *Media, Anthropology and Public Engagement* (2015 Berghahn), *Elusive Promises* (2013 Berghahn).

REFERENCES

Abram, S., J. Waldren, and D.V.L. Macleod (eds). 1997. *Tourists and Tourism: Identifying with People and Places*. Oxford: Berg.

Adey, P. 2006. 'If Mobility is Everything Then it is Nothing: Towards a Relational Politics of (Im)mobilities', *Mobilities*, 1(1): 75–94.

Chiva, I. 1985.'Georges-Henri Rivière: Un demi-siècle d'ethnologie de la France'. *Terrain* 5:76–83.

Chodkiewicz, J.-L. 2014. *L'Aubrac à Paris: Une enquete d'ethnologie urbaine*. Paris: Comité des travaux historiques et scientifiques, CTHS.

CNRS. 1970–1982. *L'Aubrac: Etude ethnologique, linguistique, agronomique et économique d'un établissement humain*, 6 vols. Paris: CNRS.

Cresswell, T. (2006). *On the Move: Mobility in the Modern Western World*. London: Routledge.

Hsu, W. 2013. 'On Digital Ethnography', *Ethnography Matters*. Retrieved from http://ethnographymatters.net/series/on-digital-ethnography.

Ingold, T. 2008. 'Anthropology is *Not* Ethnography', *Proceedings of the British Academy* 154: 69–92. Retrieved from http://www.britac.ac.uk/anthropology-not-ethnography-british-academy-review.

Ingold, T., and J. Vergunst. 2008. *Ways of Walking: Ethnography and Practice on Foot*. Aldershot: Ashgate.

Murthy, D. 2008. 'Digital Ethnography: An Examination of the Use of New Technologies for Social Research', *Sociology* (42): 837–55.

O'Reilly, K. 2012. *Ethnographic Methods*. Abingdon: Routledge.

Pink, S., and S. Abram (eds). 2015. *Media, Anthropology and Public Engagement*. Oxford: Berghahn.

Postill, J. 2015. 'Public Anthropology in Times of Media Hybridity and Global Upheaval', in S. Pink and S. Abram (eds), *Media, Anthropology and Public Engagement*. Oxford: Berghahn, pp. 246–73.

Powell, M., and C. Rishbeth. 2012. 'Walking Voices: Flexibility in Place and Meanings of Place by First Generation Migrants', *Tijdschrift voor Economische en Sociale Geografie* 103(1): 69–84.

Smart, C., J. Hockey, and A. James (eds). 2014. *The Craft of Knowledge: Experiences of Living with Data*. London: Palgrave Macmillan.

Strathern, M. 2011. 'Sharing, Stealing and Borrowing Simultaneously', in V. Strang and M. Busse (eds), *Ownership and Appropriation*. London: Bloomsbury Academic, pp. 23–42.

Index

www.ingramcontent.com/pod-product-compliance
Lightning Source LLC
Chambersburg PA
CBHW062108040426
42336CB00042B/2554